The College Union Idea

SECOND EDITION

The College Union Idea

SECOND EDITION

Edited by

Porter Butts
Elizabeth Beltramini
Mark Bourassa
Patrick Connelly
Robert Meyer
Sue Mitchell
Jeannette Smith
TJ Willis

First published in 1971. This edition published in 2012.

Association of College Unions International
One City Centre, Suite 200
120 W. Seventh St.
Bloomington, IN 47404-3839 USA
www.acui.org

ISBN 978-0-923276-64-5

Library of Congress Cataloging-in-Publication Data
2012903753

Design by Larry Buchanan

TABLE OF CONTENTS

PREFACE

When I came to the University of Wisconsin as a freshman in 1920, students were just beginning an intensive campaign, among themselves, to raise funds for a "Memorial Union" building. Two or three months later, through some unlikely happenstance I cannot explain but for which I am grateful, I was on a downtown stage doing a song and dance act in what was called "Union Vodvil," a variety show produced by the Union Board for the benefit of the building fund.

This was my first exposure to the union. In this sense, therefore, the year 1970–71 (when "The College Union Idea" was first published) represents the 50th anniversary of my first venture in the union field.

There followed, after that first union show, a continuous association with the Wisconsin Union: assignment, as a sophomore, to produce a float for the homecoming parade promoting the union fund drive; appointment, as editor of the campus newspaper, to the campaign publicity committee (then, as now, one way to get press releases on the front page and reasonably favorable editorials); a job, upon graduation, as assistant to the union campaign director to organize the publicity effort, and to find out, for the first time, who Wisconsin's 80,000 alumni were and where they lived—so they could be asked to subscribe to the fund; appointment, as campaign director in 1926, and as director of the soon-to-open building itself in 1927.

About that time, I met one of the more willing student volunteers who showed up to help get out the mail in the campaign office, and married

PORTER BUTTS, '24

her (a half dozen years later, that is). As it turned out, the union fervor, within the family, was contagious. My brother, and later a nephew, ran for Wisconsin's Union Board and were elected; another nephew became president of the Minnesota Union; and when our two daughters went to college, one became a member of the Wisconsin Union craft committee, the other president of Carleton College Union in Minnesota. (No generation gap here.)

This is all by way of indicating that, in my case, the union has been an absorbing presence from the beginning, and for 50 years.

When the Association of College Unions, prompted by some generous impulse, chose at its 1970 conference to take note of these 50 years—or, more precisely and particularly, of the conclusion of my 34 years as editor of the Association's publications by presenting a special fund contributed by colleagues in the field and to be used in whatever way I might decide, there were a number of felicitous references to the importance of "perpetuating the ideals, the philosophies of college unions," and the value of the "medium of words." Apparently to make the point clear, a corps of friends went to the trouble of reproducing some of my writing in a special publication. I began to get the message.

In conferring with union associates later, it seemed it might indeed be useful to show where the union idea came from, how it was evolved, changed, and expanded—why and when. Because it is still quite evident that many university people, not to mention others, have heard little about what, conceptually, the college union has been, is, or might be. And most union staff members and student leaders have not had an opportunity to see, readily, their own union, or the work they do, in a reasonably comprehensive historical or ideological perspective.

Now such a project could have been undertaken by carefully examining all that has been written about the nature of unions by everybody over the time span of 155 years since the first union appeared in England, trying to synthesize the findings. But that would be a formidable two- or three-year task, or more. So I have chosen the more manageable alternative of letting already published observations about unions—principally my own—speak for themselves and for the era in which they were written. And perhaps there's a certain merit—of story unity and of personalization of the story—in portraying how the union idea unfolded, and how it has worked out (or not worked out), as seen at the time by one who was a participant—an eye witness, as it were—during two-thirds of the 75 years since the first union was built (in 1896) on this continent, and during all of the period of the main union development, both here and abroad.

While in many ways this is a personal statement of the union idea and its ramifications, it is not entirely so by any means. Interlarded are the commentaries and beliefs of many others—writers who knew something of the origins and significance of the 19th and early 20th century unions, of course, and certain thoughtful observers of the general education scene and speakers at our association conferences whose messages have been especially influential in shaping thought about the union, including my own, and in giving new thrusts to the union movement. Then, too, whatever I've had to say about unions has been conditioned, not just by the experience with one union (though this conditioning, obviously, has been considerable), but also by visits to some 250 unions here and overseas, and by the flow of articles, special union studies, surveys of student attitudes and needs, correspondence, noteworthy innovations, criticisms, frustrations, and hopes that cross an editor's desk during a third of a century. So, in this sense, the observations in this book are reflective, at least in part, of the union trends of the time.

A principal problem, of course, was the familiar one of selection. What to include of hundreds of articles, monographs, talks, and some full-length books written over a period of almost 50 years? The attempt has been to choose those excerpts which might best illuminate the nature of the union, or explain how or why a shift of emphasis came about, or show what hindered understanding and progress, or otherwise illustrate, not all there is to know about the history and functioning of unions, but, mainly, the evolution of the idea of the union.

Sometimes an excerpt is included not only because of what is said, but, more especially, because of when it was said—to help identify when a germinal idea arrived, or to confirm, in later years, the continuum of an early concept. At other times, excerpts were chosen which serve as examples of an idea successfully at work, or, on the other hand, suggest potentials unrealized—buried treasure still to be searched out.

In arranging what was said, and when, in near-chronological order, some minor modifications in the original text were made to accomplish a somewhat easier, more intelligible transition from one statement to another—or, often, simply to omit surplus phrases.

Throughout, this publication does not propose to be a research document, complete with full footnotes and all the evidence, affirmative or countervailing; but rather to tell, decade by decade, the story of an adventurous idea in education, and of the forces which have shaped it, diminished it, and enlarged it—to be read as an adventure story.

Porter Butts

SECOND PREFACE

After its initial publication in 1971, "The College Union Idea" became known as the foundational text for our profession. It was used in new employee orientation and training, student affairs graduate coursework, countless facility dedications, and more. However, as it aged and the final chapter of the 1960s slipped farther into history, there became a call to update the manuscript. That call grew louder over the decades, and ultimately this is the response.

No one before or since Porter Butts has dedicated his life more passionately to documenting the philosophy and evolution of the college union. Therefore, the decades added to his original do not draw from one individual's work. Rather, a crew of ACUI members, doctoral students, and self-styled historians volunteered to collaborate on this project. They spent countless hours reviewing Association materials, publications about specific unions, major media, speeches, higher education magazines and journals, governmental reports, and campus newspapers to collect excerpts that best represent the college union idea throughout the past half-century.

In developing the updated sections, each of us felt a kinship with Porter and wanted our work to be worthy of standing next to his original. The group began by reviewing his earlier decades and laughingly pointed out to each other statements that while written in the early 20th century remained true today. Upon beginning our research into the more recent decades, we appreciated all the more what Porter had accomplished. Given how technology has coddled us, we were grateful to those libraries that had digitized some of their collections, but

realized they were the exception. To amass the story of the college union from the 1970s on, we carefully perused musty, brittle, yellowed pages. We were reunited with Microfiche, slides, and cassettes. We called government offices, colleagues, and sister associations for bits of history they might have on hand. We drove to nearby institutions to visit their archives. It was, in some ways, a scavenger hunt.

With the clues in hand, we began to piece together the chapters. Each draft provoked thoughtful critiques and advice for improvement. "Porterize" became a verb as we tried to emulate his writing style. A mighty task, but perhaps more bewildering was how to best fashion a collection from the vast array of information discovered. Knowing that Porter observed this same challenge, the team took his lead, crafting chapters that are true to the era, continue the drama unfolding from the beginnings of the movement, and help modern-day readers reflect on the cyclical nature of trends. One theme that remains steady throughout the book is the belief that the college union's primary purpose is to educate, that it is not just a building that houses auxiliary enterprises; rather it is an organization representing a "well-considered plan for the community life of the college." The contributing editors thank Porter for his commitment to perpetuating that message and hope the new book serves to do the same.

Elizabeth Beltramini
Mark Bourassa
Patrick Connelly
Robert Meyer
Sue Mitchell
Jeannette Smith
TJ Willis

FOREWORD

ADDED IN 2004

Since its first printing in 1971, "The College Union Idea" by Porter Butts has served as the definitive work in answering three important questions for college union professionals: Who are we? How did we get to this point? What is the philosophical base for our profession? Today, this book stands alone as the primer for us all.

Beginning in 1812 with the founding of the Attic Society, which was the precursor of the Oxford Union, Butts takes us on a historical journey tracing the evolution of the college union idea. Throughout the journey, the reader is privy to the challenges, the questions, the issues, and all of the other ingredients that shaped and strengthened our profession.

It has always been difficult for me to understand where we are and, more importantly, where we are going without first gaining an understanding and appreciation of where we have been. Butts answers many of those questions in "The College Union Idea."

As Butts states in his preface, the book is not a research document. Its purpose is to tell "the story of an adventurous idea in education, and of the forces which have shaped it, diminished it, and enlarged it—to be read as an adventure story." When I first read the story, I gained an appreciation and understanding of those ideals that attracted me to the college union profession and became the foundation for my beliefs.

In developing my personal philosophy of what a college union should be, I remembered my undergraduate union as my "home away from home" and the living room or community center of my campus. I remembered the lessons I learned in leadership and citizenship through my involvement with my program board, and I decided I wanted to be a part of the college union and student activities profession. "The College Union Idea" was an amazing discovery for me. It not only authenticated a lot of my personal beliefs about college unions; it also gave me a historical context for how those beliefs developed. I have spent a career promoting college union staff as educators and the college union as a laboratory of real-life experiences for students. Butts' book has been a valuable asset in those discussions.

Today, on many of our campuses, the traditional college union is undergoing a great amount of change. Many of its retail and programming services are being decentralized, while increasing pressure is being applied to generate more revenue and become less dependent on general campus and student fee support. Many see the union as nothing more than a service center with major roles in hospitality, recruitment, and retention of students. With these pressures, it is important that we not lose sight of our values or philosophical foundation. Given the current situation, I find some of the concepts presented in the book—educating, community building, connecting, unifying, student development, citizenship, and student-staff partnerships—just as relevant, if not more important, today than when first introduced.

I believe this book should be required reading for anyone who is considering entering the college union and student activities profession and an important resource for those of us who might occasionally need to take time to rediscover our sense of purpose and refocus on why we selected this rewarding and fulfilling profession.

Winston Shindell
Former Executive Director, Indiana Memorial Union/IU Auditorium, Indiana University
Past President, Association of College Unions International

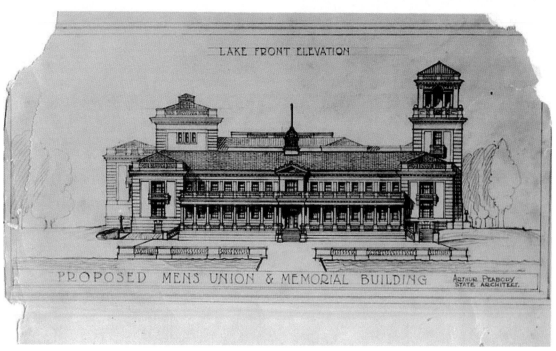

LAKE FRONT ELEVATION

PROPOSED MENS UNION & MEMORIAL BUILDING

Arthur Peabody
STATE ARCHITECT.

Porter Butts was instrumental in the fundraising effort for the University of Wisconsin Union, which broke ground Nov. 11, 1925. He later would become the facility's first union director. UNIVERSITY OF WISCONSIN-MADISON ARCHIVES

"

Forty-three years ago, in 1926, about this time of the year, in the dusk of the evening I walked along a path of the Cornell University campus with Burgon Bickersteth, warden of Hart House, and we talked at length about Hart House and college unions. We had attended sessions of the Association of Unions all through the day—I a recent graduate attending my first union conference, he already a kind of legendary figure in the then small union world.

It was then I first learned something of the nature and tradition of Hart House; it was then that I decided, inspired by what he said, that if this is what a union is like and this is the kind of man who is devoted to the idea, I would like to be a part of such a venture. ...

Two years after our talk at Cornell I found myself— incredibly—director of the new Wisconsin Union.

— From an address at the University of Toronto, on the occasion of the 50th anniversary of the formal opening of Hart House, 1969.

"

Where authorship of the statements which follow is not shown by name, the article or address referred to is by Mr. Butts.

Beginnings

The Oxford Union Debate Chamber, founded to offer "unity through diversity."

ACUI ARCHIVES

Out of the 19th century comes the genesis of the college union at Cambridge and Oxford. These debating societies are formed based on the primacy of free discussion, unity through diversity, and preparation for leadership of public affairs. The unions then facilitate for students a certain art of living.

FREE AND OPEN DISCUSSION—
THE FIRST GOAL

"In 1812, Augustus Hare founded the Attic Society (precursor of the Oxford Union). ... Hare was imbued with an almost mystical belief that discussion was both the road to truth and the only justification of a university education. ...

"Despairing of Oxford as a home of lost causes, he moved over to Cambridge, where he had hopes that the Cambridge Union, newly founded in 1815, would have freedom of life denied to such enterprises at Oxford. ... Returning to Oxford from Cambridge, Hare attempted to collect some of his old friends of the Attic Society. 'A miniature Parliament,' as his biographer puts it, 'was the Elysium.' ...

"The union debates, it was thought, played their indirect part in education—sharpened wits—taught young men how to get on with their fellows. ... In the end it was neither schools nor religion which put his (Gladstone's) feet on the first rung of the ladder of success, but the union. ... (Premier) Asquith, looking back to Gladstone, treated his union career as of equal importance with his schools."

— Christopher Hollis. The Oxford Union, 1965.

"It is not difficult to discover what has always been the most important of those characteristics which make of university life a thing apart. It is a free discussion. ...

"The contest of mind against mind is the greatest benefit which a university can confer. ... Behind formal systems, above teachers or examiners, the interplay of fresh discussion holds an important place in every country, but of a value more highly esteemed amongst ourselves than elsewhere. ... Thus, to focus these interests of free discussion—to give them name, local habitation, permanency—became the object of several enterprising spirits who succeeded in founding a debating society for the whole of the University of Oxford, in the spring of the year 1823. ...

"The new entity, to be known within a very short time and ever since, almost affectionately, as 'The Oxford Union,' did not spring spontaneously. ... Thoughts of such a unity had been in the air for some years, and the fine idealistic view persisted that this should be unity through diversity. ... Originally, debate alone seemed reason enough for founding an institution which should reach the heights.* It was meant to grow. In the minds of the pioneers were many elevating and expansive ideas. There was the love of books. There were the claims of philosophy. History might enter it. ... Politics allured, not theoretically, but as a likely occupation of freedom in any democratic sense. It was by no means intended, in these early days, to unloose the chains of a traditional exclusiveness. The idea of a general club had not yet dawned.

"And yet, as an antidote to this conception of privilege, reckoning had to be made with the gregariousness and adaptability of young men as such. ... Oxford had always cherished humor and the sense of fun. High spirits could be relied on to prevent intellectual endeavor from degenerating into pretentiousness or

16   BEGINNINGS

dullness. Unity could come from, or be stimulated by, the understanding of differences. Even conversions were possible. And to these points the importance of good manners, and the plans of the founders might be considered, as in fact they have proved, of far-reaching value—even to the nation. ...

"The policy of opportunity for public debate scarcely demands an apologist. But, for debating, the period following Waterloo was somewhat inauspicious. Nevertheless, in spite of discouragement, Cambridge had set the pace, and Oxford really desired to follow suit. ...

"Persistently the idea that open discussion, of urgent political questions especially, should be attainable in a university, held its own against all checks. ...

"The Cambridge Union Society of 1815 had actually attained, within two years of its foundation, the distinction of a decree issued by the vice chancellor, abolishing the debates on the ground that they interfered with study.

"This issue joined, it had to be fought out. By 1821, the prohibition was withdrawn, grudgingly, yet of necessity. Everywhere the truth was being established that open discussion is the greatest of safety-valves. ... **

"The mention of 'democracy' in the very first (debate) motion seems at this day significant. It hints at the radical changes coming into English life. And it is obvious, underneath these tentative forms and rather timid suggestions, that Oxford youth was seeking to understand and to cope with the restlessness of the world it would have to live in. ...

"The eight men who during the year 1823 occupied in turn the presidential chair save Bramston, who became a dean, were on the way either to the House of Commons or the House of Lords."

— H.A Morrah, president of the Oxford Union in 1894. The Oxford Union, 1823-1923, 1923.

*While the rules and regulations governing the conduct of the Oxford and Cambridge Unions and their debates were set forth, from the beginning, in lengthy and meticulous detail, nowhere is there an official statement, so far as I can learn from reading the union literature of the 19th century, of the overall purpose, or raison d'etre, of forming these earliest unions. It may well be that the purposes were so well understood that no one considered an explicit or formal statement necessary.

**Thus, in a rather real sense, the union movement of the early 1800s was a student "free speech movement," antedating the Free Speech Movement in the United States—beginning at the University of California in 1964—by 150 years.

Training for Leadership, Statesmanship

"The Debating Societies provide several outlets for political energy. Foremost of these is the celebrated union. ... A successful union orator has of necessity acquired many qualifications for speaking. Many of our present statesmen have been trained in this school."

— A.M.M. Stedman. Oxford: Its Life and Schools, 1887.

"The Union Society (at Cambridge) forms another distraction well calculated to turn out the English ideal of a university man—a man, id est, ready for public affairs."

— M.A.R. Ruker. Cambridge, 1907.

"If you wish to read the names of those who have been foremost in serving their country in church and state during the same period (1823-73), you must read the lists of the Oxford Union Society. ... It is surely no small matter that the leaders and directors of public opinion should be trained in all the learning of our ancient universities; and I claim for the Union Society that it specially represents one characteristic of Oxford training. ... Her students have not forgotten that they are citizens."

— H.A. Morrah. The Oxford Union, 1823-1923, 1923. R.G.C. Mowbray, student president of the union, speaking at the Oxford Union Jubilee, 1873.

"The union—the most famous of all university associations—was founded early in the 19th century. ... For many decades now, it has been open to all who care to join, and its aim has been to provide place and opportunity for airing political views. ... Many men who lead the political and diplomatic destinies of the Empire received a first lesson of confidence and debating skill in the union—among such have been Asquith and Lord Bryce. ... The proceedings of the evening are conducted in a dignified, or even pretentious manner, in a large hall arranged like the House of Commons. It is not surprising that prominent men of the nation—from ex-prime ministers and Cabinet members to Labour M.P.s—feel it worth their while to address the union in debate.

In 1889, the first freshman class at North Carolina College of Agriculture and Mechanic Arts, now North Carolina State University. NCSU DIGITAL COLLECTIONS

A men's union debate in 1887. ACUI ARCHIVES

... Probably the greatest undergraduate honour is to be chosen president of the union."

— Laurence A. Crosby and Frank Aydelotte. Oxford of Today, 1923.

"Nothing concerning the great English universities is to me more interesting than the way they train leaders for national life. ...

"The Oxford Union is perhaps better known than the Cambridge Union. Both are debating societies, where young men debate the most critical subjects of state and society. They are collegiate Houses of Commons. The presidency of either union is regarded as the highest undergraduate honor.

"Members of the union debate not only with each other but with the foremost statesmen and thinkers of the country. Prime Minister Lloyd George accepted an invitation to debate with an exponent of the Oxford Union an issue on which his government was tottering. After the debate, the members of the union made a division (voted) on the issue. The prime minister won by a bare majority. Winston Churchill also was taken on by the Oxford Union.

"Scouts for the political parties—Labour, Conservative, Liberal, etc.—keep an eye on union debaters. A young man who shows outstanding readiness on his feet, mastery of facts, wit, logic, and power to convince, will likely be offered a job in some government office. If he develops, his party will in time offer him as candidate in some district holding a by-election to fill a vacancy in the House of Commons. ...

"The standard of British statesmanship probably owes more to the system of training at Oxford and Cambridge than to any other one factor in British life."

— J. Frank Dobie. "A Texan Teaches at Cambridge." National Geographic Magazine, 1946.

More than a Debating Society

"The union is a kind of large literary club, where every opportunity is afforded to those desirous of improving their minds. Apart from the debates, which are naturally a very important feature, every facility is afforded for universal reading. ... There is a large library where every work likely to assist the studies, or amuse the leisure hours of students, may be found, unless dishonest members have appropriated these volumes to their own use."

— A.M.M. Stedman. Oxford: Its Life and Schools, 1887.

"The Society has a set of buildings and grounds just off Cornmarket Street, where are the debating hall, an excellent reading and reference library of more than 50,000 volumes, periodical, billiard, and dining rooms."

— Laurence A. Crosby and Frank Aydelotte. Oxford of Today, 1923.

"The university ideal is to promote the art of living, the amenities of civilized society as well as knowledge. ... In the clubroom after-dinner wine, coffee, and the pipe came in the order named. ... Young men sharpen each other's wits, have their best instincts developed by association. ... Cambridge still thinks that education which leads to the art of living is as 'practical' as a course in salesmanship."

— J. Frank Dobie. "A Texan Teaches at Cambridge." National Geographic Magazine, 1946.

"No Educational Instrument So Valuable"— and Students Created It

"I believe there is no educational instrument so valuable to the large class of students as the Union Society; yet it is a voluntary association which has never received any sanction or recognition from the university; indeed in a certain portion of its career it has received that gentle stimulus which is always given to any English institution by the disapproval of those in authority. ...

"It is a great honour to the independence and self-governing instinct of the English people, that a society, having had so great an influence for good, and producing so many distinguished men among its members, should be founded by the spontaneous action of the undergraduates themselves. ...

"Though not established by the laws of the place, though not under the sanction of public authority, the Oxford Union Society has proved itself by its fruits to be one of the best institutions of this university. ...

"This at all events is certain, that in every union which breathes the atmosphere of freedom, eloquence has at all times been one of the most potent influences of society, from the days of Pericles and Demosthenes to those of Cicero, and from the days of Cicero to those of Pitt and Canning.

"Well, this society was founded to cultivate this power."

— H.A. Morrah. The Oxford Union, 1823-1923, 1923. Chancellor of Oxford University, speaking at the Oxford Union Jubilee, 1873.

Students as University Defenders. And as Advocates of Change—but through Discussion, not Revolution

"Influence of the union became in Oxford much like the power of the press in larger life. ... The university of the 19th century (and after) has smarted under the lash of current criticism. ... Not through (the lecture room) could the university make out its case when attacked. Herein, it is the union which (kept) open the channels of communication between idealism and action, between politics theoretical and practical, between Oxford and the world. ...

"Links are forged in some countries between the universities, professions, and even commerce. At Oxford things are differently arranged. ... It was the union which really began a constructive advance away from this position, sometimes by encouraging the frankest criticism of the university itself. ...

"Such questions as the ultimate usefulness of universities, of Oxford more especially, were prominent for a long series of years. ... To those who complained that a living touch with affairs was largely wanting, the union's own success supplied some striking evidence on the other side. ...

"On the surface, many an Oxford custom seemed indefensible from any point of view. That is why there was a perpetual clamor for reform, and that is why special commissions were so often appointed by the state. But somehow it followed that in the union, which did not lack zealots who could speak forcibly, the general vote on anything resembling governmental interference took the form of a vehement 'Hands off!' The importance of all this lay, not in the vote, but in the discussion, whereby it was nearly always proved to zealots, who urged sweeping changes and reforms, that ventilation of the subject was enough; changes might come, might even be overdue; but, on consideration, these changes should be slow. ...

"The most ardent reformer hesitated, as he tested facts and views by contrasting them with others, to side with the iconoclast. He learned that to try to rush things forward too fast is equivalent to pushing them back. It dawned on him that if you wanted to build Oxford again, you would have to begin by unbuilding it, and that though destruction might be relatively easy, even that could not be accomplished in a day. This means that the union training brought a sense of proportion and the gift of patience.

"And yet, (new ideas) did their work in time, like seed which travels on the wind and plants itself. ...

"These changes may be good or bad; the union mind sees in them subjects for ever-fresh developments; for the great thing is to keep consideration open. The wisdom of gradual change has been proved specially applicable to Oxford. There have been no violent revolutions. ... The policy of open discussion has been vindicated."

— H.A. Morrah. The Oxford Union, 1823-1923, 1923.

"

THE WISDOM OF GRADUAL
CHANGE HAS BEEN
PROVED SPECIALLY
APPLICABLE TO OXFORD.
THERE HAVE BEEN NO
VIOLENT REVOLUTIONS. ...

THE POLICY OF OPEN DISCUSSION HAS BEEN VINDICATED.

"

TURN OF THE
20th Century

With the first U.S. unions at Harvard and Pennsylvania, there is a shift to the club concept. The unions serve as a common meeting ground, offering comradeship. The pervasive influence of Hart House shapes ideas about education and the course of the union's development.

Students at Victoria College, University of Toronto, in 1911.

Metamorphosis at Oxford

"Of late years the university has begun to feel its unity more strongly, and in social and intellectual life, as in athletics, it has become the first time since the Middles Ages an organic whole.

"The first formal organization of the life of the university was, as its name records, the Oxford Union, an institution of peculiar interest to Americans because our universities, though starting from a point diametrically opposite, have arrived at a state of social disorganization no less pronounced than that which the union was intended to remedy. Harvard, which has progressed farthest along the path of social expansion and disintegration, has already made a conscious effort to imitate the union. ...

"The Oxford Union was founded in 1823 and was primarily for debating. ... Its members were carefully selected for their ability in discoursing on the questions of the day. In its debates Gladstone, Lord Rosebery, the Marquis of Salisbury, and countless other English statesmen of recent times got their first parliamentary training. Its present fame in England is largely based upon this fact, but its character has been metamorphosed.

"Early in its history, it developed social features; and though it was still exclusive in membership, little by little men of all kinds were taken in. At this stage of its development, the union was not unlike those vast political clubs in London in which any and all principles are subordinated to the kitchen and the wine cellar. The debates, though still of first-rate quality, became more and more an incident; the club was chiefly remarkable as the epitome of all the best elements of Oxford life. The library was filled with men reading or working at special hobbies; the reading and smoking rooms were crowded; the lawn was daily thronged with undergraduates gossiping over a cup of tea; the telegram board, the shrine of embryo politicians watching for the results from a general election, was apt to be profaned by sporting men scanning it for the winners of the Derby or the Ascot.

"In a word, the union held the elect of Oxford, intellectual, social, and sporting. This is the union remembered by the older graduates, and except for a single feature, namely, that it was still exclusive, this is the union that has inspired the projectors of the Harvard Union."

— John Corbin. An American at Oxford, 1902.

For Harvard— "A Comprehensive Club," "A Large General Society"

"From a Harvard circular, dated Nov. 26, 1895, we note an invitation to an informal meeting at the University Club of Boston ... to discuss 'the project of organizing at Harvard a large and comprehensive club, which shall do for Harvard what the unions of Oxford and Cambridge have done for these universities.' ... At the meeting, a committee was appointed to consider the plan for a union. The committee reported in favor, stressing the experiences at Oxford and Cambridge 'where social organization has adapted itself to a more gradual increase in numbers, proves completely the feasibility of such an institution.'"

— Edith Ouzts Humphreys. College Unions, 1946.

"The revival of the name 'Harvard Union' in 1880 was accidental and related even to the Oxford Union more than to the Society of 1830–40. ... Col. Higginson in his address March 2, 1897, referred to his visit to Oxford which suggested the founding of a Harvard Union in 1880. ...

"We chose the name union in the hope that out of the Debating Society a large general society, like the unions at Cambridge and Oxford, would grow."

— From the Report of the Historical Committee of the Harvard Union, 1897.

"Excellent as are the existing clubs, they do not furnish the required field. ... Hence the need to you of this house for meeting each other, for meeting your teachers ... and for meeting the older graduates. ... Perhaps you may establish here, as at Oxford, an arena where you can thresh out the questions of the day. ... Let this house stand a temple consecrated ... to friendship."

— Maj. Henry L. Higginson, donor of the Harvard Union Building. From his address dedicating the union, 1901.

"Its (the Harvard Union's) object shall be to promote comradeship among members of Harvard University, by providing at Cambridge a suitable club house for social purposes."

— Constitution of the Harvard Union, 1901.

74. HOUSTON HALL, UNIVERSITY OF PENNA., PHILADELPHIA, PA.   81873

Houston Hall at the University of Pennsylvania, the first college union in the United States. UNIVERSITY OF PENNSYLVANIA

Houston Hall— "Where All May Meet on Common Ground"

"The purpose of Houston Hall is to provide for all the students of the various departments a place where all may meet on common ground; and to furnish them with every available facility for passing their leisure hours in harmless recreation and amusement."

— Catalogue of the University of Pennsylvania, 1896.

"The object of this club shall be to draw together students, officers, and alumni of all departments of the university in a wholesome social life, and to provide for them suitable amusements and recreations."

— Constitution of the Houston Club, 1898.

Emphasis on Recreation, Student Involvement in Governance

"When completed, it (Houston Hall) proved to be the most beautiful and artistic building in the university, with every appointment of good taste and convenience and suited to a very great variety of student uses. It contains a swimming pool and baths, gymnasium, bowling alleys, billiard, pool and chess tables, lunch counters and facilities for more extensive repasts, reading and writing rooms, an auditorium and smaller rooms for religious services, and a large number of separate rooms for the use of committees, the Athletic Association, the Young Men's Christian Association, for the college papers, for the musical clubs, and a dark room for photographic purposes."

— Edward P. Cheyney. Universities and Their Sons, 1901.

"Historically, it is interesting, rather surprising, to find that from the very beginning (in creating Houston Hall) a concept of student government was injected, the facility pattern of the college union of today established, and the environmental influences of the union on the life of students recognized."

— Edith Ouzts Humphreys. College Unions, 1946.

The Ideas about Education that Nurtured the Union

"American colleges at the turn of the century saw in the British unions an element needed in American education.

"President Charles Van Hise of Wisconsin, in what turned out to be an epoch-making inaugural address in 1904, was one of the first to advance the British idea in this country. He said:

"'If one were to name the most fundamental characteristic of these English institutions (Oxford and Cambridge), it would be the system of halls of residence, commons, unions, and athletic fields. The communal life of instructors and students in work, in play, and in social relations is the very essence of the spirit of Oxford and Cambridge. It might almost be said that this constitutes Oxford and Cambridge. ...

"'If the University of Wisconsin is to do for the sons of the state what Oxford and Cambridge are doing for the sons of England, not only in producing scholars but in making men, it must once more have a commons and union. For when a student goes out into the world, no other part of his education is of such fundamental importance as capacity to deal with men. Nothing that the professor or laboratory can do for the student can take the place of daily close companionship with hundreds of his fellows.'

"Then came President Woodrow Wilson of Princeton, propounding in his famous Phi Beta Kappa address of 1909 a similar idea—a proposition that largely reshaped the course of educational emphasis at Princeton and at many other institutions:

"'The chief and characteristic mistake which the teachers and governors of our colleges have made in these latter days has been that they have devoted themselves and their plans too exclusively to the business, the very common-place business, of instruction, and have not enough regarded the life of the mind. The mind does not live by instruction. The real intellectual life of a body of undergraduates, if there be any, manifests itself, not in the classroom, but in what they do and talk of and set before themselves as their favorite objects between classes and lectures. ...

"'Contact, companionship, familiar intercourse is the law of life for the mind. ... So long as instruction and life do not merge in our colleges, so long as what the undergraduates do and what they are taught occupy two separate, air-tight compartments in their consciousness, so long will the college be ineffectual. ...

"'If you wish to create a college, therefore, and are wise, you will seek to create a life ... and fill it with the things of the mind and of the spirit. ...

"'My plea, then, is this: that we now deliberately set ourselves to make a home for the spirit of learning; that we reorganize our colleges on the lines of this simple conception, that a college is not only a body of studies but a mode of association; that its courses are only its formal side, its contacts and contagions, its realities. It must become a community of scholars and pupils.'

"Note how this conception spread. This from an address by President Lovett at the dedication of Rice Institute (Houston) in 1912:

"'It was at Princeton that President Wilson proposed the reorganization of the social life of that ancient seat of learning. The program there suggested was an adaptation of the English residential college to American undergraduate life. ...

"'It is hoped that ultimately all students (at Rice) will be housed in halls of residence ... in a great quadrangle whose main axis terminates at one end by a great gymnasium and at the other by a great union club. ... The union will offer many opportunities to members of all colleges ... the liveliest sort of rivalry in musical, literary, and debating activities. To those students who for one reason or another are obliged to live in the city, the union will afford many of the opportunities of the residential hall. ... Side by side with the building of these collegiate homes for human living.'

"And most educators know of the much quoted pronouncement by Stephen Leacock, McGill University, of the same era:

'As a college teacher, I have long since realized that the most that the teacher, as such, can do for the student is a very limited matter. The real thing for the student is the life and environment that surround him. All that he really learns, in a sense, he learns by the active operation of his own intellect and not as the passive recipient of lectures. And for

The early home of the Wisconsin Union. UNIVERSITY OF WISCONSIN-MADISON ARCHIVES

"

NOTHING THAT THE PROFESSOR OR LABORATORY CAN DO FOR THE STUDENT CAN TAKE THE PLACE OF DAILY CLOSE COMPANIONSHIP WITH HUNDREDS OF HIS FELLOWS.

"

this active operation what he needs most is the continued and intimate contact with his fellows.

"'Students must live together and eat together, talk and smoke together. Experience shows that this is how their minds really grow. ... If a student is to get from his college what it should give him, a life in common with other students is his absolute right. ... A college that fails to give it to him is cheating him.'

"It was into this climate of ideas about what constitutes an education that the union came in America. I think you can see why the union became what it did, and, in large measure, still is—a place for students to get together and talk among themselves, a place for comradeship."

— "Goals of the College Union." Union Summer Course, University of Wisconsin, 1962.

The Student Instinct: A Central Place for Social Association

"It cannot be doubted by any person who is at all acquainted with campus life in a great university, that there are serious problems confronting faculty and student agencies in their attempts to induce leavening and fusing influences into the complex social organism of the student body.

"Moreover, one who knows conditions at the University of Wisconsin is well aware of the fact that while the Wisconsin Union has for several years successfully carried out a number of social functions, ... the facilities for some forms of social ministration are so limited as to negate any attempts.

"There is no central meeting place for the men; there is no large dining-hall or commons; there is no auditorium large enough for convocation or mass-meeting purposes; there are not sufficient meeting rooms for the many student organizations; there is not an available stage and theater for the production of the amateur dramatic productions.

"Certainly, from the standpoint of the undergraduate body, there is no other need so urgent as that for a union building, which will combine in one place the facilities at present so entirely lacking."

— Crawford Wheeler. Report of the President of the Wisconsin Union, 1915-16.

"The prime objective of the early American union was (more) like that of the union at the University of Glasgow. ... As the late Professor R.M. Wenley, of the Universities of Glasgow and Michigan and founder of the Glasgow Union, once pointed out, the order of importance in the Oxford and other English Unions was (1) debating, (2) affiliation of societies, and (3) a club. At Glasgow, a nonresidential university, the order was (1) a club (with dining commons), (2) affiliation of societies, and (3) debating."

— Edith Ouzts Humphreys. College Unions, 1946.

"Unions followed, as men's clubs, at Brown, Michigan, Wisconsin, Minnesota, Ohio State, Illinois, Indiana, Case, and Toronto, in about that order. The debate activity tapered off; greater provisions were made for games, for meetings, and for food. The American union took on more the aspect of a social center, a place to meet friends, and a place to eat. For a time—the first quarter of the century—this seemed to be a good idea only for men. Again, the British influence, no doubt."

— "Goals of the College Union." Union Summer Course, University of Wisconsin, 1962.

Hart House— A Unifying Force by Way of a Common Life and Fellowship

"The bricks and mortar are but the bones; the community of Hart House must provide the spirit. ...

"It is perhaps not incorrect to say that the House as it now stands is intended to represent the sum of those activities of the student which lie outside the curriculum. These activities are not unimportant; indeed, I would submit, Sir, that the truest education requires that the discipline of the classroom should be generously supplemented by the enjoyment, in the fullest measure, of a common life. A common life, of course, presupposes common ground. ... Even if Toronto were to accomplish a completely developed residential system, there would still be the need, indeed the greater need, for the unifying force which it is one purpose of this House to introduce into the university. ...

"Let us hope that not only will the House serve the interests of the active members of the university, teachers as well as undergraduates, but that it may help to bridge the gulf of time and space which too often separates the graduate from his university. Here will be a place where the present and the past generations may meet, and here, let us hope, may be fostered the lasting loyalty and the esprit de corps which are essential to the welfare of any seat of learning."

— Vincent Massey, Oxford graduate and ultimately governor general of Canada. From his address at the formal opening of Hart House, University of Toronto, 1919.

"Very much has happened with respect to unions, of course, since those early years. ... Growth in numbers is not all. There also has been growth of an idea.

"Where unions prior to the 1920s had been student-only unions, devoted, as in the United Kingdom, primarily to debate and refreshments at the union bar, or concerned, as in the United States, largely with social life and dining, they have become social-cultural centers embracing the interests of the total university community of students, faculty, and graduates. And for this Hart House has largely been responsible.

"At a crucial juncture this House showed what a union might be. It became a mecca for all of us in the States who were considering union buildings. Its facility provisions, in kind and scope, went far beyond anything seen before. Its emphasis on the arts opened our eyes to the ways of lifting the quality of student life. The eloquent Prayer of the Founders that the House might draw the teacher and student, the graduate and undergraduate into a 'common fellowship,' a 'true society,' inspired the concept of a union as a 'unifying force' in the life of the university—a concept which has been carried into the statement of fundamental union purpose adopted by our Association, investing the name 'union' with a deeper, more universal meaning than was ever imagined when the English student debating societies chose the union name a century earlier. ...

"By way of this happy amalgam of unparalleled facilities, the strength of an important idea, and the superlative leadership of the staff, Hart House, unquestionably, has shaped the course of the union development, on this continent and abroad, more than any other single union.

"And it stands for us today as the kind of civilizing influence unions everywhere ought to be."

— Mr. Butts. From his address at the University of Toronto on the occasion of the 50th anniversary of the formal opening of Hart House, 1969.

This 1902 poster for Columbia University features an undergraduate surrounded by pictures, beer steins, tobacco pipes, and a pennant. ILLUSTRATION BY JOHN E. SHERIDAN

THE

1920s

Following World War I, the ideals of the 1920s include a fuller life through fellowship, through service to the university, and through arts identification. The educational significance of purposeful leisure activity is better understood, and the "club" becomes a self-governed community center for all.

As in this 1921 photo, students typically led the fundraising efforts for college union facilities projects.

AT WAR'S END:
CONCERN FOR CAMPUS DEMOCRACY AND UNITY, STUDENT MORALE, AND A "LIVING MEMORIAL" TO SERVICE

"Along in the 1920s, when women's suffrage appeared and the ancient tradition of education for men only began to dissolve, students saw that it was odd for men and women to eye each other across the campus from their respective strongholds, when they really wanted to be together; so unions turned into social centers for everybody, and have, with few exceptions, been thoroughly coeducational ever since. The idea of campus unity, of a union for all, became an even stronger motivating force.

"At this juncture, in the '20s, two circumstances came together to launch the massive union development we have seen in the last 30 years. There was a great post-war upsurge in enrollment then, as after the second war, and as now. Students were forced into rooming house hovels and a fairly grim social existence. It was hard to find a place to eat. Colleges had seen what the war canteen and recreation centers had meant to the servicemen away from home. A counterpart on the campus—a union—now loomed importantly as an answer to the many problems of life on the campus.

"And the answer to the problem of how to get a building also came out of the war. What better type of living memorial to honor those who served in the war? What better way to serve the cause of democracy they served than to create a new campus democracy? The memorial theme was joined to the felt need, and this fund appeal coming in a time of prosperity gave a sudden and successful impetus to the slow-maturing union movement on a wide front."

— "Goals of the College Union." Union Summer Course, University of Wisconsin, 1962.

Duke University's West Campus Student Union. RICHARDSON'S PHOTO SERVICES

Students toboggan in a "moment of glorious play" in 1929. UNIVERSITY OF WISCONSIN-MADISON ARCHIVES

A Finer Kind of Student Life

"So inseparably linked is the new union with the future of the university, that a campaign for the Memorial Union is, properly speaking, a campaign for the university—to make the lives of those who come to her vital and vigorous. ...

"The union is not a building. There will be vital parts of the organization which can never be seen with the eye nor laid out in floor plans. The union in its fine building will become the community center for Wisconsin men, fostering and developing the best traditions and ideals.

"Because it will possess the equipment and facilities, it will take the leadership in the development of a finer and more patriotic type of student life. It will draw all men students to it by virtue of its ability to serve all their needs, and by bringing them together it will increase opportunities for the making of friendships between widely different types of men."

— John Dollard, secretary of the University of Wisconsin Memorial Union Committee. Wisconsin Union Annual Report, 1922–23.

The Author's First Perception of a Union, as a Student

"President Van Hise first suggested 'facilities for communal life' for the men of the university in his first biennial report to the legislature almost 20 years ago. ... He meant a place where friendships, the glory of college days, could be formed—where senior and freshman could sit in the same great circle around a fireplace. ...

"He planned a place where student leadership would be vigorous and concerted student opinion could be given voice and brought to bear on issues ... where Wisconsin students can take in their own hands and as their responsibility the future of the university and make of it a growing, glowing thing."

— Student editor Butts. An editorial in the University of Wisconsin student newspaper, 1923.

"Best of all you are sure to find the meaning of Wisconsin in your free and natural activity in association with other Wisconsin men and women—in the moments of glorious play—at times when you are working for her unselfishly, and giving yourself without hope of gain. ...

"The union, then, is a fellowship. It stands for the very highest things that belong to the realm of friends—mutual service, ideals, hard work, pure fun, life inspiration. It is intended to be the means of bringing all the men in the university together in order that they may cooperate in every way that is to their special advantage. ... It is self-service of the most unselfish nature, for every man who takes part is working primarily for the enjoyment of others. ...

"For the most part the union is and always will be an ideal, necessarily falling short of absolute realization, but always striving toward the goal of being of greater service to the university and the student body."

— John Dollard and Porter Butts. "A Message to You from Wisconsin Men." A booklet sent to all incoming University of Wisconsin men by the Union Board, 1924.

Full Living, Inducing Full Learning

"The Memorial Union has always meant to me a good deal more than a building project. It has been, together with the dormitories and an all-inclusive physical education program, the embodiment of a fundamental idea in education—the idea that only full living induces full learning, and that full living comes only where and when there is the opportunity for comfortable living, cordial and frequent human give and take, complete self-expression, and a certain feeling of unity of purpose and action with one's neighbors and friends."

— A statement in the Wisconsin Alumnus, following appointment as a secretary of the Memorial Union Building Committee, 1926.

"To remove social distinctions, to provide the congenial living which is necessary to easy and productive mental activity, to give the opportunity for full self-expression and the realization of one's self as a social being living in a community with other social beings and working towards a common goal, the university is building dormitories and the alumni and students are building the Memorial Union. This for the social health of students, a necessary complement of physical and intellectual well-being."

— An address to the University of Wisconsin. Chicago Alumni Club, 1927.

TOWARD A STATEMENT OF PURPOSE

1 THE UNION WILL EXIST TO MAKE WISCONSIN A MORE HUMAN PLACE.

"A community building like the union is the result of a desire that is reaching universal proportions—a desire to enrich the barren hours outside the classroom, to bring human relations in education into their proper place of importance and usefulness, to restore personality to the university.

"Every university which has experienced the pains of size realizes the need for the restoration of education to its former personal basis, for the elementary physical facilities where the contagion and compulsion of a common purpose may be felt—to the profit of the intellectual and spiritual life of the university. ...

2 THE UNION IS THE RECOGNITION OF THE IMPORTANCE OF THE LEISURE HOUR.

"It is a place to meet, to eat, to talk, to work, and to play—under friendly conditions.

"It provides the facilities for creative work not afforded by the ordinary college plant: student activity rooms, the theater, sketch rooms, debate halls.

"It provides the facilities for productive play: good books to read, good music to hear, good pictures to see, good games to play.

"It provides a natural and informal meeting place for faculty and students, where the student may be initiated into the fine art of consequential and inconsequential conversation, where the appetite for the independent search of knowledge may be stimulated, and where the teacher may learn what a student really thinks about."

— "What a Union Is For." A Wisconsin Union fundraising booklet, 1927.

The Union as a Unifying Force and Center for the Arts—Further Inspiration from Hart House

"Here then, is an instrument of no ordinary kind, sensitive and delicate to handle as all fine instruments are but capable of creating new forces in this university. What are these forces? I believe they are two.

"1. In the first place this house will become a great unifying force in the university. In these days when vast numbers of students throng our universities, it becomes increasingly difficult for the individual to realize he is part of a great academic brotherhood, bound together by common traditions and common ideals. ... This house will provide a meeting place, a rallying point for the undergraduates, faculty, and alumni, affording an opportunity for that common life which is one of the outstanding characteristics of the colleges of Oxford. It will bring into touch with one another men of different schools in the university, men of different ages, and men of different interests.

"There is one point which should not be lost sight of. If this house is in actual fact to become a meeting place, it is clear that it must attract. And it will only attract if there is a proper and reasonable provision for the material comforts of its members. Efficient management, a sane government, a spirit of good cheer, of warmth, of life—these things are necessary if the students of this university are to be found within the walls of this house. Good cooking and comfortable chairs are fine incentives to congenial intercourse.

"2. The second force which this house will create is a spiritual force. ... After all a university is preeminently 'a center of taste and beauty, concerning itself with all the large and enduring things of life.' If this house comes to be looked upon merely as a convenient place for eating and smoking and games, then it can never rise above the merely commonplace. Indeed it will sink to the level of a mere club and nothing more. A great foundation such as is being dedicated this evening should cherish ... a far greater ideal than this. From the first it must aim to widen the interests of its members and to form their tastes.

"A house devoted to student life, if it is to justify its existence, must stand preeminently for the cultivation of the arts, for the encouragement of the undergraduate's interest in public affairs through the medium of speakers and of debates ... for the introduction of a certain old world dignity and courtesy into daily intercourse, and for the formation of lasting friendships."

— J. Burgon Bickersteth, University of Toronto Hart House warden. From his address dedicating The Wisconsin Union, 1928.

The Importance of Leisure Hours

"We all know how lonely a person is likely to be at first when he goes to a strange town among strange people—how empty the hours are, after the day's work is over. The student who goes away to the university also experiences a lack of friends, a certain loneliness. ...

"It is with all these hours outside the classroom that the union proposes to deal. These hours of leisure are important; they can be used productively or they can be wasted. The union proposes to make them as valuable to the student as possible. It proposes to make the university a more human and personal and friendly place; it hopes to become a kind of living room for students and faculty, where friends are easily made and where each student's experience can be richer. ...

"We look on the union as one of the valuable educational workshops of the university—a laboratory for the close study of all our complex social relationships—the equipment for experimentation in the very slightly cultivated field of the students' leisure hours. Here on the campus we believe that the university's educational function does not end with classroom hours. We earnestly hope that the university, through the union and its informal kind of education, may add, in a natural but comprehensive way, a few more productive hours each week to the cultural interests of each student. If this can be done, it will be called a great achievement in education. ...

"A letter written by a student and published in the campus newspaper this year indicates perhaps more clearly than anything else what changes are taking place in student life because the union is here. The letter reads: 'For the span of one year, a narrow room was the extent of my domain in Madison, and now with the union here, the Rathskeller, a place to read and to write, I feel as though Madison has grown larger, more free. Wisconsin's campus for me has suddenly become more spacious, and my life here is richer than it was before. For me it is something of a home, something of a club—which symbolizes that life may be made better than it now is.'"

— From an address over the University of Wisconsin radio station, 1929.

"The most interesting thing about unions to all of us is not the physical plants themselves, of course, but what the plants were built to do, and what they are doing. ...

"In our own articles of organization we have stated, as articles usually do, a purpose, which is: 'To provide a common life and a cultivated social program for the members of the Wisconsin Union (students, faculty, and alumni).'

"It may be put another way. We find coming into the university picture in America now, a university department which is set up expressly to deal intelligently with all the student's hours outside the classroom. I think it is somewhat startling, when you analyze it in its bare terms, that universities too long have undertaken education only through the medium of classroom hours; and that it was not until the beginning of the 20th century that they turned to some means of assisting in the student's education outside the classroom.

"There is a Hindu mark of respect for the man who is a scholar and a gentleman. Neither qualification alone is sufficient.

"This ancient standard of appraising the worth of a man perhaps points to the case I am making, namely, that our universities have been dealing with scholarly matters perhaps too much. But they are now turning to the other half of the picture, the cultured social side of our life, and are seeking a means, through the union, as a kind of foster home, to teach naturally and effectively—by example, by fellowship, by subtle standards, and by an active social program—as does the student's own home."

— Opening address, 10th Annual Conference of the Association of College Unions, 1929.

In 1929—Four Basic Objectives

"1. The union exists to make the large university a more human place. Or, in the words of our President Glenn Frank, 'The union is a living room, which converts the university from a house of learning into a home of learning.' Every university which experiences the pains of growing size realizes the need for the restoration of the personal relations that once graced and fructified education, and for the elementary physical facilities, such as are in a union, where daily the contagion of a common intellectual purpose may be felt.

"2. The union can provide, in addition to the physical facilities where personal relations among students and teachers may naturally find expression, a comprehensive and well-considered program for the a social life of the university. The Faculty Committee on Curriculum, in its recent report, said: 'It is apparent from the purpose and the history of the American college that the curriculum is but one of the problems essentially involved. For a complete adjustment to changed conditions there would be necessary a program for the social life of the college.' ...

"3. The union stands as the university's recognition of the importance of the leisure hour.

"The union makes a signal contribution to the scope and objectives of the educational approach. Through a union of students, in a building devoted to recreation and an informal cultural and social life, the university can undertake to deal helpfully with all the hours outside the classroom ... a time-area most important in every student's development, but hitherto virtually neglected. ... Now the students themselves, with the university's approval and help, propose to create—first, the physical facilities for enjoying leisure time, and second, a social and cultural program—with benefit of intelligent faculty and student guidance—aimed to make leisure as satisfactory and as productive as possible. A student should find in the union ... in its concerts, art exhibitions, library, and discussion groups ... the opportunities to manifest, take pleasure in, and make a matter of habit the cultural interests which the university painstakingly sets out to develop in the classroom.

"4. The union is a genuine student cooperative enterprise, aiming to give students experience in managing their own affairs and the opportunity of reducing their living costs."

— "The Four Objectives of the Union." The Wisconsin Union Director's Annual Report, 1929-30.

Students gather around a bonfire in 1923. UNIVERSITY ARCHIVES, UNIVERSITY OF TOLEDO

Modus Operandi: Student Self-Government with Staff Aid

"In proceeding toward these general union objectives we travel by way of the student self-examination and self-government route. There is always a lot of curious and optimistic talk about student self-government. We have tried to keep free from any illusions on the subject; we have two definite feelings about it: First of all, if there is to be student direction, there must be something to direct; often we have on our campuses—we did on our own—student government which governs nothing. Second, no sizable self-governing body operates successfully without a full-time administrative branch; we should not expect more of students. So, we look to the student to provide policies and purposes and inspiration, and responsiveness to student needs and to building needs; but we also provide a good many full-time staff members to see that what the student governors have asked for is carried through. They do a lot for themselves, of course; but in general the only sure safeguard of a system of self-government is to have a continuing group of officers who are acting in an administrative way for the governors, and, in the last analysis, are subject to their control."

— Opening address, 10th Annual Conference of the Association of College Unions, 1929.

A felt silk-screened souvenir pennant of Heidelberg University. WIKIMEDIA COMMONS

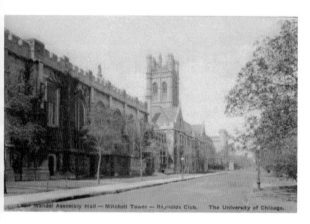

Above: A 1922 postcard features the University of Chicago's Reynolds Club.

COURTESY OF JOHN CHUCKMAN

Right: Plans for the East Wing of the Purdue Memorial Union, eventually added in 1936.

ACUI ARCHIVES

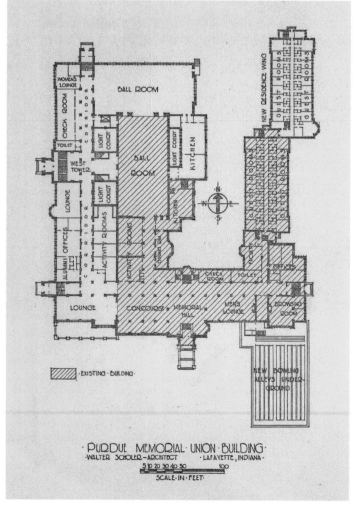

"

The Prayer of the Founders is that Hart House, under the guidance of its Warden, may serve in the generations to come the highest interests of this University by drawing into a common fellowship the members of the several Colleges and Faculties, and by gathering into a true society the teacher and the student, the graduate and the undergraduate; further, that the members of Hart House may discover within its walls the true education that is to be found in good fellowship, in friendly disputation and debate, in the conversation of wise and earnest men, in music, pictures and the play, in the casual book, in sports games and the mastery of the body; and lastly, that just as in the days of war this House was devoted to the training in arms of the young soldier, so, in the time of peace its halls may be dedicated to the task of arming youth with strength and suppleness of limb, with clarity of mind and depth of understanding, and with a spirit of true religion and high endeavor.

— Founders' Prayer, carved in stone at the entrance of the Hart House Great Hall, University of Toronto.

"

1930s

Unions search for enduring values and harmony with the purposes of education. While a communal life remains its goal, there becomes mounting interest in how leisure time is used. As the Great Depression intervenes, there becomes a socio-psychological basis of the need for the union as substitute for home and neighborhood. Following new attempts to decide what a union building is for before building it, the union emerges as a community center of the first order.

No cheating! Students at Hamline University take a final exam.

HAMLINE UNIVERSITY

45

RESTORATION OF COMMUNAL LIFE, OF AN IDEAL OF SERVICE— THE ORIGINAL APPEAL OF THE UNION

"One of the first effects of the phenomenal increase in the size of our universities was the disintegration of social and communal life on the campus. The college, once one of the most homogeneous and intimate of American communities, has threatened to become one of the least so. The social agencies which once seemed to humanize and enrich college life—the chapel, the debate society, the boarding house, the literary and music club, the informal and spontaneous gathering of teachers and students— confronted by a ten-fold increase in students, became inadequate or impossible.

"Wisconsin, in company with many other American colleges, saw that whatever the difficulties involved, the communal living which had grown naturally and spontaneously in the fledgling college ought not to be lost in its populous successor. That new agencies and facilities were necessary to its rehabilitation was obvious. ...

"The war delayed the project; but from the war eventually came a new and powerful impetus to the creation of a union.

"From the fusion of this old determination that the personality of the university need not be the price of its growth with the new desire for a memorial to service came, in 1919, the concrete beginnings of a union. ..."

The Members of the Union Determine Its Course

"How well such a house as this can be made to minister to the individual and to the common needs of so large and so diverse a group as is here will always depend, of course, upon its students and faculty members. To develop studios and workshops in which students interested in the arts may find a place to work and to play happily; to bring lively discussion into the daily experience of students; to discover the satisfactions of friendly books on the library shelves and good pictures on the walls; to color and enrich daily life on the campus with concerts and dances, games and tournaments; to so invest the house with things and with traditions that it may increase in pleasure and profit the extra-classroom hours of every man and woman who comes to Wisconsin—these are the purposes of the union and these are the tasks which can only be done by those who use it."

— "The Story of the Wisconsin Union." A souvenir pictorial booklet, 1930.

Challenges from Two Conference Speakers: How Inculcate the Wish to Serve? How Preserve Enduring Values?

"There is another thing wrong with the American college of today. If there is one thing the American people are sick and tired of, it is the self-seeking college graduate. ... The ordinary American graduate has agreed that he should work for the greatest good of the greatest number, but by the greatest number he too often means 'number one.' ... Most men go to college to make more money. I think we have about reached the point where we realize that isn't a valid reason for coming. ... The fact that a person wants to make more money is not a reason why the state (or donors to private colleges) should give him an education.

"Let us look at some of the older university charters. They all have some such phrase as occurs in the Yale charter: 'to train men for service to church and state,' not to train them to make more money. ...

"What has been lacking is a socialized attitude toward life. We in the colleges have done too little really to develop it. ...

"When you say 'my town,' you are a part of it; when you say 'my country,' you are a part of it. ... But you do not get that (feeling) out of the study of mathematics or even the study of philosophy. ...

"It is the purpose of the union to cultivate that socialized attitude toward life."

— Christian Gauss, dean of Princeton University. "The Need for a Union in the Social Life of the Campus." Opening address, 12th Annual Conference of the Association of College Unions, 1931.

"There are probably no persons (other than union directors) who purely by virtue of the office they hold are brought into closer personal relationship with the student body as a whole. And, insofar as that is true, we are fortunate, as there can be no more delightful and fascinating work than ours, and let me add none more exacting. Even in normal times 'youth loves to masquerade in mind and in body' and press for revolutionary changes. That is only natural and if it were not so, there would be something wrong.

"We are passing through a period of great perplexity: everywhere our national institutions are being questioned and there is a spirit of criticism and unrest. ... I would say that hardly a day goes by without our being called upon in some form or other to reconcile the old and the new, to strike a true balance between tradition and experiment. Therein lies, to my mind, the remarkable difficulty of our work. I believe there is no building in a university where this problem comes up in a more acute and practical form than in the building devoted to student life.

"This then is the problem as I see it today:

"We wish these great buildings for student life to be properly developed and wisely used. We wish them to be a meeting place—a center of friendship and personal relationships and good cheer. Without ostentation we wish them to stand for all that is distinguished in the finest things of life—for music, art, and wide reading, for an intelligent concern in public affairs, so that the interests which a man forms here may remain with him for all time as a possession of priceless value. ... And for the realization of these ideals we need on the one hand a true understanding of the priceless legacy of the past, and on the other sympathy, patience, and a genuine enthusiasm for the aspirations and ideas of the rising generation."

— J. Burgon Bickersteth, University of Toronto Hart House warden. Closing address, 12th Annual Conference of the Association of College Unions, 1931.

Impact of the Depression

"The most significant change this year is the increase of persons attending small gatherings for discussion and the decrease in attendance at dances and parties. Such trends reflect, we believe, a general tendency among students in these troubled times to meet and consult with each other and with faculty members on the problems of the day. Activity outside the classroom generally has taken on a more serious cast. Dances are no longer the only accepted form of social recreation; it is partly a matter of money, of course, but it is equally the case that students are finding other satisfactory, and perhaps more productive, means of social recreation: games, informal outdoor sports, discussions, music. ...

"The Union Council will do well to analyze month by month the social trends on the campus and elsewhere, keeping in mind, however, that its function is not only to observe and provide for social expression but, more important, to shape and lead social expression."

— The Wisconsin Union Director's Annual Report, 1931-32.

"Until 1932 the union, still very young, was busy working out the ideology of a university social center and experimenting with a program for the extra-classroom life of students. Money matters were in the background. Then came the impact of the Depression and the consequent shifting of energies away from the union's social and educational functions to economic functions and problems. This has not only arrested the normal course of the union's growth but has obscured its social purposes and educational character in the minds of observers both inside and outside the university. ...

"The essential character of the union as a student self-governing, cooperative, and educational enterprise, it seems evident, has not yet been sufficiently established, especially with some commercial interests, who have raised a cry of unfair competition. ...

"The dining rooms of the union are hardly commercial competitors in any sense, fair or unfair. The university is concerned with such departments only as they are incident and necessary to the larger goal of providing the elements of an educational home. Dining rooms are natural and necessary daily gathering places where the influ-ences of conversation and of group life work out most effectively. The dining table is universally the symbol and center of family social life; it has become equally the center of the college family life, binding students and faculty together socially and stimulating cultural growth through informal and personal association. The university wants to determine the conditions of its own family life the same as the home does; it has that responsibility to the people who send students here—and so it builds its house with a dining room in it."

— The Wisconsin Union Director's Report, 1933-34.

The New Leisure Gives the Union New Meaning

"There are other larger values in the union, which now, more than ever before, must not be obscured by immediate financial concerns; they are the educational and social values that reside in the ways that leisure time is trained for and used. The American drive for leisure and the growing use of machinery have insistently brought the problem of how to use spare time into the foreground of the modern scene, and now widespread unemployment has tremendously emphasized the problem. ...

"Wickham Steed, English author, recently wrote: 'Of this problem of the use of leisure, even the present crisis of unemployment gives only a foretaste. ... Hitherto education and training have gone to fit human beings for work. In the future they may have to fit them for creative, ennobling, and unselfish play. ... These things cannot be done by command. They should be done by the voluntary coordination of effort, under the stimulus of high ideals in truly democratic communities.'

"Mr. Steed has, in effect, stated the case for the college union. The union is an attempt in the education scheme to provide just what he describes—a voluntary and democratic community at play and learning how to play. Music, art, literature, discussion, social gatherings, crafts, games, and outings are the materials with which it works. In the union the university has taken the first bold step to equip its students to live satisfactorily a life that now holds for everyone an unprecedented large share of earned or enforced leisure."

— The Wisconsin Union Director's Report, 1932-33.

Northwestern University programming board students gather for a formal dinner. COURTESY OF ELIZABETH BELTRAMINI

"

STUDENTS
WANT OF
A UNION A
SECURE AND
LIBERAL
GROUP LIFE,
INGENIOUSLY
ARRANGED TO
SATISFY THEIR
REAL NEEDS.

"

A Social Psychologist's View of the Union's Significance

"We have seen, then, two factors emerging (for college students) as crucial ones—first, release from primary group control, and second, sexual maturation. Their joint operation results in a rather widespread degree of confusion and disorientation. (Naturally, also, uncertainty about the world after college which confronts our students now in an additional factor in unrest.) ...

"I suggest that not the mere size of our universities, not the loss of the old 'intimate' relationship between faculty and student, not the 'poor' teaching by young instructors, is the cause of student disinterest—but rather, and simply, they are not interested in study because it is so hard to sit still. ...

"Now here's where, in my opinion, you come in. You are trying, as I see it, to give an orderly frame to college life, to minister to the need for distraction productively, to allay insecurity by restoring a degree of group solidarity and to provide productive outlets for suddenly decanalized energies. ... You are doing what I think of as a piece of constructive social organization. ...

"I will make one more try at saying it. Students want of a union a secure and liberal group life, ingeniously arranged to satisfy their real needs."

— John Dollard, Yale University social psychologist. "What Students Want of a Union Building." Opening address, 13th Annual Conference of the Association of College Unions, 1932.

The Union as "Home"

"Recall with me that we all regard school and home as the two great educational influences. Recall also, that the college student is away from home. Then you see the place of the union. It aims to be the home pro tem, and to shape the neighborhood environment—which affects the student just as realistically in Madison as if he stayed home in Green Bay. And I draw your attention to the unique opportunity this circumstance gives to the college, not duplicated at any other school level—the opportunity of being both school and home at once, of affecting both working and nonworking hours of students. At Wisconsin we regard it as a precious opportunity; hence the union and its program. ...

"I sometimes think too much emphasis is placed on college as a preparation for life. We overlook that college also is life—four precious years of it. And so we aim to make it pleasant and productive. ...

"Should the university concern itself with such matters? If it is concerned that a student stay in school, if it is concerned that a student make a success of his college experience, then the answer is 'it should.'"

— "The Union and Its Place in the Educational Program." An address to the Association of Wisconsin Admissions Officers, 1934.

The Education Students Find in Their College Family Life

"And so today the union, as great house sheltering the social and cultural life of the college community, has changed the design of college living ...

"Of course, such a program costs money—much of the budget is spent on it directly or indirectly, much of the staff time is centered here. The question must naturally come: 'What of it? Just why is the money spent and the energies of students and staff used on such extracurricular things?' There are, I believe, three reasons."

Substitute for Family, Neighborhood at a Crucial Period

"The first is that it's fun—fun to work together, to work and play with other students and with faculty members on projects and hobbies of common interest. The university can do worse than make students happy in days when there's all too little of happiness. Or, if one seeks a deeper-going account of why the fun of social activity is a matter of importance, he may find it in fundamental sociological and psychological considerations of the following kind:

"The primary social group in America, family and neighborhood, protects and nurtures the child, shapes his beliefs and characteristics, and normally presents to him a world of security and ordered activity. ...

"Sent to the university, he finds himself pushed from a relatively secure existence into a new position in life, fraught with insecurities. He is on his own, but seldom does he have preparation in the family for being on his own. Uncertainties and anxieties present themselves. They are intensified by psychic and sexual strains. He engages in random activity, not finding any familiar field in which to express himself. It may be helpful activity, but as often it may not be. ...

"Such are the problems that the normal student brings with him to the university, and hence is there a sound need for a social center and extracurricular program which will substitute in this period of trial for the primary family group, provide a source of security, an outlet for useful activity. ...

"The findings of authorities in mental hygiene point powerfully to the fact that hobbies, social recreation, outdoor sports, music, and art activities provide two elements necessary to mental health: first, a sense of being of value to somebody, and second, a sense of being able to do some one thing well. And this problem of mental health isn't something apart from the college. Aside from the normal problems of the normal students mentioned above, 15 percent of college students, President Angell of Yale reports, suffer from decided mental difficulties—emotional and personality maladjustments which in their most aggravated form may find expression in suicide and which, at best, seriously diminish the benefits of his college experience."

Students, Like Their Elders, Don't Work All the Time

"If this first reason for the union program is important psychologically to the individual, the second is important to society. We've heard much of the new problem of leisure. It's both a new problem and an old one. People have always had many nonworking hours at their disposal; now they have, or will have, more, and so the problem, by degree, suddenly bulks larger and challenges attention. The point is: it makes a difference to society what people do when they're not working. It makes a difference in the delinquency courts, in the penal population, in risk or safety for the community. ...

"But the problem isn't only one of crime. How people spend their spare time makes a difference also in what the level of our culture is to be. A generation that has cultivated a taste for good books, that has sufficient training in music to listen with enjoyment or to play an instrument, that likes outdoor life, that has built up hobbies, that has early acquired skill in sports and games which can be enjoyed throughout adult years, that has developed ease and facility in social relationships in youth, will not drift into habits socially dangerous or culturally cheap. This is the view of Professor Jesse Steiner who wrote the studies of leisure for President Hoover's Committee on Social Trends. 'Our great danger,' he says, 'is that proper facilities for wholesome public recreation will be insufficient to meet the new strain that will be placed upon them.' He might have added that our leadership, too, may be inadequate.

"This is where the union, as the recreational laboratory of the university, has an obligation to society, the same as any other university laboratory. It proposes not only to teach its own students how to play as well as work, but to set standards and produce trained leaders who will be of service to other communities as they meet their problems of providing for leisure. ..."

"Saving Souls" at the Dinner Table

"The third reason why the union spends its energies on a long list of social and cultural ventures is an educational reason. ...

"The activities of the union are not sponsored merely to make the undergraduate years pleasurable and picturesque, nor even solely because they equip students for intelligent use of leisure. They engage the attention of the college because they are necessary complements of the classroom.

"A student cannot be educated in an academic vacuum; he must be cultivated as a person as well as in intellect. As President Conant of Harvard said, addressing his first class of freshmen, 'More souls are saved around the dinner table than through courses.' ...

"Quite aside from such opinions ... there is factual evidence that such social and activity interests, when wisely directed, actually improve the quality of academic work."

— "The University of Wisconsin as a HOME of learning."
University of Wisconsin Bulletin, 1934.

The University of Cincinnati's Tangeman University Center, as it looked in 1937. ACUI ARCHIVES

The Idea of a Liberal Education

"A world famous surgeon, one of Wisconsin's most distinguished alumni, sat talking with friends on the union terrace not so long ago. He had just received an honorary degree from the university.

"Turning to his friends, after watching students talking, reading, and dining, he said: 'This is my idea of a liberal education. If I were a student again, I'm sure I'd spend most of my time right here on this terrace, just talking.'

"Wisconsin believes its distinguished surgeon is right. There is an education in the everyday association of a student with his fellow students. ...

"Here daily life on the campus is enriched with concerts, forums and art exhibitions, traditions, and good fellowship. ...

"Here, indeed, are the makings of a better liberal education."

— "The Student and His Campus Neighbors." Wisconsin's University, 1935.

How Most Students Actually Spend Their Time

"Recently, Wisconsin had the opportunity of exploring with some thoroughness the broad area which embraces most of what we do not know about our college undergraduates' student life and activity outside the classroom. ...

"The study was predicated on the theory that the college which takes seriously its function as 'alma mater' and cares seriously to make recreational activity blend with classroom activity in furnishing a total, and perhaps better, education for its students needs to know in detail what the substitute for home and neighborhood environment on the campus is, what students do with their nonworking time, and how the one affects the other. The college has an extensive methodology for recording and appraising academic achievement, but it is not so well informed concerning its students outside the classroom, though it is often demonstrated that home environment and play life, at other school levels, shape personal habits, social attitudes, and even intellectual performance as importantly as does academic experience.

"Until comparatively recent times when colleges have undertaken dormitory housing and social center plans on a large scale, the college administration has registered its student and then followed the medieval tradition of turning him loose, fresh from a family protectorate, in the college town, hoping, if they thought about it at all, that everything would turn out all right and that the college standards of intellectual and social behavior would somehow continue to be a guiding star after the classroom bell rang. ...

"And so it was to the leisure sector of student behavior that this study turned, hoping to reveal by examining student daily endeavors how well classroom education was 'taking,' how serious students, as learners and practitioners of culture, really are. ...

"When students added up the hours they spent each week on leisure pursuits, it turned out to be, on average, about six hours a day.

"Most of this six hours a day goes into, and most students by far are occupied by, what writers on recreation sometimes classify as largely passive, sensory leisure: movies, radio, 'bull sessions,' dating, drinking, watching sports events, and just plain loafing. Motor activities, including outdoor exercise, competitive sports, dancing, and games take a middle place, and intellectual or cultural recreation is a poor third. ...

"No functional group of play occupations—and we have the student's own word that this is so—receives so much attention as the most aimless amusements of 29 forms of leisure which characterize college life. Together they occupy a third of the total leisure of all students. Sheer idleness, random conversation, and the radio rank second, third, and fourth in point of time consumed and each is common to more than 75 percent of the student population. ...

"All this is said not to discount or soften the applause given to the large if minority group of alert and thoughtful students who deserve it, nor to level blame on students for being like everyone else, nor in advocacy of eliminating pleasure in an era when downright fun has been at a premium, but simply to call to the center of the stage the average undergraduate and let him speak his piece, that his problems and his potentialities may receive their due share of our attention.

"It is little wonder that the college student performs in leisure not much differently from his lay brother. He has as yet, though the secondary schools are beginning to work consciously in leisure fields, no training for being on his own, recreationally. He misses almost all the implications of what informal, leisure-time recreation is or can be: hobbies, community service, exploring the countryside with fellow students, testing his own capacities for music, art, literature, the theater, and discussion. ... He actually has the time for purposive leisure, probably more than the high school student or the business man, but just because his total time when younger was so planned and ordered by his family and his school, he is at a loss when he comes to college and feels true freedom for leisure for the first time. He is not prepared for independence of action; and unless his group or some outside agency calls or persuades, he doesn't act. ...

"And most regrettable, but significant, of all, the college usually provides no scheme for leisure of its own nor encourages or trains students directly in the productive use of it. ...

"Some may say it's not the college's business to concern itself with other than academic performance. I would have the college consider its enormous and unique opportunity. At no other school level can the school authority so feasibly affect factors of home environment and student play life. The college has all these factors within its purview and within its possibility to affect. ...

"A start was taken by the regents at Wisconsin this year by designating the union as a Division of Social Education, to complement the Division of Physical Education in studying and ministering to the social and recreational welfare of the student body, authorizing it to counsel and instruct students in the professional aspects of planning recreation, and to utilize its facilities in conjunction with other departments as laboratories for practical experience in such fields as music, art, forensics, personnel work, journalism, social studies, and self-government. The union thus reinforces its program of external activity with research and teaching. I mention this because it indicates one possible place of usefulness for the union in campus recreational planning, and suggests that colleges can advance from a position of laissez-faire in matters affecting social health as they did a generation ago in the field of physical health."

— "How College Students Spend Their Time." Annual Conference of the Association of College Unions, 1935.

ONCE, THE FACULTY WORRIED THAT THE UNION INTERFERED WITH STUDY

"I have no doubt some think that heavy use of the union may be inimical to scholarship. Again our study of how and where students spend their time serves us by showing that this is not the case; on the contrary, quite the opposite. More than 700 students were covered in that survey, the sampling taking into account all classes and conditions of students. ... Scholarship rises, roughly speaking, with frequency of the use of the union, and the non-users of the union, both men and women, have the lowest scholastic averages of all. One may not say that using the union causes good scholarship; nor that good scholarship necessarily causes a student to use the union. What we can say for sure is that the one goes along with the other, whatever the causes, and that, in the main, one need not fear that the union will challenge or compete with scholastic performance.

"It is more likely, indeed, to broaden horizons and stimulate cultural interests that might not otherwise exist, demonstrated again by the survey, which shows that a substantially higher percentage of students among the frequent users of the union display more interest and participation in lectures, concerts, forums, plays, reading, and art exhibitions than the infrequent users."

— "Seven Years of Progress." Wisconsin Alumni Magazine, 1935.

Apathy in the '30s, Too

"The American college student has come in for such a flood of praise for his increasing seriousness since the darker days of the Depression fell upon him that we are in a fair way of having a new caricature of student life, as overdrawn for the middle '30s as it was for the '20s, when the typical student was presumed to be spending most of his time raising general extracurricular devil, and life on the campus was considered about as zippery as in a night club. What is the true picture? ...

"While students feel the demands of their studies as an omnipresent potential burden, they nevertheless devote as much or more time to leisure as the average adult in civil life, and this holds for the student who does some wage-earning work no less than for the nonworker. The total hours spent each week in leisure pursuits by the average student—42—almost equals the whole time he invests in study and classes, and is second only to the time given to sleep. ...

"He enrolls in courses in social sciences, but it never occurs to him to accept a responsibility in his own self-government or to attend a free symposium on the New Deal, a forum on modern dictators, or an argument on the political issues in his own state. He gives only an hour and a half a week at the most to the organized pursuits of the campus.

"Extracurricular activities, contrary to a common misapprehension, are neither extensive nor intensive enough to constitute a real threat to academic performance; the threat, if there is one, lies within the broader area of aimless amusements.

"When one comes to the more purely cultural interests, it is difficult to find a large enough time investment by the average student to score it at all. ...

"College leisure, altogether, reflects too much that of the lay public and the fashions of the hour instead of being a primal influence for the reorientation of community leisure habits. The classroom in four years adds to the student's information, but the pattern of intellectual and social conduct he brings with him from home remains essentially unchanged. ...

"Here, then, if as Harry Overstreet says leisure time may be the seeding ground for an American culture, is one of the prime challenges to the college: to bring its strategic role of alma mater, its admirable recreational facilities, and its trained leadership to bear more positively in producing students who are on speaking terms with culture and who are good citizens in their leisure hours as well as scholars in the classroom, and to make recreation support and enrich the processes of formal education."

— "Undergraduate: A Case Study." New York Times Magazine, 1936.

One Response of the Union

"A course of instruction is being evolved with the aid of national recreation associations and university departments, using the union itself as a demonstration center. Thus is the union beginning to join with the physical education departments in supplying the rapidly developing and keenly felt need for a university-trained leadership in the field of community center work and the guidance of leisure.

"Great impetus to this endeavor, and to the hopes also for effective recreational service on the campus, comes in the announcement this spring of the decision to complete the union building with a theater and concert hall."

Community Center of the First Order—Led by Students

"It becomes abundantly apparent, both here and elsewhere, that the days when the union was merely 'a place to meet' and a place to eat are long since gone. The union is now a community center of the first order. It is a library, art gallery, art workshop, theater, billiard room, dance center, sponsor of campus concerts and forums, informal sports headquarters, office building, public relations department, hotel, ticket bureau, general campus information booth, convention headquarters, book exchange, and post office.

"It is also, or hopes to become, a laboratory of student management and self-expression; caterer to the campus at large, housing the bulk of its meetings and serving its dinners; advisor to student organizations; troubleshooter in problems of student personnel; teacher of the arts of leisure and recreation. It concerns itself with the whole area of student life and interests outside the classroom, exploring all the possibilities of making study and play cooperative factors in education.

"Students of 1927 and 1917, who remember their solitary daily path from rooming house to classroom and back again, could tell you more—more, especially, of the poverty of campus life once upon a time.

"The course of change, naturally, has not always run smooth. Roses still come equipped with thorns. The tug and stress of contending forces are here in miniature that are everywhere.

"Especially is this so because the union touches vital economic interests of students. It deals with meals, the first ranking item in student expense, and with recreation, the fourth ranking item. ...

"Student government in such an institution is no theoretical vagary, no gallant gesture. Students have a chance to share in and cope with the pressing problems of the day; we have an instrument through which we can genuinely affect the economic welfare of the campus. The typical problems posed for industry and governmental agencies everywhere become ours: Shall wages to students be raised or shall prices to students be reduced? Can both be done? Shall benefits be arranged for some at the expense of others? Who shall pay the bills? They are not easy questions. But this is precisely one of the things that makes the union experience rich in value for students. Here, in the most realistic and challenging terms, is a training ground for good citizenship and self-government. To have such opportunity is a precious asset. ...

Students attend a formal dance in 1935. JOHN OXLEY LIBRARY, STATE LIBRARY OF QUEENSLAND

Students in their turn have two important responsibilities: one, to establish beyond doubt that freedom of action is accompanied by careful study of a total situation and by the genuine self-discipline of a university-trained mind; and second, to remember that economic problems and programs are not the only values to be reckoned with in our time, either in the campus social center or in government broadly.

"The Depression has left us with a heritage of surpassing concern over economic problems. But in a university, of all institutions, we need to guard and nurture also the values of spirit, intellect, and character, of constructive social and cultural gains for our community and the communities the university serves. We need have no misgivings concerning the student committees intimately associated in the union program. They have given excellent account of their stewardship. We have only to be sure that the fundamental educational purposes and values of the union are not obscured by financial issues in the minds of students less intimately associated.

"Financial issues are transitory. Friendships, social adjustment, the wish to serve the commonwealth, the sharpening of one's personal abilities in the give and take of group activity are of enduring importance. They determine the course of men's lives as largely as do books and degrees. ...

"I want to add the union's applause to the recognition given by the university to our leading students in union activity—for scholarship, for constructive service to the community, for intelligent and effective leadership.

"The union has a long and reassuring tradition in this respect. It is not uncommon for more than half the seniors of the Union Board to be members of Phi Beta Kappa; five of the 13 to receive the Kenneth Sterling Day Award for leadership have been members of the board; in 10 years it has contributed two Rhodes scholars; with regularity the board and committee members after graduation turn up as the leaders of alumni activity and civic enterprise—first-class examples of the first-class citizens a university aims to produce."

— The Wisconsin Union Director's Report, 1936–37.

A University of Connecticut world student relief fund drive.

Administratively, It's Not a One-Man Job

"Anyone who has watched the course of union development in the past 15 years is quite aware that the programs and functions of unions—even the physical plants in some cases—have expanded enormously. The union, perhaps more nearly than any campus agency, is becoming all things to all people. ...

"But there is no use holding the illusion that the union, as presently organized, is doing or can do all it's expected to do well. Every director knows why. Challenging as the new opportunities are, and good though our intentions may be, there simply are not enough hours of the day to go around. ...

"The answer becomes clear that if unions are to do what they want to do and if the directors are to lead reasonably normal lives, the building must be manned by a larger supervisory staff.

"There will have to be a realization of the fact that the union operates from seven in the morning until midnight every day of the week and almost every week of the year, that managing its business functions is a full-time job for one or more persons and that guiding its social and educational program is an equally full-time task for still others.

"Until there is genuine recognition by the university administration that this is so, any satisfactory achievement of a union's great expectations will have to wait."

— "One-Man Job?" Editorial in the The Bulletin of the Association of College Unions International, 1937.

"

UNTIL THERE IS GENUINE RECOGNITION BY THE UNIVERSITY ADMINISTRATION THAT THIS IS SO, ANY SATISFACTORY ACHIEVEMENT OF **A UNION'S GREAT EXPECTATIONS WILL HAVE TO WAIT.**

"

There Are Physical Means to Social-Cultural Ends

"In drawing the plans for the Wisconsin Union, the basic objective was to organize under one roof facilities which would make possible a community life for students and faculty members. Halls for the large group activities of the campus, and rooms for the day-to-day informal use of individuals, were indicated.

"The dining table, universally the symbol and center of family social life, was seen as the natural and necessary daily gathering place where the influences of conversation and of group life might work out most effectively. ...

"The living space of the building was so organized as to ... supply the elements of a congenial home life, which students cannot readily reconstruct on the campus for themselves: a place to meet with friends, newspapers from home, periodicals, radio, writing tables, afternoon coffee.

"Recognizing the value of well-used leisure in education, the university placed in immediate proximity to the informal living quarters of the house, where the stimulation to productive recreation would be felt daily, a small art gallery, reading room, a piano and a record player, and a library of classical music.

"In other parts of the house these more definitely cultural opportunities were extended by a craft workshop and photographic darkrooms. In addition, the ballroom and other social rooms of the house were so planned that they might be given over several times each week to large concerts, educational motion pictures, forums, and lectures.

"Nothing was considered foreign to the building's purposes that ministered in any helpful way to the hours spent outside the classroom. ...

"It seems clear that what is now most needed are the community values supplied by an auditorium where large groups of students can feel the inspiration of common thought proceeding from a speaker, and share in common the recreation and the cultural development provided by student-created or professionally presented drama, music, motion pictures, pageantry, and dance. ...

"The ultimate goal is to develop a community center with congenial accommodations for virtually every type of group activity, save athletic, that students may have the maximum opportunity for the profitable cultivation and leisure time and that the university may continue to be an authentic community of teachers and students."

— "A Union for a Large University." The American School and University Yearbook, 1938.

"The almost unanimous centering of student activity in one place has given to the union, perhaps more than to any other single university agency, the chance to recapture the important social and educational values of the intimate, informal relationships in the small college."

— "For a Finer Wisconsin." University of Wisconsin Bulletin, a union fundraising booklet, 1938.

"Next year, about this time, we move into a larger house. It will be a great adventure, a grand climax for our first 10 years. When we open the new rooms (of the theater wing), we open also new frontiers of activity in experimental stagecraft; in the special technique of radio drama; in the making as well as the showing of sound moving pictures; in the development of music as an everyday recreation through listening rooms, practice pianos, and formal concerts; in the development of photography, craft hobbies, and industrial design. ...

"This new building is a community center for the arts—one might rightly say for the arts of living."

— The Wisconsin Union Director's 10th Annual Report, 1937-38.

This new building is a community center for the arts

A Student Personnel Service, in a Sense

Postcard depicting Indiana University's Memorial Union bookstore. ACUI ARCHIVES

"Among the many personnel services that characterize the contemporary American college-faculty advising, deans of men and women, health science, guidance and testing bureaus, dormitories, employment services—the union is a comparative newcomer, appearing on most campuses after 1920.

"But the union idea is old, historically antedating almost every other personnel enterprise. The first unions appeared at Oxford and Cambridge in 1815 and early came to be known as the cradle of the British parliament. Undoubtedly they started and flourished all unconscious of their role as 'personnel' agencies. The word probably wasn't known. But they embraced the root idea which almost everyone considers the primary aim of personnel effort: the student's personal development through means other than curricular. ...

"As the baseline objectives of the Oxford and Cambridge Unions—student self-development and practice in real-life situations—have been elaborated and refined, unions have come to ask themselves such further questions as these:

"How can the widening area of leisure and social association be made an effective channel for a student's self-expression and self-realization?

"How can play be made a cooperative factor with study in education?

"How can the union be made valuable as a laboratory for social living as science laboratories are valuable for scientific discovery?

"How can the countless special interest groups of the campus be encouraged to contribute to the social whole?

"How can a student be provided example and practice in social relationships—consideration of others, the wish to serve the common good—so that he may live harmoniously with others?

"How can students be given ample opportunities to develop and exert leadership?

"These are exciting challenges. ...

"The union cannot operate with complete effectiveness isolated from the social life of the rest of the campus. The union may be a kind of hub, but the wheel won't go 'round unless there are spokes and a rim.

"When the union is able to concern itself with the total social life of the campus, both inside and outside of the union building, relating the one to the other, the service of the union to its college and student body will enter its ultimate phase."

— "The Union's Place in Personnel Work." The Bulletin of the Association of College Unions International, 1939.

—one might rightly say for the arts of living.

"

WHEN THE UNION IS ABLE TO CONCERN ITSELF WITH THE TOTAL SOCIAL LIFE OF THE CAMPUS, BOTH INSIDE AND OUTSIDE OF THE UNION BUILDING, RELATING THE ONE TO THE OTHER, THE SERVICE OF THE UNION TO ITS COLLEGE AND STUDENT BODY WILL ENTER ITS ULTIMATE PHASE.

"

March 31, 1938 groundbreaking ceremony for the University of Louisiana at Lafayette Student Union.

Above left: University of Idaho Student Union in 1934.

Above right: University of North Carolina Graham Memorial Union in 1936.

Right: University of Utah Union in 1931.

THE ▶

1940s

"Social education" becomes a developing concept of how the union fits into the academic experience. This is highlighted by a growing awareness of the significance of the arts and the prevailing concern of social issues and social responsibility. Experiments in informal and formal teaching promote good citizenship and students as partners. In the aftermath of the war, campuses seek to reappraise the purpose of education and the relevance of the union. Along with this comes more evidence of the value of community centers and first attempts to define the union and its mission.

Students walk outside the University of Texas at Austin Student Union Building

BY KARL GEBHARD

ANOTHER WAR— AND THE UNION SERVES MILITARY TRAINEES

"Out of World War I came the compelling evidence from military camps here and abroad of the need for recreation centers wherever large numbers of young people are gathered together away from home.

"One out of every four who ever attended the university subscribed voluntarily to Wisconsin's Memorial Union fund. ...

"Now, as military units are established on and near the campus, this same war memorial center is emerging in the new and singularly appropriate role of serving directly the young men of the military forces.

"Its rooms and its civilian employees are rendering post recreation and dining services equivalent to those the Army and Navy provide elsewhere themselves and staff with military personnel."

— The Wisconsin Union Director's Biennial Report, 1940–42.

New Thrust: Creating an Audience for the Artist

"'To have great poets there must be great audiences, too,' Walt Whitman said. ...

"An audience for art does not spring up over night in response to a call for art support, however spectacular. The process is slower than that. An audience needs to be cultivated with at least some of the painstaking care that we bestow on our artists.

"Who is to do the job? ...

"I do not believe that an audience sufficient for the arts to thrive can be created merely through the usual pattern of art history or appreciation courses. The number reached is too limited, the period of influence too short, and the approach too abstract for many people. ...

"Bringing into being an esthetically informed and art-minded audience calls for a special approach and special facilities. At the college level one potential aid that I think ought not to be overlooked is the campus social center. ...

"The union of its very nature is a center of artistic as well as social experience. As the scene of daily living for thousands of students, the building's architectural form, its decoration and furnishings, and its pictures have subtle and continuing influence on the standards of taste of its young users. It is, in this respect, whether you will it or not, an art center—for better or worse.

"Our first task, therefore, is to see that the architecture of a social center is honest, fitting to the purpose, creative rather than imitative, and hopefully, inspirational. ...

"The next proposition I offer in making the union an effective training ground for an art audience is: it should exhibit good works of art. It doesn't matter if it is already done by someone else. There is never too much, and there are many roads to salvation. Besides, a little competition would be a tonic, and a good thing.

"The social center is in a strategic situation to do the job rather better than anyone else. Art, if it is to have real vitality, must be identified with daily living—not the occasion for a rare and unwilling visit on Sunday afternoon to a silent, hollow classroom gallery or to a barred museum, to look over

A student at Xavier University works on a charcoal sketch.

the shoulder of a gloomy guard at the great but untouchable picture. The untouchable picture usually leaves the spectator untouched also.

"Where the museum imprisons art and makes it a curiosity to students, the union can bring it into the main stream of campus life. ... In the union, seeing art can be, and often is, as natural and normal a matter as seeing your friends or taking your meals. And I would remind a hesitant university administration that for every 10 who see an exhibition in a museum, a thousand will see it in the union.

"It isn't enough, of course, simply to hang an exhibition on the walls ... because then the union also runs the risk of giving students those tired museum feet and adding to general boredom. This is a disservice rather than a service to art and poor training of students for a long-time interest in pictures.

"Any art gallery, in the best sense, is a theater, for the dramatization, not of plays, but of pictures. The exhibition room, therefore, should be treated as a volume of space, instead of our fixed walls, and used flexibly in setting off the artist's work to the very best advantage, as a theater stage sets off and creates the mood for an author's play. We wouldn't think of presenting every play, regardless, in one standard square, drab stage set, or if we did we wouldn't imagine that the play or the audience's interest would be helped thereby.

"So it is with viewing pictures. The way we arrange the material, light it, develop new backgrounds (or scenery) for it, and label it to tell a dramatic story counts heavily. It can be done, without too great expense, by building portable wall units and arranging them anew each time.

"Instead of the spectator trudging around the perimeter of a four-sided room, wondering what to look at first, thinking he ought to hurry on to the next picture in the long row, and leaving remembering nothing of what he has seen, he now enters a small space where his attention is confined perhaps to a single picture or to a statement about an artist. ...

"The color of the backgrounds actually changes as he proceeds (it is easy to repaint wall units with casein colors); dramatic spotlighting picks out the centers of interest; a stage direction in large letters drives home two or three salient points. ... He experiences personally the story of an artist's work on an artistic idea. This will stay with him, and he will come again. ...

"As it proceeds this way, the college social center gives art a real place in the daily life of its students, increasing their taste and understanding if the work shown is really good, instead of perpetuating the notion of art as a refined luxury designed for the initiated, the museums, but not for us. ...

"The next proposition I have to offer is that the union should buy pictures. Nothing gives the artist such real encouragement as the purchase of his works. They are made, above all, to be owned, not just seen. And the social center, in purchasing itself, can set an example. ... It should encourage fraternities and dormitories also to offer purchase awards, for original work which will replace the chromos on their living room walls. It should set up a purchase fund in the union budget and forthrightly establish in student minds the principle that their union money, tax funds if you will, should be used for art purchases quite as legitimately as it is used for ping-pong tables or dances.

"But the works purchased shouldn't be stored in the attic or even kept on the same walls for years on end. The pictures on the walls should be rotated, changed frequently, so that the student has a new and fresh impression occasionally when he enters a familiar room—and more important, has his attention drawn to a picture that wasn't there before instead of simply accepting it, and ignoring it, like the old rug on the floor. The union can use its surplus pictures—and it should have a surplus—to form a rental collection available like books in the library for students to borrow, without charge, for the walls of their own rooms. After all, there's no art experience quite equal to living with a picture. And if it can be a good one, replaced at intervals by another, it will be an art education accomplishment of the first order.

"Finally, the union should provide the facilities for producing art. I refer particularly to the workshops which unions are rapidly adopting. This is another way of blowing the dust off art. If a student actually makes something, he is no longer afraid of it. The chances, rather, are that he becomes an enthusiast for it and its kind, and possibly, in proportion to his talent, even a creative contributor to the field. And this is what you want. ...

"An artistic environment; good exhibitions in the traffic center of the campus, dramatically presented and student-managed; purchases; and informal, readily available workshops—these are the contributions a college social center can make, and which the college would do well to encourage if, pursuing its cultural purpose, it is to play a part in furnishing a sensitive audience for the artist and the arts."

— "Creating an Audience for the Artist at College." Parnassus, 1941.

THE UNION AS A TEACHING RESOURCE

"The union is not just a service station for meetings and dining, nor does the provision of a recreation program for the campus end the story. These are important parts of its function to be sure, but the union plays a considerable role also as one of the teaching and laboratory resources of the university.

"There need be no barriers between instruction and the recreation program of a university if a good educational result can be obtained by joining them. ... The union building thus becomes at many points a vitalizing demonstration laboratory for the otherwise theoretical work of the classroom. ...

"A few examples (at Wisconsin): Sociology students do 15 hours of field work weekly at the union under the supervision of the union staff, and are thus afforded an opportunity to try themselves out in 'real life' problem situations. ...

"Women in physical education taking a camp leadership course are taught camp crafts in the union workshop by the union staff. Dance majors assist in teaching the union's social dancing classes.

"Hundreds of men meet their basic physical education requirement by learning bowling from the union staff.

"Students in stage design get their practical experience by building in the union stage shop. ...

"Students in art education discharge their practice teaching requirement by leading informal classes in the union workshop. ...

"More than 400 students serve on 17 union committees. Staff members serve as 'coaches,' preparing these 17 teams to do a year-round job of community program planning and administration in the fields of music, art, drama, films, reading, crafts, outings, public discussion, social gatherings, games. ...

"Eight hundred students enroll annually in the 'Friendship and Marriage' lecture course, a guidance venture organized and led by the union staff in collaboration with other departments.

"Appreciative of the fact that a student will do in his leisure what he can do well, the union has undertaken on a rather wide scale the teaching of recreational skills. The aim has been to give students satisfying leisure interests that have lifelong implications. Informal, short courses of instruction are regularly offered (either by union staff members or specialists engaged for the purpose). ...

"The hope is that the state will collect a dividend on this training program as well as students. Whether credit or noncredit, the union instruction program is designed to invest students with both the desire and the ability to serve their communities either as good volunteer citizen leaders or through a vocational career in community service. ...

"The test of success, of course, lies in whether or not anyone does find a place of usefulness by reason of such training.

"Enough evidence is at hand from students who have found a service vocation or a special volunteer leadership role in their communities as a direct outcome of their experience at the union to give reassurance that such training efforts do help guide students into public and social service careers. ... There are countless volunteer leaders who write us they are running community forums, organizing local art associations, serving as camp counselors, acting as War Chest chairmen, forming outing clubs, managing army recreation programs, serving as alumni club officers, or running for public office—usually commenting that their activity stemmed from interests developed at the union and often asking for further aids in carrying through their local programs. ...

"The union would not presume to say that all these abilities as leaders have derived only from the student's experience at the union, but it has, perhaps, done something by way of giving a final cutting edge to the foundation work of other departments. And in this way it is helping the university advance its prime objective of providing a future leadership for the community life of the state."

— "The Union as a Teaching Resource." The Bulletin of the Association of College Unions International, 1942.

In England, the Union Moves Beyond Debate, Building Administration— Toward Bringing about University Change

"By far the most powerful of all the organizations are the various student unions ... whose purpose is to represent the students, guard their interests, and promote the social and cultural life of the university. ... In the past, unions have mainly concerned themselves with administrative problems. In recent years, however, they have increasingly taken their place as the leading body of the students, actively taking up the interests of students, and concerning themselves far more with the wider problems of both the students and the universities ... such questions as university reform, the defense of the universities, and the maintenance of freedom of discussion. ...

"There are two ways in which students may effect changes in the universities: by expressing a point of view with a united voice, and attempting by negotiations, publicity, and other means to have it accepted by the authorities; by directing day-to-day activity into such progressive channels that they themselves increase the scope and effectiveness of the universities.

"In the latter sphere the ideal is a student community actively concerned with the social, political, and cultural issues of the time."

— Brian Simon, president of the English National Union of Students in 1939–40. A Student's View of the Universities, 1943.

The Developing Concept of Social Education

"The union for 10 years has been described by the university as its Division of Social Education. What does the term mean?

"It includes a concern for personal social competence. But it includes more ... the making of effective citizens. Good citizens are not made through the advancement of science or through the spread of literacy, still less by precept or by laboratory experiments. Citizens are made when men begin to feel a responsibility for the general welfare; when their interests include not vocational matters merely, or personal gains, but the destiny of the group to which they belong; and especially when their capacities include effectiveness among other men in making their influence felt. Citizens are made by the experience of citizenship.

"In short, then, social education means cultivating in students the desire and the ability to bring their personal talents to bear as social forces.

"All that we do is intended to conspire toward this end. The building and the program within the building give students the chance to try out and practice in their daily lives with other students what they learn in the classrooms. Much of the outcome is a matter of self-education. Much is done by way of informal education and example in the voluntary group associations between students and staff. Something is attempted also by way of formal education, especially for those students professionally interested in group leadership and community service.

"In the university, of all places, we see no barriers between a study of the good life and good citizenship and the practice of it. ...

"The union's role is to aid students in perfecting their practice and to sharpen a realization of how to work successfully with others and how to make a contribution to the common good.

"And now the union has been asked by the president of the university to join with other departments in seeing what can be done to enlarge the university's services to the cause of good citizenship in the state, in terms of planning an interdepartmental major in community leadership."

— The Wisconsin Union Director's Annual Report, 1944.

Students at Fullerton College in a performance of "Fly Away Home." FULLERTON COLLEGE LIBRARY ARCHIVES

Students as Partners

"It is students who have shaped the course of this enterprise. And they have been perceiving enough, throughout, to know that a student doesn't go on through life dealing only with persons his own age. They have themselves become adults and are ready to deal with other adults, retaining their independence when they differ and voting their sentiment into union policy, and not hesitating to agree when they do agree. In the long run it is this mutual sharing of experience and aspirations, this friendly give and take among the older and younger members of the community, that has made the union a thriving, exciting, and rewarding institution."

— The Wisconsin Union Director's Annual Report, 1944.

The Union as Community Center—Its Highest Value

"To talk about the union means talking about several kinds of things. The union probably couldn't be, even if it wanted to be, a specialized department with a single meaning, like, say, chemistry. This is because the union, at bottom, is just another name for the people of the university at leisure. Whatever interests them, whatever is important to them outside their working time becomes interesting and important also at the center of their campus life we call the union.

"So we have in the union, in effect, a microcosm of the university itself, changing and evolving, meaning different things to different groups, and with several roles to play. ...

"It may well be that the union has its highest value as a community center.

"The main task of the war, and the task in peace, in broadest terms is to achieve a better world in which men can live and work together peacefully and fruitfully. This achievement is an individual and a world task. But above all it is a community task. Only a community is both large enough and small enough to assert a pattern of fruitful living which influences deeply the individual citizen and to forge the common will to have the kind of a world we want.

"But so often in this century the community has been impotent to do these things because the community itself has been shattered. Mass production industry has built great populations but deprived the people of the communal and creative life which human beings need. The dispersive influence of the automobile, the telephone, and the radio all have hastened the disintegration of community life. People have been separated from responsibilities for the general welfare and left untouched by any community purpose.

"So, if a community is to play its part in the building of a better world, it must first of all be a true community. And as a starting point it needs to be sure there is a focus, a home, for its community life—in short, a community center. ..."

The Community Center Historically

"The community center is not a new idea, and its contributions to the good life are not theoretical. We need only to recall that it was on the acropolis of the Greek city that men discussed and matured their civic and ethical ideas; that the Roman forum was the vitalizing center of the Roman republic and later of a world empire; that in the church and its introductory square in the medieval town every person shared in the pageantry and neighborliness and spiritual dedication of the age; and that in the town meeting houses our early American villages found the focus of much of our own democratic community life.

"These were not necessarily governmental centers. It is especially instructive to us who are searching for the thing that serves the community purpose best that they were centers where people employed their leisure hours.

"Greek towns selected convenient sites outside the town for sports fields, later erecting theaters and gymnasia on the same sites. These buildings came to serve as meeting places, even as universities, the whole forming a social and cultural center.

"The Roman town was deliberately planned from the beginning to include a recreation center, with the forum and theater often placed at the center of the plan. In the medieval town all is centered on the church and its square. The church is the shrine and the theater. Sometimes, as at Salzburg, the church facade, indeed, forms the backdrop for open-air plays in the square.

The cornerstone of the original Boise State University Student Union was laid in November 1941, and the building opened in 1942. It was renamed the Music-Drama Building after the new union opened in 1967. BOISE STATE UNIVERSITY DIGITAL COLLECTIONS

Officers of Associated Men at Fullerton College pose in 1946. FULLERTON COLLEGE LIBRARY ARCHIVES

"Rarely were these centers of the town life confined to one activity. They remained community centers because they served a diversity of interests. The 17th century English tavern and 18th century 'pleasure garden' also provided comparatively fully for the free time activities of the people who frequented them: theater, dance hall, restaurant, music hall, concerts, the pub, and social clubs.

"In the pleasure gardens of 18th century London, the same building which saw the first performance of a Greek play or a personal appearance of Mozart also served as a breakfast room, a fashionable promenade, or the setting for a masquerade. In the surrounding gardens popular and cultural entertainment were successfully combined in a fireworks display of Mt. Etna in eruption, accompanied by the music of Gluck, Haydn, and Handel.

"The earlier town centers and the English tavern and the pleasure garden had the special virtue of drawing people into close contact with each other, and often into participation in the entertainment provided.

"In our contemporary world of specialized commercial entertainment and single-purpose cultural activity it is this element of intimacy, participation, social interchange, and communal feeling that is particularly lacking.

"And as each activity withdraws into a building of its own, isolating itself from others—which is largely what has happened—all sense of the interrelationships of the social and cultural life is lost and at no point, really, do all members of a community have the occasion or the inducement or the pleasure of coming together, except as they pass each other on the sidewalks of our Main Streets.

"We have not let it happen this way at Wisconsin. We have brought together in one place dining rooms and meeting rooms, game facilities and social halls, library, art workrooms and galleries, theater and concert hall—all forming the great social-cultural heart of the life of the campus. Here in the union are joined the learnings of the classrooms, the practice of the arts, and daily social life in an art of living. Here we forge our common will and common purpose."

— The Wisconsin Union Director's Annual Report, 1944.

And the Center that Shelters the Arts Endures

"Here, then, in history's confirmation of the service of a center for recreation and cultural expression is a clue to what a community can do to bring about the kind of a world men want. It can see to it that its own community life is good. One of the essentials, history says to us, is the physical embodiment of its ideal and the physical means of carrying the ideal forward.

"A community center, with concert hall, theaters, art workrooms and galleries, could form, in Joseph Hudnut's phrase, 'a great cultural heart out of which will flow the currents which inform the life of the city with dignity and meaning.' ...

"There is a further special appropriateness in a social-cultural center as a memorial significant of our purpose in this war and in the impending peace.

"How better than through the arts to asset the ascendency of the free human spirit over the oppressive regimentation which the dictators of World War II stood for?

"From the beginning, Hitler attacked and weakened nations, including the German nation, by destroying or controlling their schools and their arts. He did it because he knew that the arts were potent and that they stood in his way.

"So Hitler told men what they could paint, what kind of music and books they could write. He destroyed what didn't suit his purpose in a calculated plan to erase the memory of a culture and, therefore, of a people.

"What more triumphant statement of victory and self-dedication to the ideal of free expression than to erect a building which says: 'We cherish the freely created works of all men everywhere?'

"How better than through the arts to communicate our aspirations to the peoples of other nations and to understand theirs? Painting and music have no difficulty of vocabulary. Blue is blue in any country. And so is the key of G. Music and art encounter no tariff barriers. They are among the few of men's work that are freely interchanged.

"Employing the arts in the cause of internation understanding would be no idle, passing gesture. The communicative and cohesive power of the arts has been realized through long history. They nurture a broadly tolerant spirit of world citizenship and a healthy regard for other peoples.

The Texas State College for Women Student Union Building in 1946. ACUI ARCHIVES

"In the last analysis what we remember about a people or about an age is its art. Few know the past distinction of a people in trade, in war, in sports, or in government. But we know the temples of Greece, the painting of the Italians, the music of Bach and Beethoven, the plays of England's Shakespeare. These are the works of men that inspire us with respect and understanding. They guard our common culture, not merely by reminding us of ages past, but as forces present and active. Theirs is the message that endures. So will the building that shelters the arts endure."

— "The Milwaukee War Memorial." An introductory discussion presented at a planning meeting of the Trustees of the Metropolitan Milwaukee War Memorial, 1945.

The Arts and Recreation Interlocked

"The Wisconsin Union theater project started with the assumption that formal education, recreation, and cultural expression are inevitably and deservedly interlocked in every scheme of civilized living. It was considered important that the arts should not exist in specialized isolation as so often occurs—a separate theater for drama only, a tomb-like art gallery open only at certain hours, a remote workshop—but rather that they should be associated with the vitalizing daily social life of the campus community and thus establish a creative and recreative center that would be alive from top to bottom almost every hour of the day and evening.

"The theater was built, therefore, as an integral part of the campus social and recreation center, the union building. Brought together under the single roof of the union, the theater and shops of the cultural center and the lounges, dining rooms, meeting rooms of the social center supplement and fortify each other—with obvious economies in building cost and administration and with enormous convenience and satisfaction to student and faculty participants."

— "The Wisconsin Union Theater." American School and University Yearbook, 1945.

The Centre a Part of National Educational Policy in England

"Neighborhood does not, of itself, necessarily constitute a social bond; but if, by grouping its leisure activities around a recreative and educational centre, a neighborhood can develop into a socially conscious community, learning, through managing the affairs of the centre, to participate intelligently in the work of local and national government, then education for democracy will have made a real advance. ...

"The immediate aim should be to foster a sense of community through the service of the social and cultural needs of a neighborhood."

— Community Centres, publications of the Ministry of Education, England. Explaining the national Education Act of 1944 providing for community centers as a "necessary and important" part of the educational system in England, 1945.

A Broader Conception of What Recreation Is

"Too long has recreation been thought of as physical activity—especially as sports and games for the young. ... Just ask the average person. To him recreation and sports and games are synonymous. The arts are over in some quite separate, distant category.

"And what a pity! People miss so much that could be important to them and satisfying to them if they also thought of art as 'recreation.' But they rule out music, drama, art, literature because they sound high-brow; crafts because they suppose crafts take some God-given skill.

"The inescapable fact is that most people past their 20s aren't as competent in sports as they used to be, and they grow less interested as the years go by. If these folks are not to be left with the radio and the movies and their cars as their only leisure resources, then the arts are a must. But the arts do not find their rightful place in a recreation program just to give something to people who can't do anything else, valuable as that may be.

"Granted that no effort should be spared to have physical well-being, over the sweep of time and considering the widest implications for the community, the nation, and for people everywhere, what is more important than the arts? Leonardo da Vinci said, 'A nation's art is its soul.' ...

"From the time of the first elemental human activity, when the cave man pictured his world and his hopes on the walls of his cave, creation and self-expression in rhythm and music, pictures and words have been a universal longing and satisfaction of men.

"If we are to satisfy this universal impulse; if we are to understand the peoples of other places and times, when understanding is so desperately needed; if we are to win any distinction by which we will be remembered ourselves, we'd better have the arts. ...

"And this is where the recreation agencies of the community have an important role to play. ...

"First, let's not call them 'fine' arts. That scares people. It means uplift, the unattainable, the ivory tower, something not for me. I don't mind if we don't even call them arts. Let's say 'recreation.' And we will open the doors to what otherwise may be closed minds. Fortunately, people have no inhibitions about recreation.

"Second, let's have art for the sake of people rather than for art's sake. Too many leaders, especially those trained at universities, get all wrapped up in the techniques of music, art, and drama. Perfectionism in the play, concert, or painting becomes the important thing, and giving individuals a chance to grow and an interest and a satisfaction they can pursue for a lifetime falls by the wayside. ...

"Third, personal participation, learning by doing—as we all know—gives the greatest satisfaction, the lasting appreciations. But let's not undervalue the usefulness of the spectator program. Many great art and music centers which believe firmly in 'doing it yourself' also have as their purpose making people aware that other art or music exists, and to lead them to see and hear the works of artists far greater than the local people are likely to become. Inspiration from others, hand in hand with personal performance in the arts, makes an impression more lasting than does either approach alone.

"Why not major concerts, important art exhibitions, big names in the theater world presented by the recreation department? Let's play second fiddle to no one—just because we are 'recreation.' Don't undervalue, either, the prestige-giving benefits of an important program. It will help you win attention and respect for everything else you do. ...

"Fourth, let's not wait for people to 'express an interest' before we try something. We tie ourselves to a stake sometimes, letting, as we say, 'the program grow out of the interest of our clientele.' There's an old proverb: 'Whom you don't meet you do not marry.' ...

"There's the case of our workshop at the union at Wisconsin. Students did not ask for one. One student came to me with a proposition to start one, and she wanted a job. We gave it a try. The girl was put on the job. She hung a sign over the door, 'Each one to his own bad taste,' and a few students wandered in. That was 13 years ago. Now there are 30 to 50 students in the shop every afternoon—on the pleasantest sunny days, during football games, and even when they should be in class—painting, modeling in clay, firing ceramic jewelry, making Christmas presents in leather, felt, and metal. You couldn't pry them loose. The shop filled not an expressed need but an unrealized need. ...

"Taking all the evidence and potentialities together, I am encouraged to believe that an emphasis on art as recreation, a broad program of self-made music, arts and crafts, and plays enriched by ample opportunity of seeing and hearing the best that others can do, and an inventive and good leadership which shows the way, can produce a great cultural enterprise."

— "The Arts as Recreation." Recreation Magazine, 1946.

Touchstones of a Good Center for the Arts

"1. The good art center should illumine the interrelations, the unity of the arts. All should be there—music, drama, the dance, the visual arts, literature—all mutually supporting and enriching each other, all at the heart of community life and woven together with it in the seamless continuity fundamental to genuine culture.

"2. The good center should be for creation as well as for appreciation. The building should incite activity and encourage the congeniality that comes from working together. This means providing for self-produced plays, self-produced music, self-produced art.

"3. The kind of art facilities should be provided which make it possible for the center to be a contributing participant in the creative activity of its own community rather than only the storehouse of creative activity of the past and of other places. This means planning thoughtfully to dispel the museum gloom—galleries that are bright, the air fresh, the exhibits small and often changed. It means employing the good offices of photography, the motion picture, and the arts known to industry and the home. It means an art gallery which is a theater, for the dramatization, not of plays in this case, but of pictures. It means, in short, blowing the dust off of art.

"4. The building should be a center for the arts, yes. But even more it should be a center for people. If it is to be for people, we will provide for the things that human beings do in their more elemental daily activity: places and means for meeting friends, for conversation, for lounging and smoking, for reading the newspapers, for dining and refreshment. ...

"Provisions for personal and social needs will populate the cultural center, introducing new thousands to the arts, and increasing and prolonging the visits of other thousands. The presence and the message of the arts will add grace and purpose to social activity. Coming to the center for one activity, people will be exposed to, and perhaps inspired by, another activity. Art and daily living thus may blend into truly an art of living, one and indivisible. And we will avoid the error of labeling the cultural center with UPLIFT, in capital letters, which makes people enthusiastically stay away."

— "Goals of a Good Center for the Arts." Lecture for the University of Wisconsin course in gallery administration, 1946.

A 1948 photo of the University of Washington's Husky Union Building. ACUI ARCHIVES

Student artwork on display at Howard University. U.S. NATIONAL ARCHIVES AND RECORDS ADMINISTRATION

"

THE UNIVERSITY AS A COMMUNITY PLAYS A SPECIAL ROLE: **THE MAKING OF USEFUL, EFFECTIVE CITIZENS**—ONE OF THE MAJOR PURPOSES OF A LIBERAL EDUCATION.

"

Planning the Union Building— Early Cautions

"The college social or community center is one of the most highly complex and specialized kinds of building. In the first place, there is nothing elsewhere quite like a union; a club, hotel, or civic community center will afford no safe pattern to go by, though the union embodies characteristics of all of them. A union is much more inclusive and unique in its facilities; it may house club facilities, restaurants, hotel, theater, art galleries, post office, hobby shops, radio studios, stores, and a battery of offices all under one roof—a special combination of these functions or all of them.

"In the second place, any union to be valid and of maximum use for a given campus needs to reflect and strengthen the traditions and life of that particular campus and to serve the special recreation interests and community living needs of a particular campus population—always a highly individual thing. In other words, a good union is a tailor-made job. So a good union cannot be arrived at merely by consulting the plans of other unions. And it cannot be designed by an architect out of the top of his mind; it represents an architectural problem of the first order, requiring the maximum imagination and care."

— "Before You Build a Union." 23rd Conference of the Association of College Unions, 1946.

The American University Community— Contrasts with Europe

"Attention to the student outside the classroom, to the welfare of the college community, and to the student as a functioning leader in his society, all came comparatively slowly because of the grip of the German scholastic and research tradition on educational thinking, from which we borrowed heavily. The point of departure for the German university has been a body of knowledge, and not the student as an individual, what happens to him, or what he does with his new-found knowledge. The approach, if I may use a colloquialism, was: 'We have the experts in science and art. Come and get it, if you can.' No provision for shelter, food, social life, recreation. No campus, in fact. No student employment opportunities for those who couldn't afford college. No student government. No implications of using university training for the benefit of anyone but yourself. Just more expertness in specialized subject fields, if you could survive.

"Continental Europe has had occasion to regret bitterly the German tradition of scholarship and research as an end in itself. When the supreme test of the years before and during the war came, the nation's leaders, especially in Germany, were not, as in England and America, university graduates and faculty members. The products of the German university were men who functioned by and large as highly trained intellectual machines moving about doing an assigned job without any sense of social responsibility or practice in discharging it. So the uneducated or half-educated hoodlums ran away with the show. ...

"So we see that the thing that perhaps most conspicuously distinguishes an American university from the European is that the American university is not just a group of buildings where teaching takes place; it is a functioning community with a life of its own. ...

"The university as a community plays a special role: the making of useful, effective citizens—one of the major purposes of a liberal education. ...

"So the university provides a means for the practice of citizenship—among other things a student-faculty governed community center, the union, where opportunity is made for all who will to have a part in the direction of community enterprises.

"In other words, we have in the union what the students of German universities never had—real opportunities for the exercise of citizenship in a going community.

"If students can help make their university community strong and good, they will have attained practice and skill and the ideals that will help them to do it again another time in another place."

— "The University Community." University of Wisconsin Freshman Forum, 1946. (Reprinted in part in the The Bulletin of the Association of College Unions International under the title "Background of the Union's Purpose," 1946.)

The Role of Students in Community Government

"It needs to be remembered that student boards and committees have responsibilities to the college faculty and regents who are charged ultimately with the well-being of the university. ...

"To ignore the necessity of working with other duly constituted self-governing groups is to miss one of the essential elements in learning and strengthening the democratic process. This idea of fiercely maintaining our independence and sovereignty against all comers, whether as students or as a nation, is one of the prime reasons for fruitless conflict and why we don't get to where we want to go. To learn how to share our group sovereignty, how to work cooperatively with other organizations with interests different from our own, is the fundamental, most important lesson to learn in democracy.

"What I would like to suggest as a way out of this campus complexity is the possibility of community self-government. Not just faculty government of matters interesting to the faculty and not just student government of matters interesting to students, but a genuine overall community government embracing the whole university population, student and faculty. Actually, I can think of few areas of student interest and activity that do not impinge on some university responsibility or some faculty rule. Or of few areas of faculty policy making with regard to students that don't vitally interest and affect students. Why shouldn't we have both students and faculty share jointly in the planning and the decisions?

"If students are reluctant to call in faculty aid and counsel, I must say there has been just as much restraint on the part of faculty in bringing students into their councils. Personally, I think there's much to be gained in accepting a student as a full-fledged, responsible member of the community, as a partner in the governing enterprise. The faculty is likely to learn a lot from students and to be stimulated with a new respect for what students can accomplish. And it will be the best possible preparation of students for their role as self-governing citizens. They will be then in a situation more nearly the counterpart of self-government elsewhere, seeing community problems as a whole and not just a segment, and having effective means at hand of carrying out decisions made. And among other things they will learn to work with people older than themselves. After all, a student doesn't go on through life dealing only with persons his own age."

— "The University Community." University of Wisconsin Freshman Forum, 1946.

The Staff a Union Requires

"There are—as in the conduct of the college as a whole—two staff functions to be performed in every union, large or small, each paralleling and supplementing the other and both under one directing and coordinating head: (1) the educational function which includes the direction of a recreation program for the campus and the counseling (even organized instruction) of students, individuals, and groups, in social and recreational fields; and (2) the business and administrative function of operating the building plant and its varied services. ...

"A clue to the relative sufficiency of the union staff at a given college will be given by an examination of the number of staff members appointed to care for the physical health and physical recreation and sports program of a student body in comparison to the number appointed at the union to care for the social health and social-cultural recreational program of the same student body.

"One important practical consideration often overlooked by college administrations in staffing a union is that union buildings normally operate seven days a week, including holidays, from early morning to late evenings—in other words, two eight-hour work days each day of the week. The requirements for staff supervision during a 16-hour day and a seven-day week should inevitably lead to an increase in the number of supervisory positions in a union over those provided for the normal eight-hour, five-and-a-half-day operation of other college departments. Otherwise injury will either be done to the program or to the staff members who are given supervisory responsibility during these long hours. One of the greatest weaknesses in union staff organization in the past has been due to the failure of the administration to recognize that when the usual five o'clock office closing time comes on the campus another full work day is just beginning at

The cast of "He Ain't Done Right" performing as part of a the Annual Blue and Gold Day at Fullerton College.
FULLERTON COLLEGE LIBRARY ARCHIVES

the union, with the heaviest load often falling in the evening and on Saturdays and Sundays.

"Important as it is to select union staff members for their special abilities to direct particular activities, it is of even greater importance to take account of their general qualifications. Training or experience may be too specialized, with the result that workers cannot adapt themselves to rapidly changing situations. In the field of informal education, attitudes, interests, and potential capabilities are of even greater importance than technical skill in directing a given activity. ...

"All members of the union staff should have a conception of the community center's place and purpose in the college educational scheme, a sympathetic comprehension of the recreation needs of students, and an interest in making a student's experience within the union of educative and self-development value."

— Standards in College Union Work. Association of College Unions, 1946.

Reappraisal of the Purpose of Education—and the Union's Role

"There is a ferment of self-criticism in the educational world, a ferment of change and impending change. We are troubled with the thought that our kind of education hasn't done enough to help avoid the disaster of war, or the new disasters of self-interest and disunity that plague us and thwart us on every hand. We are troubled by the evidence that even the student veterans, who have more reason than anyone never to want to see war repeated or to see our society ineffectual in taking care of human needs, are turning, nevertheless, largely to the self-centered, job-getting studies of engineering, commerce, law, or other specialties in making a living. Though the destiny of society and every one of us is at stake, we seem dangerously on our way to producing still more 'me first' Americans.

"So there is hardly a college that has not started in the last 10 years a reappraisal of its purpose and curriculum to find something better, more effective for our times.

"President Truman has appointed a national commission on higher education calling for 'an examination of functions of higher education in our democracy ... and the adequacy of curricula, particularly in the fields of international affairs and social understanding.'

"Listen to almost any commencement address and you will hear the wistful hope that graduates will be the leaders of a new and better day, but everyone knows that only a few will be.

"Consult the older, more thoughtful students on any campus and you will find serious questioning of whether what they are getting from college is right or good.

"'Educational institutions,' one writer puts it, 'have been making Grade A physicists and Grade D humans.'

"The concern throughout is with the kind of person the student is becoming and what he will do with his learning.

"Ralph Waldo Emerson once wrote: 'The true test of civilization is not the census, nor the size of cities, nor crops—no, but the kind of man a country turns out.' Equally, the true test of excellence in education now, if not always, is certainly not the number of students enrolled, the adequacy of building and equipment, whether or not a graduate gets a well-paid job, or even the worth of the faculty—but the kind of man the college turns out. The kind of man he is as a person and as a citizen.

"How does the union fit into all this?

"First, with regard to the student as a person. The union, as the center of the social life of students, is in an especially strategic position to contribute at least a little, perhaps a great deal, to the personal social competence of students—to his ability to work and live congenially among other people, with confidence and personal effectiveness, and with a decent concern for the rights and feelings of others. ...

"Second, with regard to the college's increasingly great and central purpose: the making of effective citizens. ... The union can be one of the important educational resources in this job of surpassing necessity—the cultivation of social mindedness.

"This may point to a changing function of unions in terms of emphasis, but it is not a new function of unions. Rather it is a return to the most ancient of all union functions. Unions, you will recall, were first brought into being in the British universities as debate and discussion centers, in support of the twofold British educational aim of promoting the art of living and of infusing students with the idea that they are responsible for their country. ...

"The British emphasis on personal development and leadership responsibilities has been obscured in our American unions by the increasingly large demands upon our buildings for dining services and lighter social recreation. ... But many unions have nevertheless carried on, in varying ways and degrees, the British union tradition and, particularly in recent years, have turned their attention more and more to programs of educational and citizenship significance. ...

"Whatever may have appealed to us in the union program before, there is now so much at stake if we are to have the kind of a world we want, where men live and work together peacefully and fruitfully, that no effort of a university agency can be spared, the union's included, in the job of producing students who want to use, and know how to use, their university training, not for themselves alone, but for the common welfare.

"We cannot hope for world well-being until we have created the educational climate in which the generations of young people coming along are encouraged to care about the idea of the well-being of others, whether they be our neighbors of whether they be in Europe or Asia.

"No doubt the home community offers the greatest and most immediate possibility for the graduating student to make his contribution. But it doesn't make very much difference whether he begins in the smaller area of his neighborhood or in the larger area of international relations. It is more than likely that an intelligent concern for the one will lead to an interest and active participation in the other. The real issue is not so much where one starts out, but whether one starts out at all."

— "The Union as a University Division of Social Education." An address at the 24th Conference of the Association of College Unions, 1947.

"

HERE IS A SUPERB OPPORTUNITY FOR DEMOCRATIC GROWTH—AND IT CAN BE ACHIEVED BEST BY LETTING THE STUDENTS THEMSELVES HANDLE IT!

"

Four members of the
Interpretive Dance Club
at Fullerton College.

Summation of the Nature of the Union— As First Published by the Association of College Unions

"The union is now a community center of the first order. ...

"If a union is to respond effectively to the wide range of needs and interests of a college population at leisure, if it is to become genuinely a community center—the social and cultural heart of the campus—it will draw together under one roof those facilities and activities that will give everyone in the college family a reason for coming to the center.

"It will provide first for the things that human beings do in their more elemental daily activity. For young people especially, it will provide for dating and dancing and for activity games. It will provide rooms and equipment that will incite activity and encourage the congeniality that comes from working together on common projects. And finally, it will offer facilities that will introduce students to the enduring satisfactions of the arts, of hobbies, and of the creative use of leisure generally. ...

"From this it follows that the known unmet social and cultural needs of the college population should be arranged for in a new union. Further, that the college should provide there the means of cultivating new, worthy interests that may not at the moment be in demand locally but which, upon trial, have had strong appeal to other young people and which have inherent recreational or cultural value.

"In other words, a union is not just a certain kind of physical structure. A union, in the best sense, is a well-considered plan for the community life of the college. ...

"The general educational aims of the union are to prepare students for leisure as well as for work and to make the environment and the recreation of students a cooperative factor with study in their education. These aims have grown out of the widely held view of educators that what the college does educationally in the hours outside the classroom is of major importance. ...

"There is yet another thing a union ought to be: laboratory of citizenship. ...

"If the union, as it now sets its course, decides to emphasize this goal of active, enlightened citizenship, if it looks for all the means at hand of helping send out students who are service-minded, socially responsible, we will not be wrong."

— Planning and Operating College Union Buildings. Published by the Association of College Unions, 1945. (Reprinted in part as "A Design for College Living" in College and University Business, 1948.)

Confirmation of the Importance of the Role of the Union by Others

—A National Leader in the Field of Recreation

"The college union has at least three major responsibilities. It provides the rich recreation oasis for all the members of the great campus community. ... It provides the nucleus and the clearing house and the weather vane for all the out-of-the-classroom life of the campus. It educates the tens of thousands of students in the art of living; it seasons to a high degree their attitudes.

"And since these students are destined to be tomorrow's leading citizens whose words and deeds and manner of living and direction in civic affairs will set the patterns of recreation for all the people, community recreation will take its color and flavor through these people whose lives you nurture and shape to a degree in the unions. Thus, the union becomes a potent and far-reaching influence. Perhaps it is the most effective laboratory for the future professional leaders in recreation and allied social interest. ...

"Recreation is not a subsidiary of education, health, safety, and general welfare. It sits in dignity at the same family table with them in close family relationship. It is an inevitable part of everyone's life, an important segment of the living process. ... Recreation pays dividends of self-discovery, social adjustments, good citizenship, cultural evolution, and democracy. ...

"A fundamental responsibility of the college union is the education of tastes by exposure ... inciting activities (social, mental, emotional, physical) in environments which promote the appetite for participation. ...

"The union is not simply a building nor a place. You are not merely the keepers of taverns or hostelries or the managers of bazaars. ...

"You are daring to feel that it is just as valid to believe that people work to live as that they simply live to work. You are espousing the doctrine that recreation is not concerned with killing time but with making time alive. ... You are the educators of tastes and the mentors for the artistry for living lives. You are tenders of the lamps in the incubators of citizenship; the tillers of the fertile soil in the fine climate of the hothouse of personality development and character shaping. ... You are stewards of democracy charged with safe-guarding democracy's fifth freedom—the right of the individual to pursue his own interests in his own time off the job for the gratification of the doing.

"Yours is a beautiful opportunity."

— G. Ott Romney, dean of West Virginia University. "College Unions and the Fifth Freedom." Keynote address at the 25th Conference of the Association of College Unions, 1948. (Reprinted and distributed nationally to college administrators.)

—A Well-Known Psychiatrist

"The so-called social problems are, in reality, reactions of personalities to stress. ...

"Mentally healthy people participate in some form of volitional activity to supplement their required daily work. This is not merely because they want something to do in their leisure time, for many persons with little leisure make time for play. Their satisfaction from these activities meets deep-seated psychological demands, quite beyond the superficial rationalization of enjoyment. ...

"Good mental health is directly related to the capacity and willingness of an individual to play. ... But too many people do not know how to play. ...

"An effective community recreation program is just as important to mental health as sanitation is to physical health. ...

"In this troubled world today, so filled with unhappiness, distress, anxiety, and restlessness, to whom can one look for help? It is my firm conviction that if we could encourage and teach and guide more people to more effective recreative activity, we could and would make a major contribution to our national and international peace of mind."

— Dr. William C. Menninger, Menninger Clinic. "Recreation and Mental Health." Recreation Magazine, 1948.

—The Ford Foundation

"The evidence points to the fact that today's most critical problems are those which are social rather than physical in character—those which arise in man's relation to man rather than in his relation to nature. Here is the realm where the greatest problems exist, where the least progress is being made, and where the gravest threat to democracy and human welfare lies.

"A basic element of democracy and human welfare is social responsibility and the duty of service. Human welfare requires that every person recognize a moral obligation to use his capabilities, whatever they may be, to contribute positively to the welfare of society. ...

"At every level of government—federal, state, and local—our political system shows inability to attract adequate numbers of competent and public-spirited persons to government as a career, and the failure of a large proportion of our citizens to participate effectively in the processes of self-government. In government, as in other aspects of society, talent is in short supply. ...

"The greatest single shortcoming of our school system is its tendency to concern itself almost exclusively with the dissemination of information.

"Without question one of the most important jobs of education today is to train well-balanced citizens and leaders able to participate intelligently and constructively in the society in which we live. ...

"The Study Committee was impressed with the evidence it received of the great need to revitalize our education, particularly at the college level, so that its graduates will live more significant personal lives and participate more effectively in social affairs. The Foundation should find and assist programs in the schools and colleges which emphasize the breadth and richness of the student's educational experience, and which direct the student's attention to life, rather than to an immediate vocation, and to his responsibility as a thinking and acting citizen of democracy."

— H. Rowan Gaither Jr., director of The Study Committee. Report of the Study for the Ford Foundation on Policy and Program, 1949.

—The Secretary of the President's Commission on Higher Education

"The machines, the services, and the social skills required for modern living have automatically thrust a far greater burden upon the colleges than we had dreamed of in the past. ...

"Most important, however, is the unlimited need for better trained citizens who can operate successfully the sensitive machinery of democratic government. ...

"I am convinced that our present college programs are not contributing adequately to the quality of students' adult lives either as workers or as citizens. ...

"If our institutions of higher learning are to play a significant role in strengthening our democratic sinews, they must begin to practice freedom and responsibility as life habits. ... We have too often in the past left our education for democratic living to courses in history and political science. It should become, instead, a primary aim of all classroom teachings and, more important still, of every phase of campus life. ...

"I have given particular attention to this phase of the educational problems facing us because I believe that the Association of College Unions is capable of assuming a role of major importance in developing a broadened concept of higher education. You have under your respective rooftops practically every facet of community life the student will meet after he leaves the campus. How many of your academic administrators have recognized the opportunity for working with you in using your facilities as a kind of life laboratory? I would venture to say that there has been far more philosophy of life learned over coffee or cokes at the union than has come out of many of our philosophy classrooms.

"Those of you who are so closely identified with the union buildings and their activities know the tremendous role they play in the lives of our students. But except for random instances, in how many cases has the faculty been willing to recognize the truly massive education process which goes on in the unions? ...

"Here is a superb opportunity for democratic growth—and it can be achieved best by letting the students themselves handle it! ...

"Democracy is more than a creed. It is an activity. It is a way of thinking, feeling, and acting with regard to the associations of men and of groups, one with another. ...

"I like to think of the college unions as carrying an increasingly important responsibility for providing students the opportunities for practicing democracy in action.

— Alfred B. Bonds Jr., secretary of the President's Commission on Higher Education. "A Look to the Future - Some Implications of the Report of the President's Commission on Higher Education." Keynote address, 25th Conference of the Association of College Unions, 1948. (Reprinted and distributed nationally to college administrators.)

STATE OF THE COLLEGE UNION IN 1949

"I thought I would deal with the 'State of the Union' in the conveniently arbitrary terms of plus and minus—drawing up a kind of 25-year balance sheet and leaving out, like the accountants do, all the important explanations, or almost all. ...

"First, an easy plus for the growth of this institution we call the union.

"Fifty years ago there were two unions in this country. At the close of the first World War perhaps a dozen. ... Now there are 150 unions on this continent and there must be at least 150 more in the dreaming or building stages. The U.S. Office of Education recently reported that present plans of colleges across the country indicate an expansion of existing union facilities by 155 percent—the highest percentage increase contemplated in any field of college construction.

"It used to be thought a union was something for the large university—something that would help overcome the penalties of size by unifying the 'big' campus and personalizing and humanizing its procedures. But no longer just that. Unions now exist in colleges for 500; and as many are being planned for campuses of 1,000 students as for institutions of 10,000.

"In short, I think it is fair to say that there has come to be an almost universal recognition that wherever numbers of young people are gathered together away from home, a social center and program are needed, and that a union is as normal and necessary a part of the college equipment as a gymnasium or health service—yes, even library. And for that fast growing recognition, a resounding plus. ...

"But a building, however well planned, does not by itself create campus unity, or provide a rewarding social experience for students, or introduce them to new cultural and recreational interest. It just makes these things possible. What actually happens depends directly on the quality of the leadership of the key staff members.

"I have a choice assortment of pluses and minuses for what we do about the leadership of our unions. ...

"For some institutions I have to regretfully assign a minus when I see the lip service they give to the educational functioning of the union. The president says there is scarcely anything of more educational importance to students than what happens in the union. Faculty urge the union as the necessary complement of the classroom. You can read it in any one of a hundred college booklets. They may even appoint a director who has the stuff for doing what is talked about. And then the college classifies the union in the organizational chart as an 'auxiliary enterprise' along with the college laundry and treats the staff as housekeepers and chore boys—the people who are expected to bring off this much sought-after and most difficult-to-achieve educational result.

"An even larger minus sign goes to the administration that thinks running a union is a matter of bookkeeping and staffs it accordingly. This concept of the union is one which acknowledges the educational and social significance of the union, but assumes it will somehow come about without either a program staff or program budget. The college with this concept always wants to ask first, 'How much does it cost?' The trouble is this is the wrong question to ask. The right question is: 'What do people need?' And then, by skillful management and leadership, get it. But this kind of approach seldom comes from people trained only to interpret financial statements and not statements of human need. ...

"On the other hand, a grateful plus is reserved for the rare administration that cares enough about the needs of students and about keeping union directors off the list of nervous breakdowns to let a union have not one chief assistant but three, four, or 10. Most unions would settle for the number of staff assistants the college employs to coach 50 men on the football squad.

The Coffman Memorial Union opened at the University of Minnesota in 1940. ACUI ARCHIVES

"To the idea of student leadership of a union, jointly with the staff, I give another plus.

"In fact, I've saved space at the top of the plus column for the plushiest one of all. I can't think of another college enterprise, involving college-owned buildings and college operating staff, where students have been taken more completely and universally into full partnership than in the union. And it has been so almost from the beginning. The union student committee, with a staff member sitting in, is probably the key to the special strength of the union as a responsive, fully democratic, educationally significant institution. ...

"Now I want to suggest a super-plus to which all our purposes can contribute.

"This is a time when we need to relate what we do to the things that matter most.

"One of the things that matters most—it is hard to think of anything else that matters more—is making democracy work well, making it cherished here and throughout the world.

"Upon the outcome depends whether or not men are going to have freedom. And we are not talking any longer about a competition of political ideas in the abstract; it is plain that we are now talking about life or death of peoples, including our own.

"Democracy is predicated upon the universal education of its citizens. The whole educational process in America, fundamentally, was and is intended to prepare young people to make democracy work, to prepare them for intelligent participation and effective leadership in our common life together. This is why, above all else, is it not, that our society makes the investment it does in education?

"But the alarming evidence is that only a small fraction of those from whom we expect the most, our college graduates, have been sustaining the burden or public leadership, either at the top or the bottom of the ladder of civic affairs.

"'All too often,' the President's Commission on Higher Education recently said, 'the benefits of education have been sought and used for personal and private profit, to the neglect of public and social service. ... Teaching and learning must be invested with public purpose.'

"And yet at this critical juncture more and more college students are removing themselves as far as it is possible to get from the classroom courses that might help most in the understanding of our common problems and in producing leaders of our common life together. ...

"Until there is a realization of the desperate urgencies confronting all of us, or a change in the rewards now given for the way a student spends his time in classroom work, the job to be done will need to be done in large part through education outside the classroom. And some things can be done only outside the classroom.

"How? There are, I think, two major ways.

"First, arrange for the maximum of student volunteer service; show students that what we call extracurricular activity is not 'extra' but essential, not an end in itself to be dropped cold after graduation but the counterpart and preparation for community service and the assumption of leadership wherever they may go.

"Second, make the campus itself and all its institutions strongholds of what is best in democracy, examples of what can be achieved through our combined personal efforts, arousing enthusiasm of students for what the democratic process can do and for having in every community more of the same.

"In so doing, we will be engaged with the fundamentals of education in a democracy and will be doing what, in many respects, the classroom cannot do.

"I wish to say again, as many have said before: The basic idea at the root of American society is the elimination of reliance upon external authority at the top, and investing authority and responsibility in the ordinary person himself as a good citizen. But good citizens are not made merely by reading about it, still less by hopeful exhortations at the commencement time. ...

"Somewhere those people training for leadership in a democracy must have a chance to practice it. If they cannot practice it, where can they learn it?

"And somewhere leaders and followers must have a chance to come together to forge the common will and to take collective action. ...

"In the union especially, we have a priceless tool for shaping community solidarity and the individual student's sense of social responsibility. It is the union's job to make all this clear to the college administration. ...

"What I would like to see, in short, is a program and a process in which college graduates by the hundreds, motivated by their campus experience and equipped with know-how from well-conducted student activities, attend legislative hearings and make themselves felt, do their part in community chest drives, work on PTA committees, lead in getting a civic music association or better housing, start a community forum, join the voters leagues, volunteer to help setup a neighborhood recreation program or a teenage center, run for village, county, or state offices.

"The union's role is to manage, somehow, to enlist students in comparable activity in college and get them to see it as the natural prelude to a lifelong responsibility and a rich and pleasurable satisfaction of the educated citizen. ...

"But the question will be asked, as it is always asked: 'Do students have the time; will not out-of-class activity take away from performance in the classroom? Coursework is what students are here for primarily. Many have to work at part-time jobs to come to college at all.'

"The answers are yes, there is the time; and no, academic work, all students considered, will not suffer.

"Out-of-class organized activities are neither extensive nor intensive enough to constitute a threat to classroom work. ... The tragedy is the terrifying apathy the majority of students show toward both campus and world affairs.

"About scholarship: Actually it is often found—how much is cause and effect, and how much a pre-selection process, we do not yet know—that the busy student leaders and the frequent participants in activity like the union's have higher scholarship than the infrequent or nonparticipants. Furthermore, a high percentage of the leader group also work at part-time jobs, earning part of their living in their stride.

"I should like to remind the college administration that hesitates to encourage other than studies what Pericles, representative of a people most respected for learning in academic circles, said of Athenian institutions 2,379 years ago.

"'Our citizens,' he said, 'attend both to public and private duties, and do not allow absorption in their own various affairs to interfere with their knowledge of the city's. We differ from other states in regarding the man who holds aloof from public life not as "quiet" but as useless.'

"And lest, perchance, the 5th century B.C. seems slightly out of date, I quote Columbia's President Dwight Eisenhower: 'Only when each individual, while seeking to develop his own talents and further his own good, at the same time cooperates with his fellows for the common betterment—only then is an orderly civilized life possible. Education for citizenship is the first function of our educational system.'

"So regardless of questions of available student hours or of outcomes in other directions, we should make time for what is imperative. I repeat: We all need to relate what we do to the things that matter most. ...

"The union, as much as any, has a part in this job of surpassing necessity—the job of enlisting everyone in a personal concern for the general welfare. The union is the kind of social and service institution where it ought immediately be apparent that the ideals of democracy are practiced and that they work. The union cannot do it all but it can see to it that its own household is in order and by example encourage other college enterprises to do likewise.

"For the student, the campus is the present reality. Here he will see whether or not the basic questions of what people need—personally, physically, socially—are being faced. Here he will see whether he has a part in the process, or whether these things are settled by outside authority. Here he will see whether or not anyone really cares about the well-being of others. And what he finds in the union, what he does in the union, will be, for him, a prime example of what the methods and goals are. The union, as the community center, will exemplify perhaps better than anything else what the community stands for.

"Do we actually welcome students to a share in making the important decisions in the union? Do we reach out to the vast numbers of unorganized students when we appoint committees? Do we countenance race discrimination when we choose employees or elect officers? Do we close our meeting rooms to certain groups or our lecture platform when a troublesome issue is up? Do we show we're interested in anything that's happening beyond the borders of the campus? Do we care enough about what it costs students to eat at the union or to use its services? Do we wink at student petty graft? Do we do something about legitimate student requests and needs?

"Here, in short, at the threshold of his participation in adult affairs, the student will find out how well democracy works where it ought to work best—in an enlightened college community. And his attitudes, his feelings of personal obligation to do his part, will be substantially shaped accordingly. ...

"If we can help see to it that thousands upon thousands of students leave our doors socially minded, ready and able to serve the common welfare, contributing freely to the imperative cause of a successful, respected democracy, the union will receive, and deserve, the most important plus of its history."

— "State of the College Union in 1949." Opening address, 26th Conference of the Association of College Unions, 1949.

1950s

With the nature of the union better understood, questions of facilities and governance come into clearer focus. Campus growth prompts conversations about centralization and decentralization. Research validates training for union leadership. The federal housing program is a milestone in recognition and financing, but skeptics need reconvincing.

Candidates for sophomore class office pose with posters made for the campaign at Boise State University in 1951.

WHAT, DAY BY DAY, IS THE UNION FOR?

"What is this building supposed to do? What is any union for? ...

"We spend so much of our time and our substance—almost all of it, it seems sometimes—arranging for the necessities that let us exist, repairing the damage of past wars and worrying about the next one, being annoyed with our neighbors or our political leadership, quarreling on the economic front as to who shall get what, stalemating each other, struggling to hold things together, just keeping even with where we are—what somebody picturesquely has called just keeping the plumbing of life in order—always having to postpone to another time, for one pressing reason or another, the things that make life really worth living.

"And then one day there suddenly bursts on the scene a new institution like this one—where people can come together to enjoy each other; where people treat each other considerately; where there are a multitude of services and conveniences which make the day go easier; where the prices for doing things and for dining will probably be cheaper than anywhere else, except at another union; where one can follow the urge to make things and learn the lasting satisfaction of personal creation; where it is in order, and natural and pleasurable, to stop and to see good paintings, listen to a concert, read a book, and hear or talk about ideas; where having fun and making friends comes easily; where old feelings about race and religion dissolve on an outing or around a game table or in a committee that does things together; where students can meet readily in groups to shape a course of action; where social mindedness becomes a habit and people work together for the common welfare as a matter of course; where students by the thousands can engage in what Prime Minister Nehru calls the most important thing in the world—to get to know and to understand other people.

"I think in a very short time you will be able to say, because you have the union, this is what we've been working and waiting for all the time."

— "What that Union Is For." Address dedicating the University of Oregon Union, 1950.

How to Decide What to Include in a Union?

"The first union (at Cambridge) was literally the uniting, or 'union,' of three debate societies to get their own quarters. And that's where the name came from. ...

"But the British unions weren't only debate halls. They gradually added reference libraries for the convenience of the debaters, dining rooms, meeting rooms, lounges, and offices (and a bar). The buildings took on the character of men's clubs. They emphasized good paintings in their decoration; books of poetry and philosophy were added to the library. The unions came to be known also as centers of good taste and social acquaintanceship. ...

"Now, how do you find out what should be in your particular union?

"It is far from easy to do it, without error. But doing so is at least as important as it is difficult. For the answer which is finally embodied in the architectural plans will be frozen in steel and concrete. Errors are not readily rectified, nor are they easy to hide.

"You as students are a source of information of the first importance if the new center is to produce anything like a full return on its investment. Since it is for you primarily that the union is to be constructed, your needs, wants, feelings, opinions, and habits must be revealed clearly, or tens of thousands of dollars may be spent in erecting a monument to an unfulfilled purpose.

"Although we are all admittedly less than perfect in our knowledge of our own needs and our ability to express them, and although it is unlikely that we can specify with exact accuracy the facilities and services that would be most beneficial and satisfying to us—there is nevertheless no better source for this information."

— "Guide-Posts in Planning the Kansas State Union." Address at a Kansas State University student convocation, 1950.

"In America, unions turned up variously as men's club rooms with a large cafeteria added, or as primarily a party and meeting center, or as just a snack bar and bookstore. The principal common denominators were a ballroom and coffee-coke center. A few venturesome colleges, sometimes accidentally, sometimes with a flash of insight, added theaters, art rooms, music rooms, or a browsing library.

"Then for a considerable period (and this in a measure is still true) unions were treated merely as catchalls for just those miscellaneous college needs not previously accounted for—anything from cafeteria, student offices, and hotel rooms to quarters for the dean of men and the campus health service.

"It was in the late 1930s before anyone seriously undertook, in a careful way, to find out what a union should be before building it.

"The findings of those experimental years have now been largely consolidated. Shortly after the war there emerged a controlling concept of the union purpose to place in the hands of the architect. The planning of a union is now regarded neither as a matter of roofing over a set of miscellaneous, unrelated facilities nor the opposite: erecting a certain kind of physical structure with predetermined standard elements (as with a dormitory or gymnasium). The planning of the union, in the best sense, now means arriving at a comprehensive, well-considered plan for the community life of the college."

— "The Changing Concept of the College Union." Manuscript for the Architectural Forum, 1951.

And How Best to Arrange for the Governance of a Union?

"Some people fret about the committee way of doing things, some oppose it, in the union or anywhere else. 'It takes too much time; it's inefficient. And what do students know about it anyhow?' So they say. We would do well to remind ourselves that free self-direction and self-government of the committee kind are at the heart of the American democratic method. It may be a slow way of getting things done. Inefficient, sometimes. Mistakes are made, of course. But, as William Jennings Bryan said, 'It is far better for people to make their own mistakes than to have someone else make their mistakes for them.'

"There are some phases of self-government in the union and in other areas of student life, however, which do not help the democratic cause—especially the general campus election of committee chairmen and board members and the notion of complete independence for student government. ... There are some special characteristics of the college community which are too often overlooked when the student government system is planned, in or out of the union. We get off the track when we try to set up a form of student self-government which copies the form of city government. I know it sounds good to say, 'Students ought to have experience in self-government; so we will set up a student government like our city government and let students run it entirely themselves.' The trouble is that the situation is not the same. There are all kinds of important differences. ...

"In the first place, there is already a government set up for the college by law—usually the trustees and the faculty. And many of the important functions of government typical of the city are already lodged there. So a student government, functioning separately from the established college government, has a pretty thin slice of what city government normally does, and pretty limited final authority to do anything about even that slice.

"Second, the nature of the student community is that the population is transient. In city government, elections, to be sure, are the keystone of the democratic way. But the essence of the success of the elected representative system is an electorate and a candidate that know something about each other and a lot about the problems at hand. Student candidates, being newcomers, have no real opportunity to build up a public record of performance or even to announce the ideas for which they stand. The student electorate has no opportunity to express approval or disapproval of its representative's behavior in office, for after a year he is gone anyway. The student body itself, after a year, is half new. In many ways, asking all students to elect union officers is like asking the people moving through the Grand Central Station to get together in the station lobby and elect some of the transients among them to run the railroads. At least, it is not like having the population of a city, which has lived there long and knows its problems, choose among candidates who over a period of years have built up reputations for what they stand for and have to face the consequences if they go wrong.

"What you really have in such student elections is the appearance of the democratic process but not the substance. How good is that as preparation of students for later self-government of their own communities? It can give a completely wrong notion to students of what good, responsible self-government requires: the notion that you do not really have to know anything, do anything, or account to anybody.

"It must be remembered in connection with union government that there is more to self-government than elections and lawmaking bodies. A vast range of our public affairs—including the operation of community centers like unions—is tended to by boards and commissions which are not elected but appointed. We choose representatives of the public who are specially qualified for the job at hand and consider it in the interests of good government. ...

"The third difference between the campus and the city is that government works in the city, once the elections are over, because the city council has a formidable array of full-time paid employees to carry out what is decided, while most student government boards have no one except volunteer student helpers, who are not around when needed. This often results in dissatisfaction and cynicism on the part of other students who expect action and service, and feelings of frustration and disillusionment on the part of the governing-board members themselves. I wonder if this fosters enthusiasm for more self-government.

"Many student leaders, however, view with suspicion any suggestion that they relate themselves to the existing paid personnel of the college. When things do not go well, instead of seeking assistance from the college, they blame somebody for not granting more power, or they 'change the constitution.' ... Some students fiercely maintain their organization's independence of the rest of the college community, fearing no doubt that they will be unduly influenced by the faculty. I wish I knew how to dispel this popular fallacy. Faculty members by and large are surprised and flattered to be asked to share a student problem. They are glad to help if they can—most of them are scared to death they will not know how—and the last thing they think of is to interfere with what students want to do, or to try to control what they do."

— "The Social and Educational Goals of The Campus Center." Journal of Higher Education, 1951.

Students play a version of bingo near the soda fountain in the Boise State University Student Union in 1950.
BOISE STATE UNIVERSITY DIGITAL COLLECTIONS

Also in 1950, University of Toledo students take a soda break between classes.
WARD M. CANADAY CENTER ARCHIVES, UNIVERSITY OF TOLEDO

Working Together in Groups— the Essence of the Democratic Method

"One of the central enterprises of the union is to give students the opportunity and responsibility of planning their own community programs, to coach them in how to work well together in doing it, and more and more how to use their experience on the campus in making a similar contribution in their home towns when they leave the university. At the union, free, creative activity among students goes forward at its best. Students work for hours each week and count the time well spent. No thought of monetary reward or class credit, but of the fun of doing it, of the new friendships made, of the satisfaction of getting a good job done. Thus they learn their responsibilities for the common welfare.

"The democratic value of such group activity has brought sharply into focus recently. ... Our state department and the people who have the job of reconstruction in Europe see such committee work as central to what young people in the authoritarian countries ought to learn how to do.

"So ... the union is dealing with something of main line significance in the current worldwide clash of ideas: how to make democracy work well, at home and abroad. ..."

A Basic Question Looms: Centralization, Fostering Sense of Community? Or Decentralization?

"In all that the union does, whether providing for free, creative activity or for low-cost recreation and meals, it has an over-spreading purpose, a dominant goal in view.

"The union was seen by its founders as a symbol of unity for the university. The name 'union' itself stated the goal of 'uniting' the university population. The seal or crest—a pipe of peace superimposed upon a compass—signified: 'From the four quarters of the earth come students to the campus, to be united in fellowship at the union.' The purpose set forth in the constitution and approved by the faculty and regents was and still is: 'to provide a common life and a cultivated social program' for the university.

"In drawing the plans, the basic objective was to organize under one roof those facilities which would make possible a communal life for thousands of students and faculty members. The union planners knew what educators everywhere knew: that much of what students learn they learn from each other, and from faculty in informal association outside the classroom.

"So the continuing goal has been to develop a community center with adequate accommodations for virtually every type of group activity, except athletic—that students might have the maximum opportunity to meet and talk and work with each other during their leisure hours; that engineers might rub elbows with agriculture students, fraternity members with independents, graduate students with undergraduates, students from small Wisconsin towns with students from Chicago and from China; that the university might continue to be an authentic community of teachers and students. ...

"Now the campus is expanding and changing. ...

"The central question in all this appears to be: Will the campus service facilities and social life be widely decentralized—and must they be, should they be—or should we retain centralization wherever possible, with the union continuing to play its historic role of 'center?'

"In other words, will there, and should there, develop on the campus numbers of small islands of student life and interest centering in other campus buildings—several separate centers—or will there be a resolve to continue the goal of a major community center and a unified campus social life?

"Upon the answer may well hinge what the character of campus life is going to be in the future, the role of the union is to play, and, to a large degree, the financial outlook for the union. ...

"A center, naturally, is made for the community, not the community for the center. And it is not assumed that everyone desires, or will participate in, a community life. But if it is granted that the objectives of a community center and the unity of campus life are good, then all that can reasonably be done to establish conditions favorable to high use of the union, and to the exposure of as many students as possible to its benefits and influences, is in order."

— Report on The Wisconsin Union. Pictorial booklet published by the Trustees of the Memorial Union Building Association, 1952.

And What about the Togetherness of Students, Faculty, Alumni? Is "Student" Union the Right Name?

"What you call the union makes a difference.

"On campus after campus members of the faculty have expressed reserve about helping with fundraising for the union or using the building after it has opened. They had always heard, they say, that the union was 'just for students.' Sure enough, there's the name on the building and on all the literature: 'Student Union.'

"Alumni and college friends take the hint, too. Are they welcome, they wonder? At best, they feel they are only visitors who better have a brief look and go. ...

"And then, the students. They look ruefully around the lobbies at a college conference for visiting chemists or newspaper editors and say, 'What goes on here? I thought this was a student union!' Or they get in a hassle with the administration over some union policy that the president or business manager knows just has to tie in with college policy. The students don't see it. Why? Indignantly they protest, 'This place is supposed to be run by students, isn't it?'

"All along the way the mental road block is 'that name' and all that it seems to imply. ... How did the name get that way? Very likely the college wanted to avoid confusion with labor unions in the public mind. ... But there is little basis, historically or in the present fact, for the name 'student union.'

"Originally unions bore only the title of their institution—'Oxford Union,' 'Harvard Union,' 'Ohio Union,' 'Purdue Union.' ... The national association was organized as the Association of College Unions. Only in recent times has the modifying adjective, 'student,' crept in.

"Almost all unions, by definition in their constitutions or in their published purposes, are for students, faculty, and alumni. Some unions include faculty clubs; many include alumni headquarters. ... Many collect faculty and alumni membership fees. All want faculty and alumni participation.

"Many unions serve as the college conference headquarters. ...

"For all such unions—and this means most of them—'student union' is plainly a misnomer. No one would worry too much about it if it didn't hurt. But it does hurt. The colleges that misname their unions are likely to give students the wrong idea, to lose important support from faculty and alumni, and to miss the values that come from a sense of campus community.

"The union succeeds best—socially, financially, ideologically—when it is conceived as genuinely the community center for all elements of the campus population. The name 'union' itself implies a goal of unity for the college, all members of the college family included. Students, faculty, and alumni all gain from informal association together. ...

"It all adds up to a case for calling union buildings what they are—'college unions,' not 'student unions.'"

— "Is Student Union the Right Name?" Guest editorial, College and University Business, 1952.

A Welcome to a New Union

"I daresay this little stranger in the household (or shall we say big stranger), this newcomer to the campus—the union—will at times seem to be a mixed blessing.

"As with a new arrival in any family, there are bound to be noises in the night. The family routine is likely to be upset for a time. Older brother and sister organizations may have to adjust to a new scheme of things—may have to give way a little on longstanding prerogatives. ... And the bills—the budget—have a way of going up.

"But after all, it's a beautiful, wonderful baby. New and exciting things begin to happen. Despite the cost or the trouble, the college family soon concludes it wouldn't have missed the fun for anything—wouldn't want it any other way."

— "Best Wishes for the Washington State Union." On the occasion of the dedication of the building, 1952.

Students gather on the steps of the University of Southern California's Gwynn Wilson Student Union. EL RODEO YEARBOOK

PRECURSOR OF THE ASSOCIATION'S STATEMENT OF THE ROLE OF THE UNION

"Every college, small as well as the large, is concerned with the living problems of its students. Every college is coming to recognize that the campus environment furthers (or may deter) the fruitful use of student time and the learning process. ...

"Study in the presence of a good teacher can provide an experience never to be forgotten. But the impacts of such moments, and the student's regard for the college, should not be flurried or destroyed by overcrowded dining rooms, the lack of ordinary conveniences, cutting campus life and activity up into small unrelated segments, a poverty of meeting and discussion opportunities, or unfavorable social relationships with the faculty and other students. ...

"Further, if people are to live together in harmony, they must learn new social skills, and the meaning of serving the common welfare. In the college such lessons are often best learned where students, eat, work, and play together; where they meet to discuss freely and act responsibly to solve, as members of a student community, their own group problems. A campus is not complete without the essential facilities for such activities. ...

"The following is an attempt to assist in arriving at a guiding philosophy for the Boston Union:

"1. The union is conceived as the campus center and will represent a well-considered plan for the community life of the university.

"2. It will serve as a laboratory of citizenship, training students in social responsibility and for leadership in our democracy.

"3. It will be the 'living room' of the university, providing for the conveniences students and faculty need in their daily life on the campus, for dining together, for getting to know and understand one another through informal association outside the classroom.

"4. It will encourage self-directed activity, giving individual students and groups maximum opportunity for self-realization and for growth in social competency—assisting students in developing as persons as well as intellects.

"5. It will provide a cultivated and social and recreational program, aiming to make free time activity a cooperative factor with study in education and to blend classroom and cultural interests, community service, and daily living into an art of living, one and indivisible.

"6. It will serve as a unifying force in the life of the university, cultivating enduring regard for and loyalty to the university."

— "The Purpose of the Union." A statement prepared for Boston University to assist in guiding the development of a new union, 1954.

"An Integral Part of Education"— President Hancher's View

"I am happy to observe, as the years pass, that we are coming more and more to the position, which the British have found to be eminently sound, that education consists of far more than the hours spent in classrooms, libraries, and laboratories. ... In the years since World War I, we have had a revolution in the concept of university responsibility.

"At my own university the change came about primarily through the development of union activity. Many of you know Chancellor Rufus Fitzgerald of the University of Pittsburgh (formerly director of the Iowa Union). Much of the thinking which changed our conception of the union at Iowa must be credited to him. It was his hope and ambition that the union might become 'the hearthstone of the university,' a place where the university family would gather. It was my good fortune as a student to be associated with him. I had just returned from Oxford and had acquired a taste for college life in that university. I had seen that there was such a thing as 'education by osmosis.' ... Any alert university now knows that there is more to education than textbooks or formal lectures.

"And so in the years since unions were first started in this country, the union idea has grown and developed to the point where we now find them to be centers of good music, a good painting, of dining, and of group meetings for good conversation and pleasant association. ...

"All of us have increased our dining services, some are running hotel units, all of us have, or have heard about, bowling and billiard rooms and similar recreational facilities. All of these things are useful and necessary in their way. All of them are good, but are they good enough? Are they all that a union should be?

"It seems to me not. It seems to me that the union, if it is to be justified on a college campus, should be more than just a place to keep the students off the streets and out of taverns. It seems to me that the union should be thought of as part of the total educational enterprise, as an integral part of the institution, as contributing a supplementary form of education—outside the classroom in one sense but certainly not unrelated to it—as rounding out the student's life so that by the time he graduates he not only knows his mathematics or his history or his law or whatever else he may take, but will also have an appreciation of the great music and the great painting and the great theater of the Western world. ...

"If the union does not justify itself as an educational enterprise, in my judgment we have made a major error in our thinking. ...

"I am certain that the goal toward which each of us should work, is an educational and cultural union that is the 'hearthstone of the university.'"

— Virgil M. Hancher, president of the State University of Iowa. Keynote address, 31st Conference of the Association of College Unions, 1954. (Reprinted and distributed nationally to college administrators.)

Statement of "The Role of the College Union"—First Draft

"1. The union is the community center of the college. It is not just a building; it is also an organization and a program. Together they represent a well-considered plan for the community life of the college.

"2. The union, as the center of college community life, serves as a laboratory of citizenship, training students in social responsibility and for leadership in our democracy.

"3. The union, in all its processes, encourages self-directed activity, giving individual students and student groups maximum opportunity for self-realization and for growth in individual social competency and group effectiveness—assisting students in developing as persons as well as intellects.

"4. The union is the 'living room' or 'hearthstone' of the college, providing for the services, conveniences, and amenities students and faculty need in their daily life on the campus, for dining together, for getting to know and understand one another through informal association outside the classroom.

"5. The union, through its governing board, committees, and staff, provides a cultivated social and recreational program, aiming to make free time activity a cooperative factor with study in education and to blend classroom and cultural interests, community service, and daily living into an art of living, one and indivisible.

"6. The union serves as a unifying force in the life of the college, cultivating enduring regard for and loyalty to the college."

— Mr. Butts. First draft of a statement of "The Role of the College Union" for adoption by the Association of College Unions, 1955.

IT WILL BE THE 'LIVING ROOM' OF THE UNIVERSITY,

PROVIDING FOR THE CONVENIENCES STUDENTS AND FACULTY NEED IN THEIR DAILY LIFE ON THE CAMPUS, FOR DINING TOGETHER, FOR GETTING TO KNOW AND UNDERSTAND ONE ANOTHER THROUGH INFORMAL ASSOCIATION OUTSIDE THE CLASSROOM.

Confusion over Purpose, Identity

"As one reads through the proceedings of union conferences, he will notice a recurring theme, couched in some such terms as: 'The union shouldn't duplicate anything that is already being done.'

"This is one of our current popular union fallacies.

"If student officers and staff members say their union is only to render a service in those areas no one else is tending, it puts the union in the position of just taking on the leftovers, as though it didn't have any reason for being in and of itself.

"This is a sorry role for the union to play, indicating that union people themselves don't know what the union is for. In such case, obviously, the administration of the college and others aren't going to know what it is for, easily leading on to the situation where the union has a miscellany of unrelated, perhaps minor, activities—and even these may be chipped away at will as soon as someone else decides to enter the field. Which leaves the union where?

"Consider what happens in the organization of any other college enterprise:

"If the classics or English department has been offering a survey course in art appreciation in the absence of an art department, and a new art history department is then inaugurated, the art survey course is transferred to the incoming art history department, as essential to the successful performance of its described function. ...

"The function for which the union is designed as a community center and best equipped to handle, and which it ought to fight for if necessary, is the provision of the central, all-campus social and cultural recreation program for the student body.

"The union, to be sure, will not expect, nor will it be expected, to do everything in the field of campus community life, and there will be variations in the basic pattern, campus to campus.

"But unless the union has some distinguishable, valid function of its own, and can proceed to work at it without hesitation and apologies, why, one can rightly ask, was it built?"

— "Let's Give the Union an Identity of Its Own." Editorial in The Bulletin of the Association of College Unions International, 1955.

The Federal Housing Program— Milestone in Recognition, in Financing

"The significance of the inclusion of unions in the new federal college housing program as projects eligible for federal construction loans can hardly be over-emphasized. ...

"The fact that Congress has given legislative recognition to unions along with housing and health services stands as a landmark in the acceptance of the idea that a building for the community life of a college is normal and necessary. ...

"The Congress comes right out and says 'unions' in the federal housing act. And what's more, it brackets unions with housing, dining halls, and health as an 'educational facility' and 'essential service.' ...

"So the union, for the first time, is established in the law of the land as an identity in its own right and as an educational facility deserving governmental encouragement and financial support. ...

"College administrations which may have given their existing unions only passing thought, which may have been doubtful about adding them to their campus or kept them at the bottom of building priority lists, or which may not yet even have heard of unions, are likely to take another look. ...

"In a very real sense the federal housing act of August 1955 marks the coming of age of the union idea in American higher education."

— "Milestone." Editorial in The Bulletin of the Association of College Unions International, 1955.

Final Version of the "Role" Statement, as Adopted by the Association

"1. The union is the community center of the college, for all the members of the college family—students, faculty, administration, alumni, and guests. It is not just a building; it is also an organization and a program. Together they represent a well-considered plan for the community life of the college.

"2. As the 'living room' or the 'hearthstone' of the college, the union provides for the services, conveniences, and amenities the members of the college family need in their daily life on the campus and for getting to know and understand one another through informal association outside the classroom.

"3. The union is part of the educational program of the college. As the center of college community life, it serves as a laboratory of citizenship, training students in social responsibility and for leadership in our democracy.

"Through its various boards, committees, and staff, it provides a cultural, social, and recreational program, aiming to make free time activity a cooperative factor with study in education.

"In all its processes it encourages self-directed activity, giving maximum opportunity for self-realization and for growth in individual social competency and group effectiveness. Its goal is the development of persons as well as intellects.

"4. The union serves as a unifying force in the life of the college, cultivating enduring regard for and loyalty to the college."

— Statement of "The Role of the College Union." Adopted by the members of the Association of College Unions at its 33rd Conference, 1956.

Confirmation that Union Training for Leadership Works

"If one consults the introductory pages of almost any college catalogue, or the key paragraphs of its charter, he is likely to find a statement in this vein: 'The aim of the university is to equip students to grow in usefulness as citizens.' Or, 'The university is a community in which students participate as maturing and responsible members and in which they enrich their resources as participants, present and future, in the larger community.' ...

"Such statements of purpose will hardly be a surprise, considering that the whole educational process in America, fundamentally, was and is intended to prepare young people for intelligent participation and effective leadership in our common life together. ...

"In America, over the 50 years that unions have become a familiar part of the college scene, there have been recurring, reassuring evidences that there may be a relationship between leadership in the union as a student and leadership in community life as a graduate. Union leaders have turned up in noticeable numbers as chairmen of civic organizations, leaders of alumni activity, members of government boards, and candidates for public office. Almost every union has received letters from former student chairmen at not infrequent intervals which read somewhat as follows: 'I know that in my case the union outranks all of the other training I received in terms of influencing my life. My appetite for my present work in the community service field clearly stems from my experiences at the union.'

"The accumulation of such expressions over the years, coupled with the realization of the historic role of unions in Britain, led the national Association of College Unions to declare in 1956, as part of its basic statement of union purpose: 'The union serves as a laboratory of citizenship, training students in social responsibility and for leadership in our democracy.' ...

"But the question in all this which will occur to everyone is: 'Granted the theory is good, how do we know that it works?' ... How do we know that anything happens to a student by the way of union leadership experience that wouldn't have happened anyway, or that doesn't happen to other students by way of their campus experience? ...

WHAT IS A STUDENT?

A STUDENT IS A PERSON WHO IS LEARNING TO FULFILL HIS POWERS AND TO FIND WAYS OF USING THEM IN THE SERVICE OF MANKIND.

— Harold Taylor, president of Sarah Lawrence College. Quoted in the National Student Association News, 1957.

University of Georgia student films presents "Titanic" at the union in 1954. UNIVERSITY OF GEORGIA

"To test the theory, to learn as well as one can what happens, was the object of a recent study of Wisconsin. It is the first documentation of the relation of union leadership experience to post-college civic and political activity. The results are indeed encouraging—though it is apparent there are many opportunities for the union which are still to be cultivated.

"This study, of course, was made of the graduates of a single institution. It does not say that a carry-over of leadership in union affairs to post-college life happens elsewhere or happens as a matter of course. It does say that may have a vast unused resource in carrying out its continuing central and transcending purpose: the making of effective citizens."

— Anne Minahan. The College Union and Preparation for Citizenship, 1957. Foreword by Mr. Butts.

And Union Committeemen Quality

"You might wonder how it happens that we have such a full-blooming crop of students. I believe it's like this:

"You who are their parents do the indispensable job of planting good seed in this academic garden by sending your sons and daughters here in the first place.

"We sprinkle them with a little encouragement and turn on the sunshine of the opportunity to show what they can do. They flourish.

A 1955 photo of Southern Methodist University's Humphrey Lee Student Center. ACUI ARCHIVES

"By and by we have some top flight citizens who do exceptional service for the university. This year is no exception. ...

"All through the spring when the newspapers came out with the lists of student achievement—honoraries, Phi Beta Kappa, Phi Kappa Phi, leadership awards—we found them generously dotted, as usual, with the names of union chairmen and committee members."

— From a talk to Wisconsin Union student committee chairmen and their parents at the annual Union Recognition Dinner, 1958.

"There's a line in our color-sound film about the union that goes: 'The good life doesn't just happen by itself. Somebody works at it.'

"The people who work at it most—so far as the good life on this campus is concerned—are the ones who are here tonight. You who are parents, and who have tried to get them up in the morning, may not have suspected it, but you are surrounded by do-ers—the students who see to it that there are ready at hand for everyone to enjoy:

"The best of music, films, plays, books, and art ... exciting discussions of ideas ... adventures out-of-doors ... helping others in how to do it—whether sailing, bridge, dancing, bowling, or crafts ... and creating countless easy opportunities for making friends.

"Five hundred students on our committees engaged in doing this."

— From a talk to Wisconsin Union student committee chairmen and their parents, 1959.

Why Include the Union in a "Housing" Program?

"The case for the union phase of the federal housing program, reduced to its simplest terms, is that a house consists of a bedroom, dining room, and living room, and that on the college campus the living room and the dining room are commonly called a 'union.'

"To start with the dining room: I think we ought to be able to muster support from the Budget Bureau, the president, and Congress for the proposition that eating is not less essential than sleeping. (I believe if you asked college students, the object of all our efforts and affection, they might say eating is more essential than sleeping.) ...

"The core of almost every union is its dining facilities. And it is almost a universal truism that more students are served every day by the union's dining facilities than all other union facilities put together.

"Why, then, is there any doubt about extending the union loan program? It is because some do not understand the nature of the housing and dining needs on many campuses, and they do not understand that it is the facility we call a union that furnishes the answer to part, or all, of the need. ..."

"To terminate all the union phase of the federal program would result in a serious imbalance in meeting the living needs of students.

"It would mean that urban colleges could expect no help in handling their most crucial problem—providing dining and elementary living space for commuting students. This matter of taking care of the students who commute to college is not an incidental housing need. Looking ahead, we see that it can rightly be described as the main need. The deputy commissioner of the U.S. Office of Education, whose specialty is determining trends affecting educational planning, reports: 'Most of the students who attend college in the future will be commuting students. This trend has meaning for those who are planning housing programs for the future.' ...

"Now if someone should say, 'What about those other union facilities that aren't dining; they're the ones that make the program hard to sell?'

"I would answer: Consider your own house or apartment. Does it have a living room in it—a place to read, to talk with your friends, to play a game, to listen to music? Again, I think we could find agreement that a house consists of a bedroom, a dining room, and a living room. These are the normal, minimum requirements of meeting the basic living needs of everybody. A house, thus, is a three-legged stool. Sit on a two-legged stool and you don't stay off the floor very long. And that's hardly an ideal posture for concentration on studying. ...

"Further, the college housing law provides specifically for 'housing and other educational facilities,' such as 'dining halls, student centers, or unions.' So the housing act recognizes that housing is more than shelter for sleeping. And what is a union? The union from its beginnings in America 60 years ago, has provided—besides the central campus dining hall—living rooms, workrooms, and recreation facilities. ... These central living spaces make the family life of the college possible, which educators everywhere regard as especially necessary in meeting the living needs and sustaining the morale of young people away from home.

"The living room part of housing alone, quite aside from dining, fully justifies federal financing of unions."

— "The Case of the Continued Federal Financing of College Union Buildings." Statement presented at the meeting of the College Housing Advisory Committee and the Federal Housing Agency staff, and printed in the Congressional Record, 1958.

Another Role Statement: Role of the Union Director

"To me, these are the main functions, contributions of a union director:

"1. To provide continuity, to preserve goals and traditions. But more important: to set goals and standards—the ancient question of leadership versus followership. Is the union going to be what the *Saturday Evening Post* says it is—a 'fun house'—or something else? The director probably determines this more than anybody else.

"2. To achieve understanding of the union by the administration and faculty. ...

"3. The selection of staff. The training of staff. One of his best services is to build a competent, perceptive staff so the union's potentialities are released—especially, convincing the administration of the need for adequate staff and professional status. ...

"4. He should take his place among other department heads, the faculty—not be just a housekeeper. Not for reasons of personal prestige, but because the union and its importance is gauged in many ways by the status of its staff.

"5. He should be coordinator of total union enterprise, not just part.

"6. He should stay close to the student union board, be knowledgeable, directly, of student interests and attitudes, keeping students at the center of union decisions. This is not something to pass on to a 'program director,' not a side issue.

"7. In short, he should be a leader of the student and educational life of the campus versus a manager of a building."

— "Role of the Union Director." Outline of a discussion with union directors at the Annual Conference of the Association of College Unions, 1959.

Top left: Linfield College's Riley Student Center in 1956. ACUI ARCHIVES
Top right: The Stetson University Student Union Building under construction. STETSON UNIVERSITY ARCHIVES
Middle: The college union at the University of Virginia, Newcomb Hall, opened in 1958. ACUI ARCHIVES
Bottom: A 1951 photo of the University of Arizona's Student Union Memorial Building. ACUI ARCHIVES

"

ALL THROUGH THE SPRING
WHEN THE NEWSPAPERS
CAME OUT WITH THE LISTS
OF STUDENT ACHIEVEMENT—
HONORARIES, PHI BETA
KAPPA, PHI KAPPA PHI,
LEADERSHIP AWARDS—WE
FOUND THEM GENEROUSLY
DOTTED, AS USUAL,

**WITH THE
NAMES OF UNION
CHAIRMEN AND
COMMITTEE
MEMBERS.**

"

1960s

Amid changes in social discourse, the union focuses on the higher purpose of giving through volunteering. The proliferation of labels such as "auxiliary enterprise," "student union," and "center" do a disservice to the college union idea. U.S. professionals learn from unions overseas. The union emphasizes the potential for constructive activism in response to the shattering impact of student disruption and violence.

In 1965, a University of California, Los Angeles football player takes a break with three coeds in UCLA Student Union.

STATE OF THE UNION, 1961

"In 1949 we were congratulating ourselves that there were 150 some unions, with perhaps another 150 in the dream stage—total 300. As of now I would guess about 600 buildings are in operation, with probably another 200 ready to come along as soon as financing can be arranged. ... And the junior colleges, 700 strong and multiplying fast, are just starting to get interested—not to mention the multitude of universities abroad that are printing blueprints and turning spades. ...

"In short, we are a 'growth industry.' Why, and how, has this come about?

"Basically, I venture to say, the 'why' traces to the realization—almost unpardonably slow in coming as one thinks of it—that the student is a person as well as an intellect, that he has elementary human needs—to eat, to associate with his fellows. Many universities abroad build their unions to level down costs and make it possible for more students to get a college education. Many see the implications for better student morale. Some frankly say they are trying to ward off rebellion, subversion; it's as simple, and urgent, as that. In this country, to its concern for the living problems of its students the college adds a conviction that the campus environment can further the learning process.

"For whatever combination of reasons, the union, once on the luxury list, now assumes a high priority in the campus plan. This is most notably apparent when a new college is created or an old one moves to a new campus. The union is often the second or third building built—sometimes ahead of the library. Far cry from '49. An unexpected, but heartwarming, plus to see in the ledger.

"The way we have planned, and still plan, these buildings is another matter. A melancholy minus.

"The same university which will put a team of scientists at work to study with meticulous care for a year the potential of a research project before asking for a $50,000 grant will the next day list, by name only, a score of facilities to go in a $3,000,000 union and command an architect who has never seen a union to have the plans ready to meet a federal loan deadline next month. Incredible, but this is what happens, over and over. ...

"The concept of the union—the 'image' if you will—in the public mind is still shadowy and confused. This is probably our fault. We have talked too much about unions as 'social centers,' instead of 'social-cultural centers.'

"We have taken the important first step of clarification, concurring in 1956 in an official statement of what a union ought to be. And in pamphlet after pamphlet, one sees that individual unions have made this four-point statement their own, each time spreading the gospel, and each time adding a hefty plus in my book.

"But then the purpose gets blurred again by the other misleading labels that are tacked on unions.

"I am not one who is enchanted by the Madison Avenue reliance on creating images through words; but I do think that what you call a union makes a difference. Consider again what happens:

"We announce in our statement of 'The Role of the College Union' that it is 'the community center of the college, for all of the members of the college family—students, faculty, alumni, guests.' And then we proceed to cancel this declaration, or 'image,' by constantly referring in press, in speeches, in correspondence to the 'student union' or 'student center.' ...

"I read in the New York papers recently this choice bit: 'Harvard does not have a student union. The house activity system serves all the functions of a student union—and does so on a more intimate level.'

"Well, no doubt Harvard students gain a sense of fraternity with a few, but not a sense of community, with all—which is what society most needs to have inculcated in students. So, because of a name, a great and good university deprives itself and its students from the values of a community center. ...

"There is another label, widely used in college literature, that is even more helpful to the chances a union has of realizing its true potential. A double minus sign for the now too long tradition of cataloguing the union, along with the college laundry, as an 'auxiliary enterprise.'

"Conceived in these terms, what chance has the union got to enter into the minds of its planners and overseers as an educational force that requires educators on the staff, as a cultural center that requires a theater, art gallery, music rooms to do its job?

"The natural question for the uninitiated is: 'Auxiliary to what? In what ways?' Many assume the union is an auxiliary of the business office, whereas most unions report to the president or dean of students, and many are engaged in teaching—not to mention presenting the main cultural and recreational program of the campus. ...

"Mostly the reader is left without any clue to what is really meant. ...

"Result of all this: an ignorance of, or misconception of, what the union is and how it operates, affecting attitudes, budgeting, staff selection, and producing local misunderstanding or controversy over the goals for the union. ...

"For those who would avoid the word 'union' altogether, because it might be confused with labor unions, I have a parting minus sign.

The word 'union' is a good word. It means, lest we forget, 'joined together for mutual benefit,' 'oneness.' This country chose to call itself a union. We fought a war 100 years ago to keep it. And we haven't given up the name because Russia adopted it later.

"I think it's no less than shameful that college trustees deprive their colleges and student bodies from identity with the rich heritage of the college union because they don't like labor unions, which weren't invented until 50 years after the founding of the Oxford and Cambridge Unions. These same trustees, without a qualm or rise in blood pressure, hold their meetings in the conservative Union League Club, invest the college funds in Union Pacific, deposit the income with the Union Trust, endorse the rules of the Amateur Athletic Union, and send their telegrams, I suspect, via Western Union. To blackball the college union just doesn't make sense.

"It isn't merely nomenclature, however, that deters the realization of the union's stated purpose, not by any means. The prime road block, I think we have to say, is lack of staff, professionally prepared, to work at it.

"In comparing with the balance sheet I drew up in '49, I see I said: 'If there's one liability more damaging than any other to the successful functioning of the union, it is that the staff has far too much to do.' Unhappily, this is still the case. One of our conference sessions this year is titled: 'Staffing the Union with Professionals.' An unintended irony. Many a director will read this and forlornly ask: 'What staff? What professionals?' Because he's the staff; and while he has professed interest in the union or he wouldn't be on the job, that's as far as he's been able to go in becoming a 'professional.' You who are here are lucky. There are perhaps as many who couldn't come because if they left home there'd be no one else to tend shop. We'd be surprised, I think, if we counted up to see how many unions are one-man, or even half-man, jobs—where the director does everything but sweep out.

"Most union directors, with or without assistants, launched as they are into an infinity of things to do, have the sensation of hurtling through space day after day, with no time to look to right or left, answer a letter, or phone their wives they won't be home to dinner. Very exciting and adventurous, this insistent daily orbiting, but it's lonely up there. ...

"We have shaped a statement of guiding purpose, and in five short years witnessed remarkable concurrence in this declaration of what a union is for. This doesn't say we've fulfilled the purpose, but the indispensable beginning of knowing what we want to do has been made. ...

"Now, in recent months, the Association has turned its corporate attention to the cultivation of the arts. Why at this juncture, you may ask, the arts?

"Here we come close to the theme of this conference—'Higher Education and the National Purpose.' Because one clear national purpose, which this country has had from the beginning, is to make secure the natural right to pursuit of happiness, along with life and liberty itself.

"And this, in turn, was a restatement of enduring, universal human purpose as enunciated by the Greeks centuries ago when Aristotle and others spoke of leisure as 'the end of all labor,' 'the main content of a free life,' 'the nurse of civilization.'

"Never since history began have so many men had so many hours of leisure for high achievement as now, in America. The leisure we have gained truly could mean, social and cultural historians agree, personal happiness and a better civilization—if we could come by quality in the use of it.

"But how have we 'pursued' happiness, used our hard-won leisure? All too much, sad to say, in aimless amusement. Dreadful TV shows the current hallmark. ... 'No people in history,' says Clinton Rossiter, professor of American Institutions at Cornell, 'has ever had to put up with so much vulgarity, bad taste, and ugliness ... Let us be honest about it: we have the wealth and leisure to make a great culture an essential part of our lives, an inspiration to the world—and we have not even come close to the mark.'

"Does this make a difference now, as we search for the common national purpose which will help us survive in the death grapple with communism? It does indeed.

"In the provocative series of articles on the national purpose in *Life* magazine last year, Rossiter goes on to say, 'No great nation can be said to be worth respecting or imitating if it has not achieved a high level of culture.'

"And what may all this have to do with higher education—and our corner of the world, the college union?

"Well, colleges—and unions—are themselves not immune from the prevailing criticism of the low estate of our leisure pursuits. We all know of the widely published slighting references to campuses as country clubs and unions as 'play houses.' ...

"Why and how, when the creative and cultural use of leisure at the American university might set the influential standard, as at universities in centuries past, has this mission of the university—and its union—miscarried?

"Arnold Toynbee thinks it's because our system of education has degenerated into the formalities of book learning divorced from what he calls 'a spontaneous apprenticeship for life,' that the art of playing with words has been substituted for the art of living—forgetting that it is our experience of life that educates us most.

"Henry Commager, Amherst's professor of American history, affirms this, saying that much of higher education in America is anticultural because of 'the widespread illusion that education is something that goes on in the classroom, something that comes by way of a 'course' that a professor 'gives' and a student 'takes.' This leads to the natural conclusion that when the classroom is closed, the process of education is over, and that

the professor might as well go home and tend to his garden, the student might as well go to the union and watch television.'

"What, then, might the university now do to fill this void and assume its role of leadership in our nation's cultural life? Commager's answer is: 'It is the function of the university to provide scholars, old and young, with the environment conducive to the discovery and transmission of ideas ... physical facilities for the meeting of the minds, for social intercourse. ... Students educate each other—that may be the most important part of college education—and the university must make that possible: by residence halls, club rooms, theaters, music rooms, browsing rooms, pleasant dining facilities ... by building unions, and making them more than convenient places to install juke boxes.'

"I couldn't agree more. The union has a unique and superlative opportunity to bridge the gap between classroom and leisure, and to enhance the quality of leisure, because it is precisely in the area of a student's leisure time that it operates. But if the union is really to do something about taste and intelligence in the use of free time, it has to have the right kinds of facilities to work with. And this means, as Commager implies, an emphasis on the arts. For the arts are the starting point in lifting the quality of our life. If there are to be choices beyond juke boxes and television, students need the kinds of facilities readily at hand which point them in the direction of the better, more rewarding uses of leisure—music rooms, art gallery, browsing room, craft shop, theater. When, besides accessible cultural facilities, students receive a hand from enlightened staff and student leaders in moving toward some standards of excellence in what is done in these rooms for leisure, students rise to the occasion by the hundreds, and the university suddenly finds that it has, through the presence of such a union, a new dimension in education—a vast expansion of the time area in which it educates a new means through which it can make its contribution to the national cultural purpose. ...

"So there we have it: mounting evidence that the whole pattern and tone of student interests can be substantially changed—toward serious, rewarding cultural pursuits.

"I think I hear a swelling chorus of pluses, and they sing: 'The fine arts are fine in the union.'

"In another quite different theater of action, perhaps the most crucial of all, the union purpose—'to train students in social responsibility and for lead-

Colorado State University student body leaders from 1960 look forward to the 160,000-square-foot Lory Student Center, which would open in 1962. CSU PHOTOGRAPHY - COLORADO STATE UNIVERSITY

ership in our democracy'—comes together with the basic purpose of higher education as set forth last year by the Policies Committee of the American Council on Education—'to provide opportunity for each individual to discharge the personal and social responsibilities of life.' ...

"As John Gardner, president of the Carnegie Corporation, said in analyzing our national purpose, 'We agree on our more important aims, we know what the problems are. So what is lacking? The answer is simple: We lack leadership on the part of our leaders, and commitment on the part of every American. ... In a democracy leaders must lead. ... The survival of the idea for which this nation stands is not inevitable. It may survive if enough Americans care enough.'

"And it is in our universities, President Kennedy said in his message to Congress, that are produced the leaders we need.

"There is our ultimate mission: to help produce the leaders who care enough. ...

"Does the union do enough to help? Not enough.

"But perhaps the time has come. As a national group we have now consolidated our intent to do something about responsible citizenship. And many unions are on the way. In simple ways first, perhaps—but essential ways: like guiding stu-

dents in how to register as voters ... conducting mock political conventions ... bringing informed observers of the national scene by the dozens to discuss with students political, social, scientific, and international questions ... dedicating one union expressly to serve as a 'Citizenship Center' ... searching for the factors that strengthen a student's desire to serve his community ... and, most significant of all, patiently continuing day by day the task of coaching countless student committee members in how to use their abilities, not just for their personal advancement, but for the common good. Gleaming pluses throughout.

"And now comes affirmation of the importance of all this from the summit: 'Ask not what your country will do for you; ask what you can do for your country.'

"Here a simple, powerful paraphrase of the social responsibility purpose of higher education as proclaimed in almost every college catalogue, but largely unattended by any specific effort to inculcate a public service point of view in students month by month. Here what could well be the touchstone of the union purpose."

— "State of the Union, 1961." Opening address, Conference of the Association of College Unions, 1961.

Student leaders from Boise State University's student government and programming board gather around the Student Union sign in 1969. BOISE STATE UNIVERSITY DIGITAL COLLECTIONS

Case Example of the Union Idea at Work

"In these recent anxious times for the university at the legislature, it is not entirely accidental that the key Democratic leader in the Senate and two young Republicans in the Assembly who are heading the move to restore cuts in the university budget were officers of the union when they were on the campus.

"Certainly it is not accidental that hundreds of parents got letters from students and in turn wrote letters to their legislators about the importance of maintaining a strong faculty.

"Not entirely accidental either that last fall five former chairmen were candidates for the legislature, two for Congress, and one for the mayor of Madison. Or that a former union president has worked devotedly in the public interest on the state's tax revision plan, trying to bring some order out of chaos. Or that the chairman of the fund campaign for the Milwaukee Union is one of our former chairmen. ...

"I mention all this to give you who are new chairmen an idea of the kind of company into which you are inducted tonight, and to illustrate one of the center line objectives of the union: working voluntarily for the common good."

— From a talk at the annual Wisconsin Union recognition dinner, 1961.

Closer View of How Learning at the Union Takes Place

"What is it these chairmen of union committees are engaged in doing? In the best sense, education—for themselves and for fellow students.

"President Woodrow Wilson of Princeton, in his address on 'The Spirit of Learning' in 1909, said: 'The real intellectual life of a body of undergraduates, if there be any, manifests itself, not in the classroom, but in what they do and talk of and set before themselves as their favorite objects between classes. ... If you wish to create a college, therefore, and are wise, you will seek to create a life ... and fill it with the things of the mind and spirit.'

"This is what this company of students has been busy doing: creating a life outside the classroom that is suffused with learning.

"They have turned their attention, and the attention of the campus as a whole—between classes—to book talks and creative writing, to better films, how to sail a boat in a windy rain or climb a mountain, how to use a pottery kiln, to a better understanding of the cultures of their fellow foreign students, to the meaning of the arts, to earnest discussions of national affairs and how to win the peace, to the poetry of Robert Frost, the music and exciting ideas of violinist Isaac Stern—until such have become, in Wilson's words, 'favorite objects' of students between classes.

"It isn't entirely an accident that junior prom is no longer with us, or the Campus Carnival. Students have something better to do—other favorite objects. And the committees headed by the students here tonight have helped make it so.

"Students may come here first to eat—thankfully, because this is how we get most of the money to do all the other things. But they stay to talk, to see, to argue—about the state of the world, the arts, their personal philosophies.

"This process of exposure, and of example, reaches most of the student body—broadening horizons and bending, even changing, interests.

"I must say, in retrospect—if I may interject a personal note—this was my own experience, as a student, with the union.

"I started as a freshman in commerce. In the first few weeks I became aware that the previous year one of the members of the Union Board—Frederic March—had made quite a hit in a song and dance act in the Union Vodvil. ... March seemed to have a good idea, so shortly I found myself on the Union Vodvil stage—scared to death, and with something less than Frederic March's appeal.

"But then I discovered the union also brought concerts to the campus. Now as a boy I had cranked up the old spring motor Victrola at our house to accommodate guests who wanted to hear 'Liebestraum' by Fritz Kreisler and 'I Hear You Calling Me' by John McCormack. But I thought this was music for the old folks. For one thing, you couldn't dance to it, I had no idea who Kreisler was, and cared less. Then as a freshman at Wisconsin I found a man named Kreisler, alive and real, appearing in person on the campus. And then McCormack, Pablo Casals, Chaliapin, Paderewski, Rachmaninoff—brought not by the Music School for the old folks, but by the Union Board. Students managed concerts. Students attended concerts. Incredible! I went to my first concert.

"Well, I wound up—with certain encouragement from the advisor to the Union Board—in English, art history, and in this union business of presenting concerts.

"Something like this—this transmutation, or expansion, of interests—has happened over the years. And it has happened this year.

"Who can say what may be the ultimate outcome of a history student selling her first painting in a sidewalk art show or the state Salon of Art, of students of the Literary Committee talking intimately and earnestly with Robert Frost—spending an evening, as one of them said, in the presence of greatness—of the Music Committee dining with Isaac Stern to hear his idea of student cultural exchanges, of the Forum Committee entertaining Mr. Kubitschek, the former president of Brazil?

"Well, we know one very pleasant immediate outcome: Mr. Kubitschek invited our forum chairman to visit Brazil as his guest. And she's going. ...

"Our vice president—student of economics in the classroom—after working a year with the foreign student program, is now to be the state chairman of the college 'People to People' program.

"And our outgoing president, intrigued with music ... moved beyond his marketing classes, his major, to the student direction of our music program. And shortly, he found himself interested in, and able to direct, as president, this whole far-flung program for Wisconsin's social and cultural life we call the union. He has done so well, we've asked him to join us on the staff."

— From a talk to outgoing and incoming Wisconsin Union chairmen, 1962.

"

BUT THE ULTIMATE
JUSTIFICATION OF A UNION
IS THAT IT HAS SOMETHING
TO DO WITH EDUCATION.
AS THE UNION ENTERPRISE
HAS UNFOLDED, MANY HAVE
PERCEIVED—DIMLY AT FIRST,
BUT MORE CLEARLY THAN
EVER—THAT THE UNION HAS
SOMETHING VERY IMPORTANT
**TO DO WITH THE CENTRAL
PURPOSES OF EDUCATION.**

"

An Interpretation of the Association's "Role" Statement

"The phrase—'unifying force'—supports rather better than anything else, I think, the meaning of the word 'union' and the concept of a union as a positive contributor to college life, rather than just a convenient place to gather, or a physical facility giving service. ...

"There is always a risk, even in the small colleges, that special interest groups and the living unit groups—the fraternities, the dormitories, the church centers, the clubs, the commuters—will become insular, withdrawing into themselves, splitting the campus socially.

"One college administrator has said: 'The more students tend to be separated into socially limited units (i.e., fraternities and dormitories), the more important the union's function to assist in the integration of the student body.'

"It is here, indeed, that the union can render a special service as a unifying force. Because of its centralized social-cultural-dining facilities and because all students are members equally, the union becomes the common meeting ground for all. It encourages and strengthens the special interest groups, but on occasion, by conscious design, it brings all together. ... In such ways the strengths of separate special interest and house groups can be combined to produce a strong single student body, with all students widening their acquaintanceships and sharing the feeling of belonging to the larger college community. ...

"In an earlier era, many universities sought the values of a campus-centered fellowship principally by way of recreating the Oxford kind of residential college, with the union as the supplement which counteracted the attractions of the town and facilitated interchange among the several college residences. But the residence halls are no longer the answer—not when nonresidents are beginning to outnumber all residence students put together. For the increasing number of commuters the residence halls are simply of no significance.

"This spectacular turn of events in who goes to college assigns to the union the role of creating a common life for students that educators once anticipated the residence halls, mainly, would fulfill. For it is the union that largely now supplies the reasons and attractions for staying on the campus or returning to the campus. ...

"This all represents a very tough problem, as every union director confronted with the daily or weekend exodus knows; but when the effort succeeds, even in part, the student's college experience is extended and enriched and the union becomes one of the principal agencies through which a sense of commitment to the college and belonging to it comes about.

"And not to be overlooked is what this can mean in cultivating, as the Association role statement phrases it, 'enduring regard for and loyalty to the college.' Many unions, urban and nonurban, were built with the avowed intention of 'making better alumni while they are students,' and these institutions believe they have succeeded.

"Now we come to that part of the Association statement of purpose which says 'the union is part of the educational program of the college.'

"If one reads only the accounts of unions in the popular magazines, he is led to believe they are merely playhouses, fun factories—'a rallying point for snacking, dalliance, and amusement.'

"Well, unions are for fun, and that's all right. We can do much worse than provide a measure of cheer in these troubled times when every day the headlines announce some new morale-shattering crisis. Some fun between headlines is a way of staying sane. And the 'pursuit of happiness' in our country, in every country, is entirely legitimate—in fact, we say, an inalienable right. We don't have to apologize for this part of the union outcome.

"But the ultimate justification of a union is that it has something to do with education. As the union enterprise has unfolded, many have perceived—dimly at first, but more clearly than ever—that the union has something very important to do with the central purposes of education.

"First, with respect to the development of the student as an individual. ...

"The union, as the center of the social life of students, is in an especially strategic position to contribute at least a little, perhaps a great deal, to the personal social competence of a student—to his ability to work and live congenially among other people, with confidence and personal effectiveness. ... If he doesn't have this aptitude, all else that he knows from the classroom, or whatever he may wish to do in his vocation or as a leader, may count for nothing. ...

"So unions have had reason to be persistently watchful for the ways of assisting all students entering the union toward social orientation, personal development, and self-realization of latent interests. Hence a program of social and cultural activities through which a student can express himself fully and find personally satisfying uses of his leisure time. Hence the teaching on a rather wide scale of social and recreational skills to cultivate the social competence that helps a student in status in his group and confidence in himself. ...

"Don't discount what this means to students. Students bring all sorts of personal problems, insecurities, and confusions to college with them, or develop them there. Mental health difficulties aren't something apart from the college. ...

"Then there is the opportunity to broaden personal horizons, to shape beliefs, and to choose new goals that comes from social association with other students. You recall that a half century ago Van Hise, Wilson, Leacock, and many others were saying that much of what students learn, they learn from each other, and from faculty through informal association outside the classroom. This isn't only an early speculation—a throwback to Oxonian education—or incidental. This may be, Henry Commager, one of our most respected historians of American institutions, said quite recently, the most important part of college education. And if the comprehensive studies of today's students by Philip Jacob, Edward Eddy, and others mean anything they mean that essential student attitudes, beliefs, and values are formed not by the kind of curriculum they take, not by what the teachers say in the classroom, but by the 'value-climate' they are exposed to in their life with other students outside the classroom. ...

"What we now know is that students are learning at all hours of the day; they are becoming what they are doing and accepting at all hours of the day. In sum, the total environment educates. And since only a small part of the student's day is spent in formal classes, it follows that every campus has a vast range of learnings—an informal curriculum—which is of tremendous importance. These learnings, of course, can be poor as well as good. It takes the right sort of environment to yield the right sort of experiences which in turn yield the right sort of learnings. And the kinds of constructive and creative endeavors that are the sure sign of a good environment, as Dr. Karl Menninger has said, 'need encouragement, example, direction, facilitation.' What a challenge to the perceptive and imaginative union! ...

"The second goal of the union as part of the educational program is to strengthen our kind of society and the cause of democracy in another way—by serving as an effective community center which becomes a 'laboratory of citizenship,' training students for social responsibility and leadership.'

"We have heard a good deal about the union as a 'community center' in recent years. And rightly so. There is probably no better way to describe in two words the increasing multitude of functions the union serves—living and dining room of the campus community; center for fellowship; force for unity; active encourager of student self-expression and self-directed activity; teacher of the arts of leisure and recreation; social and cultural heart of the campus.

"But above all, a union is a priceless tool for shaping an authentic community of teachers and students of the kind which helps prepare students to contribute intelligently and positively to the welfare of each other and of society. ...

"Current studies of student attitudes show that their goals in life are couched almost entirely in terms of self-reference; vocational preparation and personal social acceptability head the rewards students seek from their higher education. Only 3 percent give top priority to being active in national affairs or being useful as a citizen; only 17 percent expect that participation in the affairs of their community will be even one of three activities giving them the most satisfaction in life; and only 12 percent expect activity directed toward national or international betterment will be among their three most satisfying activities.

"We simply can't afford any longer to have it this way, not when the common transcending purpose of us all is making democracy work, so that it survives, and so that it excels in men's minds everywhere. ...

"There, then, is our ultimate mission, as it was the original, central union mission at Oxford and Cambridge: to muster as best we can all the unparalleled resources of the union for influencing students to become the leaders who care. ...

"If I were to have to choose where the main emphasis of a union should lie, I think I would say:

"1. Associate the union firmly with the purpose of education, because of what this will do to validate the union in achieving goals your administration also seeks and to help it succeed in all its endeavors.

"2. Find the ways, modest though they be, to make a contribution to national and international well-being, for if our nation and its values, and a measure of international understanding and amity, do not prevail, it may, indeed, make little difference what else we do."

— "Goals of the College Union." Union Summer Course, University of Wisconsin, 1962.

HOW TO ORGANIZE THE BEST RESULTS

"Many unions falter or fail from the outset because there is no authoritative delineation of what it is or how it is to function. The most recent general study of unions, in 1957, showed that less than two-thirds of unions surveyed had a constitution. The other third, I'll guess, are shaky in their own minds as to what they should try to accomplish, and are free game for poaching and interference by other college agencies. Such unions are headed for trouble—when a new dean of students, president, or business manager arrives, with ideas of what his prerogatives are, or when a student government decides it would like to take over a function the union has been performing or should perform.

Recognize the Primacy of Student Leadership

"It is sometimes proposed that the dean of students, a faculty member, or even the president of the college be the head of the governing board of a union. Perhaps it may work well on some campuses, but in general these seem to me to be the reasons for maintaining student leadership:

"1. One of the greatest values that has come out of the development of unions has been the opportunity afforded the college to train students in self-government and in leadership of community affairs.

"Genuine interest on the part of students and the assumption of real responsibility, however, have been achieved only when students have been given a leading and central part in the direction of the building and its programs. When a student is president, the general student body sees him as a symbol of the student body's essential part in the success of the enterprise and of the college's confidence in students to do a good, responsible job.

"2. By giving students primary leadership, the college usually wins immediate student support for the union and many other corollary benefits of student feeling of partnership with the administration.

"3. Both the social and financial success of a union depend heavily upon the feelings of student responsibility for achieving such success.

"4. The users of the union and the paying members will inevitably be overwhelming students. Logically, therefore, a representative of the majority group would be president and, desirably, the majority of the governing board would be students.

Make the Board's Authority Real

"Whatever the composition of the governing board, or whatever its leadership, it is essential that its authority be real, reasonably complete, and spelled out, or what you are likely to have is the window-dressing of self-government but not the real article. As early as the 1949 Association conference, Foster Coffin of Cornell, after a survey of 64 unions, reported:

'There's a general trend toward independence of the union from the control of either the president or the dean; unions make their best contribution to the enrichment of student life if union boards, so far as possible, are given latitude, with a large degree of freedom and autonomy, to manage their own affairs and give students every opportunity to hammer out their own problems and make their own decisions.'

"The disposition of the college is not to give the union any real autonomy when its fate is subject to the vagaries of student elections. So insistence on

Oklahoma State University constructs a five-story addition to the northeast side of the Student Union in 1964 at a cost of $2.5 million. OKLAHOMA STATE UNIVERSITY STUDENT UNION MARKETING

elections can lose for the union the chance to be a self-governing institution.

"The union function, by definition, is essentially educational and administrative, not legislative. And it proposes to teach the uses of citizenship and leadership in the context of volunteering for service. To do this successfully it needs to bring together students and faculty well motivated in this direction. Its chances are not very secure through elections where campus politics and all sorts of extraneous issues enter in.

Lines of Responsibility

"Now it is necessary in any college structure that there be staff line responsibility to a given office—for submission of budgets and clearing staff appointments. But when you come to the question: 'To whom does the union director look for policy direction?', except for basic financial policy which is settled for all departments by the business office or trustees, this is a quite different matter. ...

"If the college really believes in the principle of self-government in community affairs and cherishes the benefits self-government of the union can produce, then the union director, at least in non-fiscal policy matters, will report directly to and receive direction primarily from the governing board of the union, his line of responsibility running through the governing board to the president and trustees, where the responsibilities of all college agencies wind up, and must.

"But the wise administration will allow the maximum latitude for the governing board to govern."

— "The Government and Staffing of a Union." Union Summer Course, University of Wisconsin, 1962.

"The rather easy assumption is made in some quarters that because the union deals with students outside the classroom it is ipso facto part of the student personnel program; hence, should be under the direction of the dean of student affairs.

"This overlooks, of course, that the union also has extensive responsibilities to faculty, alumni, conference groups, teaching departments, and many others, not to mention heavy financial responsibilities that run to the business manager. And especially it overlooks the merits of self-direction.

"There is no college office which includes an official concern with all groups and interests with which the union deals except the president's office. Hence a union governing board which represents all interests, with line responsibility to the president's office and on to the trustees."

— "Relationships with Other Agencies." Union Summer Course, University of Wisconsin, 1962.

Other Hallmarks of a Good Union

Funds for Program

"Besides funds to employ a staff, operate the building, pay the debt, a union needs money for a program, too. The sad truth is the program is often the last to be considered, and, in times of trouble, the first to be cut.

"The mark of a union that believes in what it says about its purposes is a good social-cultural program for the campus, adequately financed."

— "Financing Programs." Union Summer Course, University of Wisconsin, 1962.

Facilities for the Arts, Outings— and Room to Grow

"The union has an unparalleled opportunity to enhance the quality of leisure, because it is its great fortune to be able to reach students during their leisure time.

"But if it is to seize this opportunity and make the most of it, it has to have the right kinds of facilities to work with. This means, in my book—and in the student's book—facilities and equipment for music, art, drama, literature, crafts.

"This is not a paternal or missionary effort to roll back a competing tide of student interest. It is a matter of running with the tide. The reassuring and exciting thing is that students respond to the arts—more than to almost anything else the union offers these days, besides food.

"Throughout the colleges of the country, the interest of students in the cultural facilities a union can provide—theater or auditorium, gallery, browsing room, music listening rooms—is proving to be extraordinary. Such specifically cultural facilities are supported in almost all surveys of union needs by approximately 60–75 percent of all students, and often are exceeded in student interest only by snack bar, lounge, ballroom, and cafeteria—the traditionally acknowledged essentials. ...

"When you provide these, especially a theater, what you end up with is a truer community center—the avowed union objective—with enormous gains in usefulness and convenience for both the union and the college and with the means of making the union a principal cultural force, perhaps the principal cultural force, in the life of the college. ...

"It may seem to you I am laying extraordinary stress on the arts—more than really warranted. I don't think so. Because through the arts we are dealing with one of the most important concerns of education and of our times: student creativeness and standards of taste, student understanding of what is best in the world about them, and student understanding of something we have not given much attention thus far: the culture of other peoples and the means of achieving an international fraternity of free men. ...

"Cultural facilities, of course, are not the only ones that strengthen what the union is trying to do in providing the student experience of value and meaning. I would be negligent indeed if I didn't call attention especially to the potentials of outdoor activity, which the union can bring to life by arranging for a few facilities and applying a little resourcefulness and leadership. ...

"Unions have a logical role in the outing field. An outing program complements the normal union program. Students engaging in an outing program learn by doing; they develop interests that will carry over after graduation; they develop qualities of leadership by teaching skills; they adjust their differences with others in the free and easy give and take of an outing perhaps better than in any other situation; they form fast friendships. ...

"No one has the last word on what the union will be doing, or students will expect it to do, 10 years from now, or even five. We have seen already how student interests and needs can change—witness the declining popularity of the large ballroom, the rising interest in the theater; the virtual disappearance of lounges for men or women only, indeed the futility of almost any lounge that is just a place to sit down, while snack bars are expanding to twice or four times their original size.

"There are new, interesting facilities that are beginning to make their appearance and which just might be prophesying what may be common in the future union program. ...

"A union is on the safest ground when it starts with the assumption of growth and change, and adapts—or better still, leads—accordingly."

— "Building Facilities which Strengthen the Program." Union Summer Course, University of Wisconsin, 1962.

"While the architect cannot control what goes into the building, he can bring to the attention of the college client the numerous aids which can enlarge the client's perspective and, hopefully, improve the ultimate judgments. ...

"Especially, the architect can see to it that whatever facilities are chosen are blessed with an environment that is humane. And of course, he can see to it that the architecture is fitting to the purpose; an invitation to informality, human in scale; creative rather than imitative; and, hopefully, inspirational."

— "The College Union Story." Journal of the American Institute of Architects, 1964.

Commitment to Enlisting Student Interest in Service, Leadership

"The union is especially well fitted to develop leadership of the best kind because:

"A. It is a service institution—not a power group, not embroiled in meaningless campus politics. Its concern is what students can do for fellow students.

"B. It deals with things that count, that have lessons and meaning beyond the campus—economic aids, price policies; personal conduct, social acceptability; minority groups—shun or welcome?; current social and political issues; cultural standards, freedom; democratic, non-democratic procedures.

"And the committee system (vis a vis legislating) is the meaningful method. Eric Sevareid has said: 'By the team and committee system, he (the student) learns the doing of things together as the natural method, and since the central problem of our times is the social problem, the instinct of working together is the most important instinct a man can learn.'

"Further, the union has, or should have, a counseling, teaching staff especially devoting its time and effort to preparation of students for leadership. Where else is this true?

"It has extensive physical and program resources to work with, something tangible to lead. Leadership can't operate in vacuum.

"It operates in the time area outside classroom, is not bound by curricular requirements; so there's a wide range of opportunity for student initiative, experiment; for failure without disaster, as well as success. ...

"And it is working with students on projects they want to do something about. ...

"But the union has to give conscious attention to leadership training, not leaving it to chance. ...

"We can't hope for commitment to humane values and selfless service as an accidental by-product of education. This has to be a central expectation with which we confront students."

— "Developing Student Leadership." Union Summer Course, University of Wisconsin, 1962.

This Is the Way Things Ought to Be

"Two widely separated union incidents tell us something about the union mission, something of the difference the student-staff leadership of a union makes, why this all-important matter of your leadership counts. And is worth any dedication you can bring to your mission.

"First, an article in the current issue of *Time* magazine. This is what it says: 'On the orders of Burma's military strongman, an army demolition team marched on campus and blew up the two-story union building (Rangoon University), whose brick walls have echoed for 34 years with the student arguments of such leaders as Aung San, father of Burma's independence, ex-Premier U Nu, and capable U Thant, Secretary-General of the United Nations. A government spokesman explained that it had been necessary because "it was a haven for underground leaders, plotting the overthrow of the government."'

"This is reminiscent of Germany in Hitler days; though there the Nazis didn't destroy unions—they took them over as training centers for the Hitler youth movement. It was one of their first acts upon coming into power. They prostituted a decent, humane institution for evil purposes.

"I was in Germany at about this time, visiting the German unions. I came to know especially of the work of Fritz Beck, director of the Munich studentenhaus and one of the leaders of the new German union movement—a good friend. A month later, when I returned home, I read in the papers that Fritz Beck had been taken by the Nazis into the woods at night and shot—because he refused to exclude Jewish students from using the union. He was the first.

"What Rangoon and Munich show is that unions can be used for evil purposes as well as good.

"Who is to stand against this kind of perversion? We are the ones, if it ever came to that, God forbid. We would hope for the support of our college administrations and the enlightened elements of our society. But some issues transcend the college policy. Where basic human values and rights are at stake—social justice and freedom of speech—leaders must lead, wherever they are, and this includes us, in our strategic and crucial role of leaders in student life and thought. ...

"Then the 'good' the union can mean—the second incident:

"A while back, at the close of a summer session like this one, we received a letter from a visiting professor who had been on the campus for the summer and was about to leave. This is what the letter said: 'We don't have a union; I've been watching what happens at yours; I've been here almost every day. It's an amazing place. The food is good and inexpensive. The employees are cordial and go out of their way to help us. There's a place to leave your things. You can use the phone without hunting for a dime. There's an air of informality and cheer about the place. Everybody seems happy. We've watched Negro and white students, Japanese and Canadians, sitting on the terrace laughing and talking together as though it were the most natural thing in the world. There are paintings to see, music to listen to, good books to read. The movies are excellent. And that workshop—I framed a picture there the other day and I just wish I had had more time to putter around. We've taken in all the lectures and concerts. We sat on the floor and sang with students at almost every Sunday evening sing. And the other night we stopped to watch the square dancing and were invited in on that. We feel as if we belonged. In fact, the union has made this the best summer we've had. It's really all very wonderful. We've said to ourselves many times, this is the way things ought to be.'

"I suddenly saw that what he was saying embraced, in a simple and very special way, all of what a union is for—all of what we have been trying to say this week: 'This is the way things ought to be.' ...

"So ... you who have chosen the union field for your endeavors are the guardians of a precious instrument for good. I think, as you see the opportunities unfold, as you see how this instrument touches and enriches the lives of countless students, you will be able to say, because you have the union, 'This is what we've been working for and waiting for all the time—this is the way things ought to be, here and everywhere. And I had a part in it.'"

— "A Summing Up." Union Summer Course, University of Wisconsin, 1962.

THE UNIVERSAL UNION FUNCTION: PLACE FOR MEETING, DINING

"There are many kinds of unions, with many variations of purpose—and some, regretfully, with no apparent purpose at all. ... Because people are diverse, their life together is diverse, and colleges themselves are diverse, in what they choose to emphasize and to be.

"But nevertheless there are certain common denominators, certain unities, in this diversity. So it is also with unions. What are these more common purposes? ...

"What is perhaps the most universally acknowledged function of a union is expressed in the Association's statement of the 'The Role of the College Union' in these terms:

"'The union provides for the services, conveniences, and amenities the members of the college family need in their daily life on the campus and for getting to know and understand one another.'

"To spell this out in terms of specifics:

"Students and faculty need a common meeting ground to personalize relations between students and teachers, and to create an intellectual environment outside as well as inside the classroom.

"Students need a common meeting ground. Whenever a survey of needs for a union is conducted, students on almost every campus still register as their main request 'a central place to get together.' If students are to meet informally and to share common interests beyond drinking a coke together in an overcrowded, noisy, untidy corner drug store, a union is a 'must.'

"Commuting students particularly need a place to headquarter on the campus and an adequate place to dine. And the administration and student organizations need an effective way to communicate with them. The commuters' ties to the central student body, their participation in the life of the campus, and their satisfaction with their college experience increase immeasurably when there is an adequate social-dining-activities center.

"Serving as a 'living room'—or living space—for the campus in the above ways is an elementary function of a union. It is a function which has continuing important relevance at any college, representing as it does the answer to needs which exist regardless of the size of a college, its location, or its plan for housing.

"Sometimes obscured by that felicitous phrase, 'living room,' is the fact that the union is also the 'dining room' of the campus—usually the principal, and often the only, dining center for students who do not dine where they live. ...

"If a union were to consist of only one facility, it would be a lunch room and snack bar. Many unions on small campuses are just that. And if you take all unions together, you will find that more than half of the total building area is devoted to dining and dining-related space. ...

"Finally, besides dining and living space there are the countless other services and conveniences which a union can provide and which simply make life easier: a place to check your things, an information desk that answers all the questions, telephones, a handy place to get supplies and books, and mail.

"Now all of this is what some call, sometimes deprecatingly, the 'service station' role of the union. I wouldn't deprecate. It is the indispensable precondition to the success of a union in all that it undertakes. If a union is surely and regularly to gather together the populace of a campus, for whatever purpose, it will provide first for the things that human beings do, and need, in their more elemental daily activity. ...

"But I think we see now that this is only the beginning. If a union is content merely to be an inanimate shelter and a dispenser of service, no matter how well dispensed, its mission is only half fulfilled."

— "Goals of the College Union." Keynote address, Region 7 Conference of the Association of College Unions, 1962.

The Higher Purpose: "Putting Something Back"

"Some of you heard Margaret Mead, the anthropologist, give her perceptive address for the Forum Committee a couple of weeks ago, pointing up the prevailing, desolating fact that most of our young people live 'partial lives,' seeking only what is called 'getting something out of life'—in a hurry, while there is still time—and not much concerned with putting something back. Margaret Mead, unfortunately, is right. Recent studies of student attitudes across the country show that a job and personal acceptability (which usually means marrying well) head the rewards students seek from their higher education. Only 17 percent expect that being active in their communities will be even one of three goals really important in their outlook.

"Well, union committeemen are not living partial lives. They are clearly among the 17 percent who care. And this the union has something explicitly to do with. Because showing how to put something back is what the union exists for.

"We don't advertise it in the campus newspaper or on our posters, but the other official name for the union is the Division of Social Education. Now this doesn't mean education in the social amenities, though some of the inhabitants of the campus and this building could stand a five credit course in this. ... It means, in short, education in bringing one's personal talents to bear as social forces—learning, as Margaret Mead urged, how to help to carry civilization forward."

— "The Meaning of Union Committee Work." A talk to incoming and outgoing union chairmen, 1963.

"The question the union enterprise poses, in effect, is: 'Good grades, degree, maybe honors—so what? What does this mean to anybody else, to society? What else do you plan to do?'

"The students who volunteer for union work don't wait to answer the question some other time. College, to them, is not just a 'preparation for citizenship,' as the saying goes—something to get at sometime in the future, maybe. Taking on social responsibility is here and now.

"The union building is, of course, the great facilitator—a visible, matchless opportunity for giving as well as getting—with all the doors wide open for students to come together to make good things happen.

"But why in the end should anyone respond to the call for long hours of volunteer service without much recognition? Why should you? Why not just hit the books? Or get married, settle down, and forget it all? Some of you, no doubt, seek a sense of accomplishment, a change of pace from the workaday world, maybe self-expression, or to make new friends, or only to belong. As a Canadian writer said recently, there is no better way to avoid feelings of futility or to counter act the depressing effects of world crises, or personal crises, than by engaging in thoughtful work with or for others. Our richest experiences come when we are acting with other people to achieve some common goal. The end result is self-fulfillment—which is different from self-interest and on a higher plane.

"But there is more to it than self-fulfillment, or even the romantic idea of giving one's self to a cause. Self-fulfillment cannot be separated from the interests of the rest of the community. The contribution made by individuals and groups voluntarily is the real foundation of a democratic society. ...

"It is fundamental in democracy that citizens must take part. Every person in a free society can help in his individual way to shape it—by working with others on a social need and offering the help it is in his power to give. We do what we can because it is the right thing to do—the essence of a self-governing society. And it counts. The unofficial Peace Corps motto, borrowed from Edward Everett Hale, is 'I am only one, but I still am one. I cannot do everything, but still I can do something.' And Longfellow said: 'Give what you have. To someone, it may be better than you dare think.'

"This is the meaning of your committee work and the long hours you spend. And remember that what the leaders of the Oxford and Cambridge Unions have been able, ultimately, to give has been much more than anyone dared think. They have largely shaped the destiny of England."

— "What a College Union Is For." Keynote address, Region 9 Conference of the Association of College Unions, 1963.

IS ALL THIS AN "AUXILIARY ENTERPRISE?"

"College presidents from almost the time unions were first established in America have emphasized the importance of the union as a necessary and fundamental factor in the education of students. College and union literature abounds with references to the educational significance of unions.

"And yet, when unions are classified as to function in college business publications, in college financial reports, and in certain publications of the U.S. Office of Education, they are categorized as 'auxiliary enterprises' along with bookstores, print shops, and laundries.

"No one would worry too much about this if it didn't make much difference. But it does make a difference. The term is inadequate and misleading. It suggests only a service agency or business 'enterprise.' It obscures the primary function of the union as a social-cultural center for informal education. It affects in important ways in many quarters what the union is expected to do, how it is governed, where it appears in the college organization chart, how it is staffed, and what is spent in effort and funds to develop a program of educational worth. ...

"The principal intent of college business officers originally was to identify those college activities which are self-supporting or 'intended to be,' for accounting purposes.

"The implication of the term for this purpose is undoubtedly well understood by business officer groups. The difficulty is that 'auxiliary enterprise' has been borrowed from business officer publications and is used in other college literature and the press for quite different purposes, where it stands alone and does not explain itself, leading to misinterpretation. ...

"While unions do, indeed, produce revenue, their primary reason for existence is that they are necessary to the educational program of a college. They are accorded a high degree of self-government for the purpose of training students; they frequently present the main cultural and social-recreational program of the campus; many are staffed with staff members of academic rank and carry on credit or noncredit teaching.

"Union buildings commonly include auditoriums or theaters, art galleries, art workshops, music rooms, browsing libraries, swimming pools, faculty clubs, and even gymnasiums, which the U.S. Office of Education categorizes as 'instructional' or 'general' facilities (though classifying unions, as a whole, as auxiliary enterprises). The federal housing legislation describes unions as 'other educational facilities.' ...

"There is precedent, even in the business officer reports, for identifying separately, and by name, certain other major facilities which have unique functions, not associated solely with formal instruction—hospitals, for example (though hospitals also produce revenue). ...

"What, then, is an appropriate classification of unions in college reports? The simplest answer is to call them what they are: 'college unions.'"

— "Auxiliary Enterprise? The Case for a Better Term for College Unions." The Bulletin of the Association of College Unions International, 1964.

A 1968 photo of Longwood College's Student Union. ACUI ARCHIVES

The union at California State University, Hayward (now California State University, East Bay)
as it looked in 1968. ACUI ARCHIVES

"

You can have
no building
at all and still
provide a rich
social-cultural
experience for
students.

"

Explaining the Union in Japan

"In the United States we have union buildings with fine program facilities and no program worth mentioning, and poor buildings with exciting programs. And you can have no building at all and still provide a rich social-cultural experience for students, if you have an imaginative student-staff leadership. ...

"Some plans of organization have seemed to have special merit. ...

"The first requisite is an agreed-upon clear, controlling statement of purpose, and of authorities and responsibilities, so that the governors—whoever they may be—and the operating staff know what they are supposed to be trying for. This means a basic charter, or constitution. ...

"Once approved, such charter assures a continuing purpose and explains the reason for the union's existence. It will, or should, largely determine the kind of staff to be selected to carry out the purpose. And it will protect against change in the union character or function when governing boards and individual directors change or when other college agencies or student political groups happen to get different ideas about what the union should do. ...

"While in some Canadian and U.S. universities the general student governing body names the union committees, asking them to report to student government, most do not find that this works very well. The essence of good community organization is that the heads of operating committees should come together to consult with each other, to learn from each other, to coordinate their efforts, and jointly to make the total program decisions based on direct operating knowledge of what is good or doubtful. And students, like everyone else, just don't like to do the hard work and have someone else tell them what they ought to do. It's a matter of not separating authority from responsibility. ...

"If you consult the union literature of the last 20 years and listen to both student and staff recommendations at union conferences, you will find virtually universal agreement—at least in the United States—that it is best when union boards and student government boards work in close cooperation but are independent of each other in their jurisdiction."

— A lecture at a regional conference of university staff members at Kagoshima University, Japan, 1964.

"In most countries, including our own, there are, of course, some students—a slim minority—who are aggressively concerned with social and political problems. But so often they seem to know only how to 'demand' and not how to contribute; only how to stage demonstrations and strikes to have their way, disregarding the interests of others, and sometimes disregarding law and orderly process. This is not very helpful. It is not the kind of student initiative and leadership of which I wish to speak, and which is most needed. ...

"Student leaders of the union in America and in other countries that share the aim of training students for useful public leadership study the needs of their fellow students, arrange all sorts of services and programs that meet these needs, and spend endless hours to make sure the services are good. ... When government decisions affect student welfare, they appear at legislative hearings and present the student case in an orderly way. They plan countless social and cultural programs that promote fellowship and understanding. They arrange welcoming programs and services for new students and foreign students, aiding them in adjusting to their new life. They send gifts of books and clothing to needy students overseas. They raise funds to present literary and art programs and to encourage student artists. They thoughtfully discuss local and national issues, always making sure that all sides of a question can be heard. They look for any and all ways to help make life at the university joyful, rich, inexpensive, and profitable. In short, they work for the common good."

— A discussion at a regional conference of university staff members at Doshisha University, Japan, 1964.

"Edmund Burke, the British statesman, once said, 'All that is necessary for the forces of evil to win in the world is for enough good men to do nothing.' One of the present pressing dangers to the central principle of self-government is still that talent and concern are in short supply, and indifference on the one hand and disruptive demonstrations by small groups on the other hand are in oversupply. Not enough intelligent and competent people lend a hand in community enterprises or assist in the shaping of public policy. You may remember what our President Kennedy said: 'Ask not what your country can do for you. Ask what you can do for your country.'"

— A lecture at a regional conference of university staff members at Hokkaido University, Japan, 1964.

State of the Union around the World

"Anyone telling about college unions around the world has to start by saying which kind of union.

"Except in the Anglo-American universities, 'student union' usually means a political action student group, often left wing. ...

"There is an 'International Union of Students' behind the iron curtain as well as the National Unions of Students based in the Netherlands, but formed after World War II—130 years after the first British unions. Whether either or both adopted the union name deliberately to borrow on the prestige of the long established British and American unions, or whether it was accidental, I can't say.

"I guess we'll have to learn to live with this confusion, just as the world has had to learn that when the President of the United States gives a 'State of the Union' address he isn't talking about the Soviet Union."

In Russia, Europe, Africa

"No university in Russia or its satellite countries responded to either of two inquiries except the University of Warsaw in Poland. ... In Moscow there are no unions in the social sense. No snack bars. The cafeterias are open only at meal times and are strictly for getting food. Sounds grim.

"The political action student unions, of course, are everywhere—Europe, the Near East, Africa. But union buildings are there, too—each with an interesting story of its own—especially in central Europe, where they largely follow the Scandinavian service and welfare pattern. Buildings are fairly inconspicuous in the countries bordering the Mediterranean, except in Turkey, Lebanon, and Israel where western influence has produced American-type recreation centers. In South Africa every university has a union and they copy the British tradition in detail, but borrow a little from Scandinavia, too—offering medical service, discount schemes at local shops, tours. ...

In Latin America

"The blankest spot on the union world map— that is, our kind of union map—is Central and South America, though the Latin American countries, like Africa, are heavily populated with student political unions. ... It was the 'student union' in Rio de Janeiro which first staged a 'solidarity with Cuba' rally. Student riots in Bolivia have been called a prime factor in the recent overthrow of the American-backed government there. And so it goes.

"These unions do, in fact, have many welfare projects as part of their program—health services, better student lodgings—much in the vein of the Scandinavian unions. But they are primarily political-minded and their method is typically protest, strikes, and sometimes violence.

"In the face of all this turmoil and risk, Latin American universities have been extremely reluctant to create centers where students could come together readily, this seeming, undoubtedly, like opening the door wide to more student trouble. ..."

In Asia

"In Asia, as in Latin America, the reason that governments—and universities—show disaffection for the politically active student unions is, of course, that such unions become adversaries, and eventually, in many cases, a threat to the peace and order of the university or to the government itself.

"An aggressive political student leadership can commit the union—and presumably the whole student body the union represents—to political action on the national front—in short, to partisanship. ...

"What can happen to the kind of union development we are most interested in, caught in the middle of such a struggle, is illustrated by the incident at the University of Rangoon. The government decided that the union building was a 'haven for underground leaders plotting the overthrow of the government.' To quell a student demonstration in 1962 the military authorities ... blew up the union building.

"The university had apparently seen the subversion of the union building purposes coming. Already in 1956 it had started planning for a new structure, for student and faculty recreation, taking pains to call it the 'University Recreation Center.' ... The purpose is stated in terms of exact quotations from 'The Role of the College Union' as set forth by our Association. This building is owned and operated by the university administration, exclusively. ...

"So it has happened again that when student unions intermix partisan political action on the national front with their endeavors to do something about student welfare—and open the door through elections to let the left leaders infiltrate— students lose their chance to help direct their own welfare activities. ...

"At almost all Japanese universities there is a prevailing problem overshadowing all others: Who should control the union building?—an unresolved

"

AND, IF THIS STORY OF UNIONS AROUND THE WORLD MEANS ANYTHING, IT MEANS WE ALL HAVE A JOB TO DO IN HELPING STUDENTS LEARN HOW TO GIVE SOMETHING OF THEMSELVES TO SOCIETY—TO ASK NOT 'WHAT WILL I DEMAND?' BUT 'HOW CAN I HELP?'

"

deadlock between student governments and their universities which has seemed to bring union progress on almost all fronts to a standstill. ...

"This conflict over control, basically, traces to the student antagonism to authority in any form, and to government authority in particular. The union is identified with government authority because the government has sponsored the union development. Also, the Ministry of Education laid down the condition that the dean of students be responsible for union administration. It is to this condition in particular that students object. They saw it as a defeat for the student rights movement. ...

"I thought perhaps Japan, in looking to the union as an answer to some of its problems of student life, had borrowed too fully a western idea, adopted it too suddenly, and possibly super-imposed it on a culture with which it wasn't in harmony—until I talked to a young alumnus of Tokyo University.

"As a sophomore, in 1956, without ever having heard of a union in the U.S. and before any building existed in Japan, he became fired with the idea that there could be a better college life if there were a campus center. He printed pamphlets urging donations and distributed them personally—as an individual effort, not associated in any way with student government. 'Let's have something humane on our campus,' was his slogan. Students responded by the hundreds. The work of a few volunteers turned into a general campus movement. It was agreed that students would be asked to pay a union fee. It was not a compulsory fee, but 90 percent of all students paid.

"This is the kind of student leadership that produced unions in the first instance in England and the United States. It is the kind of leadership that was on its way to succeeding in Japan when it was blocked by the leftists. ...

"Free China, in contrast to other parts of Asia, has a long tradition of common group efforts and programs for community welfare, including centers for community social and recreation activity. These paved the way for ready acceptance and understanding of community centers at colleges, as represented by the union idea. It is no accident that the first union in Taiwan is called 'Gregarious Hall.' ...

"The support for the union has been such that each of the 29 colleges in Taiwan has either built or is planning a union, all in the space of six years. ...

"The whole approach—building facilities, primary emphasis on program and student leadership, friendly student-faculty cooperation—follows closely the pattern of the U.S. unions. ... Not only does every college have a union; many high schools do, too.

And the central College Union Service Center is providing program aids, on a national scale, beyond anything known in any other country.

"This is not to say that there are not problems. But in the main, if the unions visited are typical, Free China is well on its way—perhaps farther along, in the important ways, than any other country in the world. ..."

What We Can Learn from Unions Overseas

"What may all this mean to representatives of unions gathered at San Francisco in 1965?

"It means, for one thing, that student social-cultural well-being and partisan politics on the national front don't mix very well, and that if a union is to do much about the basic day to day needs of students and the enrichment of their lives, it had best tend to this instead of trying to change the government. Hence, stay independent of elected student governments and their militant political causes.

"It tells us that in most parts of the world a minority leadership is proposing to speak and act for all students in all things. And it suggests that it is the union that can give the large body of students a chance to make themselves heard and felt, by providing a center for free, untrammeled activity and open discussion—for everybody—equally.

"It suggests that universities might want to be reserved about identifying the union too closely with the authority of the dean of students office, or of any single administrative office. Coordination, yes—but the widest possible latitude for genuine self-direction, the union an instrument possessed and governed by the whole student-faculty body.

"It suggests the union needs to do everything it can to bring about a true community of interests and effort among students and faculty. The suspicions, the voids in personal relationships that divide students and teachers in so many other countries, the discontent and the stormy demonstrations of protest, can happen—are happening—here. Conceiving the union as only a 'student' union doesn't help.

"And, if this story of unions around the world means anything, it means we all have a job to do in helping students learn how to give something of themselves to society—to ask not 'What will I demand?' but 'How can I help?'"

— "State of the College Union Around the World." Opening address, 42nd Conference of the Association of College Unions, 1965.

Student Disruption, Violence Abroad— and Why

What happened on the Berkeley campus last fall—which shook up the American press and public and seemed to start a chain reaction on campuses across the country—was relatively mild and innocent compared to what happens right along, almost any week, abroad.

"In one Japanese university, for example, students locked up 21 faculty members in a room for 24 hours, until they agreed to hire a new cook. In another, 22,000 students boycotted classes for two weeks and refused to take final exams because of a proposed tuition increase. The increase was rescinded. ...

"On several campuses brand new, attractive union buildings have stood empty for up to a year, not a student entering—a boycott protesting a rule that the dean of students would be responsible for administration. ...

"At the University of Dacca, East Pakistan, the entire student body struck because they wanted final exams moved up—to have a longer summer vacation. They stayed away from classes until the date was changed.

"When I was at Tokyo University, students were being called out of classes in a general strike against the government's policy in Korea.

"And in Korea, four universities shut down for two weeks while 6,000 rock-throwing students battled police. They were protesting government concessions to Japan. Scores of students and police were seriously injured. ...

"This kind of thing has been going on around the world for more than a decade. So that happened at Berkeley, or on this and other campuses in the last few weeks, should perhaps not be too surprising. It's just a little late in coming, that's all.

"And why all this? The press has been full of explanations and speculations concerning Berkeley and all the rest for some months now. You can take your choice. I can give you a couple of observations on the overseas situation, which may have some relevance.

"In Asia, Latin America, Africa, for the most part, students and faculty haven't learned how to talk to each other, or how to join in a partnership in dealing with any matter of common concern. And it appears to be mostly the faculty's fault. Too busy, they say. Or they just haven't cared—over the years past—what happened outside the classroom, or though that knowing students personally or understanding what goes on in their minds was part of their job. And now they're scared.

"When I was in Japan, I could meet only with a faculty group or a student group—never together. ...

"The second circumstance abroad is that a tightly organized extremist, usually leftist, minority action group—less than 2 percent of a whole student body—has taken over student government and union leadership in many universities and sees to it that no one else has a chance to speak or act. ... Though all is done in the name of student rights, student autonomy, and democracy, there's nothing more totalitarian, authoritarian, and antidemocratic than the student government leadership of a great many of the universities abroad. And it stays in control, though the mass of students is as reasonable and sensible—and interested in good relations with their university—as anywhere.

"Now there are extremist action groups—minorities—in the U.S. who would also like to signify to the public, and the university or the government, what the student attitude is—by the similar, and now well known, techniques of sit-ins, marches, picketing, and other demonstrations—the physical spectacles that make, as they well know, good television and press copy.

"But the true situation, so far as the whole student body is concerned, as abroad, is quite another thing. The prevailing main problem, as Dean Williamson of Minnesota recently pointed out, after a year-long nationwide study, is still the student who doesn't do anything except go to class and go home. ..."

The Union Potential for Constructive Activism

"It is as a counter force between these two extremes that a college union may find its most significant and useful role. On the one hand it does indeed, in contrast to the repression of the majority student voice overseas, give the large body of students a chance to make themselves felt and heard, offsetting the minorities which would like the public to think their view is the general student view. And on the other hand, the union works around the clock to arouse the indifferent, self-centered student to an active, but constructive, part in community affairs and to an interest in the things that broaden

In the late 1960s, student demonstrations in protest of the Vietnam War became common. ACUI ARCHIVES

their experience on the campus, and lift the quality of their lives. ...

"There's a great deal of talk about giving students a greater voice in university affairs, having them on university boards and committees.

"The board in charge of this $6 million building and its program has had a majority of students, and a student chairman, since 1928. And the program board that approved last Thursday a $227,000 income-outgo budget for paid admission cultural and recreational programs, and will administer it, is composed entirely of students.

"There's a lot of current talk, too, about student rights to bring speakers of their choice. This union has had a free platform, open to all shades of opinion and affiliation, from the beginning—without urging from anyone, and sometimes in spite of pressure from the university administration to do otherwise. It was the union that led the way on this in the early years, when the university really wasn't sure how it felt.

"These policies of almost 40 years, invented long before the present stir about such matters, should say something about whether students can partici-

pate usefully, effectively in their own education and in an enterprise in which the university as a whole also has a large stake."

— A talk to the incoming and outgoing Wisconsin Union committee chairmen, 1965.

"Now I'm certainly all for the work and time that goes into getting equal rights for everybody, or doing something about the underprivileged, or trying to figure out what is the sensible thing to do in Viet Nam, and we should certainly do our part to help in both large and small ways.

"But somewhere, some place, some time, somebody should show what life can be like if some of the problems get settled—what the end product of all our endeavors and struggles might be.

"It seems to me the unique and superlative opportunity the union has—differing perhaps from all the other organizations on the campus, or in the city for that matter—is to demonstrate, here and now, what the good life is."

— A talk at the Wisconsin Union student-staff orientation retreat, 1965.

Who Will Educate the Leader? Why Not the Union?

"The union is undoubtedly thought of by many as a building, a place. It is true, to be sure—and a very useful place. ... But there's much more to the union idea than that.

"Whenever I, or the student officers or the staff advisors, pick up a newspaper, or read a report, or scan the *Saturday Review* or *Life* or *Time*—or, more accurately, the life of our times—we say to ourselves, 'We could do something about that.'

"And then, before we can talk to each about it, we're waited upon by protestors or see the complaints in the complaint box—euphemistically called the 'suggestion box'—and we say 'We have to do something about that.'

"This is the eternal dilemma facing the university itself, or any community of people: how to balance one's time and effort between what you have to do—putting out fires, as it were—and what you could do, would like to do.

"So, of all the golden opportunities that lie around us, we keep trying to choose the things that matter most.

"One of the things that matters most, in these times of continuing crisis at home and abroad, is, most of all agree, cultivating in students, those we expect to be the future leaders, the will to volunteer to do something about our common problems, small and large, and the skill for doing it. ... In a democracy there must be leaders, and those who can lead, must lead.

"Now the making of good, actively participating citizens, and of leaders of our common life together, happens to be the first function of education in a democracy, and the avowed purpose of almost every institution of higher learning.

"But the fateful fact is that universities aren't coming anywhere near the achievement of this part of their purpose. It isn't that students aren't willing and able. Rather, the curious circumstance is that universities themselves are immunizing a high proportion of our most gifted young people against any tendencies to social leadership by administering day by day what John W. Gardner calls 'the anti-leadership vaccine.'

"John Gardner is the new commissioner of education in the president's cabinet. This is what he said, shortly before taking office: 'In our colleges today, the best students are carefully schooled to avoid leadership responsibilities. They are introduced to—or, more correctly, powerfully indoctrinated in—a set of attitudes appropriate to scholars, scientists, and professional men. ... Entry into what most of us would regard as the leadership roles in the society at large is discouraged. ... 'As a result, the academic world appears to be approaching a point at which everyone will want to educate the technical expert who advises the leader, or the intellectual who stands off and criticizes the leader, but no one will want to educate the leader himself.'

"This is what the head of our American educational system said. And it reminds us at the union, as we work at sorting out what matters most, that here is our special mission—to be the one, or one of the ones, who will want to educate the leader himself, by mustering all the unparalleled resources of a community center like this—building, teaching staff, and budget—to give students themselves the opportunities to shape the conditions of their life together and thus learn the ways of leadership. This is in harmony with the original central mission of a college union. The very first ones—at Oxford and Cambridge—set out, primarily through debate and free discussion of any proposition, to infuse students with the idea that they are responsible for the welfare of their country."

— "The Union Mission." The Bulletin of the Association of College Unions International, 1966. (Reprinted in College Student Personnel. Published by Houghton Mifflin, 1970.)

Key to Success: The Caliber of Staff and Student Volunteers

"The success of a union, in the end, depends upon the adequacy of volunteer student committees and of the staff and the caliber of their leadership—just as the most important single factor in the success of a college as a whole is the faculty, and the students whom a top grade faculty attracts. ...

"The union director, in the view of many college administrators and of the Association, should hold the same status and have the same salary (granted the necessary preparation and the same effectiveness of performance) as the directors of other major departments of the institution."

— Standards in College Union Work. Published by the Association of College Unions, 1967.

Planning Buildings for Multiple Use— and Change

"The evolution of the union—from 'a large university club whose object shall be to promote comradeship among members of Harvard University' (union constitution of 1901)—is fairly clear.

"In the 1930s the leaders of the union effort, influenced greatly by the concurrent development and success of general community recreation and cultural centers where people employed their free time, began to see the union as the campus counterpart of the 'community center' elsewhere, with a positive recreational and educational mission to perform. ...

"The union has become an all-purpose community center of the first order, with an identity and meaning of its own.

"But this is not to say that evolution, or growth, is over.

"The changes in the world of education are pressing for special attention, and new emphases, in union facility planning no less than in other directions. ...

"Not only may the functions of given union rooms need to change; the campus itself may so develop that the whole union may need to double or triple in size or be built anew in another location. This is no speculation. There are a number of instances where a union, under pressures of enrollment growth requiring a much larger building, or a decisive shift of the center of gravity of campus traffic, or the development of a totally new campus elsewhere, has had to be converted to other uses five to ten years after it opened. ...

"One can scarcely plan a union at the outset for unknown other future college uses, or for simple conversion, en toto, to who knows what. But it is well to have in mind that 'it might happen here,' and so far as one can, without compromising the effectiveness of the union as such, keep an eye on what else the building might be used for—avoiding load-bearing interior walls and modifying somewhat the structural system accordingly.

"Total conversion or replacement, of course, is likely to be the exceptional case, applying only where there was some initial untoward miscalculation. The great lesson to be learned is the importance of doing the best one can to foresee which way the campus is developing and to place the union in what will be the future strategic location, allowing enough area at that site for the building to grow. ...

"The heart of this study is a showing, in more specific terms, of ways of making the facilities originally planned flexible in accommodating the known, more likely, more universal and more enduring uses of a union—and of saving, at the same time, a good deal of money.

"If the union is conceived as a general campus community center in the first place, responsive to whatever the people of the college want or need to do in their leisure time, it will have latitude for accepting change. ...

"This starting concept of what the union is, or can be, buttressed by the multi-use approaches to space planning sketched in this study (granted, of course, a strategic building location, with room to expand) can produce a more useful, relevant, and resilient building which will make conversion of facilities to new and different functions, or sudden death for the whole building, and a start-over, much less likely. ...

"Further—the most important thing about a union, by far, is not the building but the program within it. ... So any means that can be devised, by way of facility arrangements or space contraction, that converse funds for program and staffing are of the utmost significance. Else the building, no matter how ample, may substantially fail of its purpose."

— Planning College Union Facilities for Multiple Use. Published by the Association of College Unions, 1966.

"The most successful unions are those that have developed as general campus community centers. ...

"It follows that some realignment of campus facilities and of plans for the future may be necessary so that there will not be missing at the union an element essential to its functioning as a true center of campus life or a facility important as a matter of sheer convenience to the student-faculty body. The college will be richly repaid if with the creation of a new union, or the expansion of an old one, the overall design for campus living is made right, even though this involves some readjustment and shifts of existing facilities and plans.

"Certainly it is a mistake in planning if the union is treated, as it still is on some campuses, merely as a catchall for just miscellaneous college needs, without regard to their appropriateness in the union or without regard to implanting in the union the core of activity essential to a good campus center."

— Planning and Operating College Union Buildings, Seventh edition. Published by the Association of College Unions, 1967.

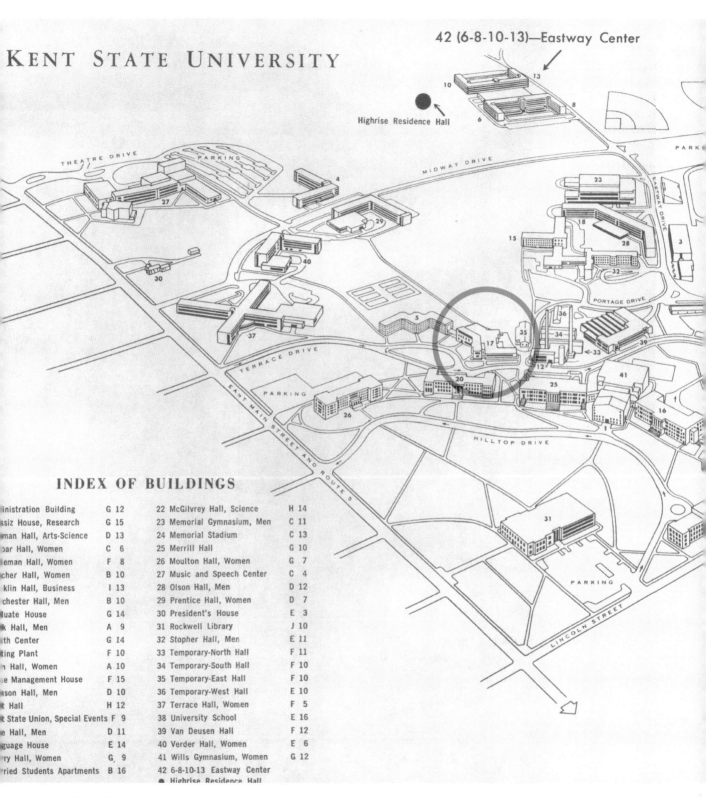

KENT STATE UNIVERSITY

42 (6-8-10-13)—Eastway Center

Highrise Residence Hall

THEATRE DRIVE

PARKING

MIDWAY DRIVE

EASTWAY DRIVE

PORTAGE DRIVE

TERRACE DRIVE

EAST MAIN STREET AND ROUTE 5

PARKING

HILLTOP DRIVE

LINCOLN STREET

PARKING

INDEX OF BUILDINGS

On this 1965 map, the union is centrally located at Kent State University. ACUI ARCHIVES

"

THE UNION NAME ENJOYS IDENTITY WITH A LONG AND HONORED TRADITION IN COLLEGE LIFE, **A RICH HERITAGE OF MORE THAN 150 YEARS.**

"

THE QUESTION OF "CENTER" OR "UNION" AS A NAME

"While the union building has been described, so far as general function is concerned, as the 'community center' of the campus, this does not mean that 'center' is recommended as a substitute name. Rather, the term 'union' is considered to be most appropriate, and of greater value and meaning.

"'Union' states directly the goal of unity among diverse groups of people which the building fosters, much as 'university,' of which a union is a part, signifies unity in diversity in academic endeavors. The word 'university' derives from the Latin 'universitas' meaning 'the whole'; union from 'union,' meaning 'oneness,' a whole made up of united parts. In the educational world the two concepts support and complement each other.

"The union name enjoys identity with a long and honored tradition in college life, a rich heritage of more than 150 years. The extensive literature on college buildings and organizations of this kind all makes reference to "unions" as the generic term. ... And the national (now international) organization is, of course, the Association of College Unions, and has borne this name for more than 50 years.

"'Center' implies only a place. It should be noted that if 'union' sometimes leads to mistaken identities, the use of the name 'center' does also, and perhaps more so. There is confusion with the growing number of campus adult education centers, research centers, art centers, recreation centers, religious centers, and medical centers. And with 'center' the college has a building name only; there remains the problem of what to call the membership organization which uses and operates the building, names officers, sponsors programs, and to which students and others belong."

— Planning and Operating College Union Buildings, Seventh edition. Published by the Association of College Unions, 1967.

The Growing Recognition of Educational Significance

"A number of unions operate almost strictly as business enterprises or service agencies without educational purposes or results, functioning more nearly like hotels or clubs than college unions, as now generally conceived. The proportion of unions without educational program goals, however, has decreased sharply in recent years. ...

"Though there are some discrepant points of view, some discrepant cases, the trend is toward greater recognition of the educational potentialities of the union and consequently toward closer relationships of the union to the college's educational program. ...

"The recognition of the value and necessity of the union has reached the point where state legislatures or college trustees, or both together, in numerous cases have made direct appropriations from general state or college funds for the total or partial financing of construction."

— Planning and Operating College Union Buildings, Seventh edition. Published by the Association of College Unions, 1967.

Student-Only Control, or Partnership?

"Some student governments (in Canada) consider the union to be exclusively their province, that is, union buildings should be completely controlled by students (i.e., student government). ...

"This view is echoed, and expanded, by the chairman of a Canadian 'Student's Union' Planning Commission:

'The argument that the union building committee must be apart from student government "to protect the programmed organization from the uncertainties of student politics" is absurd. ... If this is to be a student building, and if students are to finance the building out of their fees, voluntarily assessed, then I argue that the building should be run by students and that professional staff hired should be employees of the students.'

"What this attitude assumes is that university administrations and union staff members somehow wish to operate unions for their own purposes and to the disadvantage of students—an assumption supported by little in the way of evidence. And it overlooks, curiously, the prevailing conviction among students and citizens generally that a centralized, monolithic government, in control of everything, including the press and voluntary cultural and social organizations, at any other level is not a good thing, in fact, antithetical to the concept of the role of government in a democracy.

"There is much that can be said for multiple, and parallel, avenues of planning and action, freedom of expression, and even of self-government, especially in the campus situation. There is likely to be involvement of more students, and more opportunities for significant leadership, more latitude of initiative, more diversity of approaches and emphases, more freedom of action, and more expeditious action (by way of avoiding the severe bottlenecks of having to carry all propositions through a single student governing board, so often deeply involved in other concerns).

"The categorical demand of some Canadian student leaders for student-only control of the union (via student government) would appear to leave no room for the kind of partnership of students and faculty-staff which largely characterizes the union enterprise in the United States, or ironically, even for the kind of partnership Canadian students seek when they ask to be represented on university committees. The principle of reciprocity, and the appropriateness and possible usefulness of having faculty and staff members involved in union policy and program making if students are to be involved in other university policy making, apparently simple doesn't occur to them. ...

What Is Now Missing in the British-Oriented Unions

"The absorption of student interest (in Canada, Australia, and the United Kingdom) in 'governing' and in the causes represented by the National Union of Students to which student government belongs is not, of course, something to be regretted—except as the potentials of the union building are not realized. While the national unions are often involved mainly in organizing conferences, adopting resolutions, and joining in 'demands,' their influence exposes thousands of students to vital issues of the times and enlists an interest that might otherwise never develop.

"The trouble is that at the other end of the pole of a local student government's function—its union building—it would seem, from a reading of hundreds of pages of minutes and annual reports, that both the union building governing board and the standing committees deal largely with finance and management details—something the British-oriented unions apparently consider to be a useful educational experience, but which all too frequently appear to be minutiae of the kind that United States union boards and committees, concerned more with the social-educational and cultural purposes of a union, would consider a bore, and hence are quite content to leave to the staff.

"To be sure, one can find in the United States numbers of unions where 'the staff administers too much'—both the building and the program. But these cases are likely to be the exception to the rule. Typically the minutes and reports of union conferences in the U.S. show that both staff and students are occupied in large measure by the social, cultural, and educational concerns of the times: what contributes most to individual student development; how to advance interest in the arts; the recreational needs of students; the problems of civil rights; how to prepare for larger social responsibilities; how to involve students and faculty in meaningful joint undertakings; and on and on.

"In Australia, Canada, and Britain this large area that lies between the expression of student opinion and the espousal of political causes (via student government) on the one hand and the mechanics of administering union building facilities on the other hand—in other words, the large area representing possible endeavors of educational worth and the development of a richer community life for the university—for the most part is left, in the name of 'student autonomy,' with small special interest clubs and societies whose resources are small and whose horizons are limited. Some of them do well, no doubt. But truly substantial educational values, as represented by any sophisticated, comprehensive attention to the arts or to personal development of students through social association, or by any explicit training for leadership responsibilities, or by the creation of a favoring climate for learning outside the classroom—all of which are prime functions of, and at, a university—seem to be, except for debates and some notable forays into a few cultural ventures, left largely unattended by any one.

"So often in the universities that have developed in the British tradition there appears to be a void between the 'activities' (which the faculty tends to regard as frivolous) of the student clubs and societies on the one hand and the educational purpose of a university on the other hand. And the Australian, Canadian, and British unions, for the most part, do not attempt to bridge this void with any positive out-of-class program of their own."

— State of the College Union Around the World. Published by the Association of College Unions, 1967.

More Lessons from Overseas

"What may this story of unions around the world signify, further, to those who would hope to make a union useful and viable as the center of university community life and an effective instrumentality in higher education?

"It confirms, for one thing, that students everywhere have about the same basic personal needs and aspirations—for dining economically under reasonably pleasant circumstances, for associating socially with fellow students, for recreation, for self-fulfillment—and that the potentials of a union in meeting these needs are now of almost universal interest, after almost a century of seeming to appeal only to the Anglo-American and Scandinavian uni-

versities. In short, the union idea, though not always well understood, has now become truly worldwide, and is spreading with unprecedented speed.

"It suggests that a good union can reshape student values, enrich student social and cultural experience, strengthen the university as an educational community, and vastly ameliorate the conditions of student life, but that in many countries it is now—in contrast to earlier times—the university administration, in the main, that sees this, not the student leadership, preoccupied as it is with controversial political issues—sometimes subverted by 'professional student' agitators. ...

"It suggests that the union is best conceived not just as a building facility rendering services but as a program of widespread individual and group participation in fruitful enterprises which enhance the educational experience of students and their awareness of other interests and of the world around them—vis a vis allowing useful out-of-class activity to become by default the province of restrictive special interest clubs haphazardly serving a few.

"It tells us that there is a prevailing student suspicion of administrative or advisory help, but that a union is likely to do the most for students, by way of services and a program of excitement and worth, when there is understanding aid from a professionally trained staff. ...

"Plainly, it signifies that there is much that student leaders, reasonably or unreasonably, find wrong in their universities and in society, with the mass of students sometimes following their lead, but mostly standing by unconcerned, self-centered, or frustrated in their desire to do something of value beyond protesting. For all, the nonpartisan union can open doors to a more socially useful and personally rewarding kind of service and leadership.

"If this story of unions around the world means anything, it means all colleges and universities still have a pressing job to do in helping students—the leaders, the followers, and the indifferent—learn how to give to themselves to society, to ask not merely 'What will I demand?' or 'Why should I care?' but 'How can I help?'

"It was on the steps of the Michigan Union that President Kennedy said to students: 'On your willingness to contribute part of your life to this country I think will depend the answer whether we as a free society can contribute.'

"This was the birth of the Peace Corps idea. Singularly appropriate that the birthplace was a union—symbolic of what the union is all about."

— State of the College Union Around the World. Published by the Association of College Unions, 1967.

The Union in Retrospect and Prospect

"When I was a student in the early 1920s there was a union organization—a men's union—but not a building. Even without a building, the union made an impact—fall mixers in the gym, weekend dances with a student band in the parlors of the women's building (where the dean of women chaperoned), concerts and plays and Union Vodvil in the gym or a downtown theater, and, once every four years, an all-university exposition.

"Beyond this, students had a pretty thin time. Life revolved around the fraternities, though only one out of every 20 students was a member. No dormitories, no intramural sports. No place to meet anybody, or hold a meeting.

"This was supposed to be the era of 'flaming youth.' Don't believe it; most of us were very lonely. Students sensed something was missing. They set out to make the university more than a classroom—a very revolutionary idea at the time.

"The campaign to raise funds for a union building was just starting. 'Build a home for Wisconsin Spirit' was the slogan. ... Students organized a door-to-door campaign every year for the next 10 years. They raised more money than anybody else; one out of every two students gave $50 or more to the union fund—worth $200–$250 now, in terms of dollar value. Could we do this now?

"The university, on the whole, was indifferent. Not much help, except for a few perspective faculty members.

"In a sense, I suppose we were the activists of the time. We were out to make the university a different kind of place. And we worked at it, day and night.

"The building finally came off. It was evident to all that students had earned it. So when the building was organized, students were given a central place in the policy making, the 'government'—a majority on the board, with a student as president—not just token representation.

"At first, we only dimly perceived what we were doing, what a union was for. Then we learned about our President Van Hise's plea for a union in his inaugural address of 1904, about the Oxford-Cambridge Unions, and about Hart House at the University of Toronto. We began to see the union as a means of building a better kind of community—making the university a 'more human place,' doing something about the economic welfare of students, providing a general social-cultural-recreational program—with the building the center of campus community life in all its aspects. We did, indeed, find the building and its resources to be a remarkable tool to work with. In the Depression we maintained student wages at the former level (35 cents an hour) where others cut; we reduced meal prices to 24 cents; when the banks closed, we issued scrip so students could eat on credit—and stay in school. We created an art gallery and craft shop, the university's first; invented an outing club; organized rooming houses for social and intramural sports purposes, bringing to the residents of these bleak quarters some of the advantages of fraternity life; developed a major music-theater-film program; started forums and Oxford-type debates; brought foreign students into the main stream of campus life; started a social program for graduate students.

"The union developed by the mid '30s some types of programs and services—now more than 200—which simply didn't exist before.

"These things didn't just happen by themselves. Hundreds of students worked at it. Concert series? Most students couldn't have cared less. So union committeemen went to fraternity and dormitory dinners, night after night, to give a sales pitch. The union's Wisconsin Salon of Art? Now the state's principal competitive art show, though at the beginning nobody even knew who the state's artists were; we wrote everywhere in the state to find out. The now flourishing outing program? To get a ski jumping scaffold, students went out for gifts, and then turned out by the score to haul snow to the hill—to stage an admission ski tournament to get the money to do the rest of the outing program. To organize rooming houses? Students walked the streets, house to house, to talk with the inhabitants, encourage them to elect officers, give the house a name, enter the intramural sports program. ...

"These are some of the bare highlights—we can't cover 45 years adequately in 45 minutes. But maybe this will give some idea of where we came from, what kind of an organism the union is.

"And what, now, seem to be the prospects—for the next few years, particularly this year?

"The university is growing, changing rapidly—the most spectacular change in its history. This has brought several phenomena of special significance for the union, and for you:

"1. With the enormous turnover of personnel—administration, faculty, students—the traditions, contributions, indeed, the very purpose of the union have tended to get lost. We have spent much of our

Members of a student programming board string balloons in preparation for a Friday night dance. VISTA YEARBOOK time just rebuilding fences, trying to reassert what the union is, and is here for. A vitiating thing.

"2. The very size of the campus poses formidable problems. Our historic constitutional purpose is 'to provide a common life.' How to do that for 33,000 students, plus faculty? The campus is steadily moving away from us. Then there is the new mode: apartment living—farther away, self-sufficient. Large segments of the campus population are missing at the union altogether. But the larger and more dispersed the campus is, the more important the role of the union as a unifying force.

"We have some answers in the making: our outreach program, proposals for better access and parking, the new branch union. What we do about this will make an enormous difference. But we have to be careful, especially in the case of the branch union, that the result isn't divisive, but cohesive.

"3. The average age of students is steadily rising. The greatest growth is in the graduate school. We have to be watchful we don't have committees of teenagers planning for 25- to 30-year-olds.

"4. The other part of our stated purpose is 'to provide a cultivated social program.' We do very well here, but this, too, could change suddenly—as more auditoria and galleries and film societies come on stream, downtown and on the campus, competing for attention. ...

"5. Right now the union, in a sense, is so much a part of the scene, so established, it is taken for granted. If anyone else does anything—in the arts, with a coffee house—that's big news. The union may have been doing it right along for years, and 20 times as much, but that's not news. How will you as union chairmen create an air of excitement about what you do?

"6. In another sense, the union is so successful everybody wants to get into the act—student government, the new arts societies, the dean's office, the administration. All tend to forget the union itself was, and is, a revolutionary student movement in which students earned a place of responsibility and authority—'power,' if you will—in the conduct of many years of student affairs, and set up a mechanism for governance of the building and its program of, by, and for students. ...

"The irony is that students are crying for power. In the case of the union, they have had it, and still have it, but are not asserting it, preserving it. If you as students don't do it, nobody can do it for you.

"Then there is the kind of change that is not unique to Wisconsin, but affecting many colleges: an apparent shift of student leadership to activists with partisan political or social causes to promote. I say 'apparent,' because it is highly visible.

"The question here is whether union committees will remain simply program-oriented in traditional ways, or assume a broader role in leadership of student life and thought. The truth is that on this campus and others the extremists have seized the initiative and run with the ball. They are the innovators, they insist on what is relevant. The union groups lie back and go their accustomed ways, dealing with 'programs' instead of issues. The earliest unions were centers of debate and discussion of the prime issues of the day. The union represented the leadership in setting student goals and the intellectual environment of the campus.

"I don't mean assuming leadership of partisan political causes, but doing something more important: carrying out the purpose of any educational institution, and any union—examining the issues at hand by establishing an open platform for learning all sides of a question. In other words, educating—and in the process giving a voice to the unheard majority on the campus.

"Well, there is an infinity of things to do. And time is finite. So we have to set some priorities. As I read the signs, I think I see some that could, or should, be at or near the top of the list:

"1. Certainly one is to care about the central issues of the day—not by pronouncements and protests, but by illuminating the issues from all sides—the basic role of a university in a civilized society—and thus learning more about what, usefully, can be done—what students can do. This, I repeat, is the open platform approach, and it includes arousing the indifferent and unconcerned majority. I am thinking, of course, of such overriding issues as the war, racial turmoil and civil rights, the fate of our cities, drugs, poverty, our environment, the effectiveness of the U.N., the bomb. Union committees should be the first—not the last—to examine these questions, and in depth.

"2. We should be aware of student protests and their meaning, and make room for them in the union. But not spend so much of our time just reacting to what others do. Let's do something ourselves, constructively—not just try to accommodate to change, but shape it.

"3. And what about 'student power?' Is it a valid concept? Is it viable? Are the faculty really to be regarded as natural enemies, a race apart? Is there something students can do to seek a partnership with faculty in the educational enterprise? Is there more the union can do about the elementary matter of students and faculty getting to know each other?

"4. Generally—how can we do our part in humanizing this university? We might do much more than we do—including communicating with fellow students not by posters but by telephone, in person, or in periodic general assemblies, television assemblies if necessary.

"5. Another priority, central to the union purpose: in what ways can the union serve as an integrating, unifying force in this huge, sprawling university? What about our promising outreach program? How can we make the building itself appealing and useful not just to theatergoers, to the 'round-the-clock inhabitants of the Rathskeller, to the steady daily users of the cafeteria—but fully representative of all parts of the university?

"6. And a final priority, also basic to our reason for existing: creating opportunities for rich experiences which shape the cultural and intellectual and social environment of the campus. Do we mean to be leaders in this field? Or abdicate our leadership to others?

"As you see, this all adds up to working on the ways and means of creating a decent community, the good life, here and now. A committee chairman, or committee member, or the union as a whole can't do everything about the world's problems or the university's problems. But we can do something.

"You may recall Adlai Stevenson's memorable tribute to Mrs. Franklin Roosevelt: 'She would rather light a candle than curse the darkness.' That is the heart of all I have to say, and what I think we are here for."

— "The Union in Retrospect and Prospect." Last message to Wisconsin Union student chairmen and staff, at an orientation retreat, 1967.

Valedictory

"In all these years, and long before it became front page news, union people have been, and still are, a bunch of activists too—out to change and improve the conditions of student life. But with a sense of humor, thank God, for the kind that came through tonight. (I think this is one of the prevailing difficulties of some of the activists we know; no humor.) And I must say also that union people usually followed channels. At least they haven't tried to lock the Board of Regents in, or the president, to get what they wanted. Or set fires in South Hall.

"The leit motif of the union has been construct, not obstruct. And this has been so from the beginning, and is now.

In 1966, Mario Savio, an activist in the Berkeley Free Speech Movement, led this rally at the University of California, Berkeley, protesting the university's ban on the distribution of political material. PHOTO BY MIJOVAS

"Back in the '20s one of every two students gave $50 or more to build this building, and then gave the building to the university. With this priceless tool to work with, all sorts of good things began to happen. All together, some 200 kinds of services and programs, including an extraordinary cultural program—200 kinds of services and programs that never existed before.

"And the happy thing about it all, to me, is that this student impulse to construct, to help, seems to carry over into the alumni years. It was largely former union chairmen and union trustees who organized the Foundations which have given tens of millions of dollars to the university. Of the regional campaign chairmen for the new art center—seven former union chairmen. The head of the drive to equip the Milwaukee Union—a former union chairman. And union committee members everywhere—running alumni clubs, doing all manner of good works for the university and their home communities.

"So I guess I'd like to think of this gathering tonight as being also—to borrow a current phrase—a kind of 'sit-in,' a sit-in in support of this idea of the union as a great constructive force in the life of the university. You might even call it a love-in. Or so it seems to me, after all the embraces tonight from all my old girl friends. But by whatever name ... enduring love and regard for the university, for the union idea, and for each other.

"May there be many more."

— A response at the Union Family Dinner on the occasion of retirement as director of the Wisconsin Union, 1968.

CRISIS ON THE CAMPUS ... AND THE ÜNION

"There is no longer any doubt about that higher education is in a state of deep crisis. ...

"In 18 months, to May 1969: 427 disorders ... 25 bombings and attempted bombings ... 46 arsons and attempted arsons ... 67 cases of general destruction ... an estimated 598 injuries ... more than 600 persons arrested.

"The cost of all this is appalling. ... And the student is the loser. The money and time spent on disruptions could have gone into teaching and service.

"Most devastating, perhaps, is the indirect outcome: the deterioration, sometimes imperceptible at first, sometimes rapid, of the quality of education—brought on by the pervading preoccupation, not with education, but with disorder and crises. ...

"This widespread disaster has been caused, it seems generally agreed, by a handful of extremists. ...

"So, the big question continues to come—from the thoughtful writers, the investigating committees, the faculty, the alumni, the parents, the taxpayers, the legislators, and even student leaders—'What does the majority think about all this? They're the ones who are being hurt most. Why don't they assert themselves?'

"Why, indeed? And this brings us to the role of the college union. ...

"Union board members and committeemen, by and large, are fairly representative of the student majority. ... Despite discontent over society's failures, they have no interest in disruption, destruction, or violence as a means to any end. But when an issue begins to burn, or disruption and chaos strike the campus, what has been their response? Silence, inaction, with a few notable exceptions—as with the large 'silent majority.'

"Why is this so? There are, I believe, a number of explanations:

"Some just don't realize the seriousness of the situation—don't realize that the determined minority, as the National Commission on Violence points out, aims not at reform but at the destruction of existing institutions, like the university. Some are busy with what they're already doing and don't want to get involved in anything more. ...

"And then there's the crucial matter of what is a union, and what is its role? This is a two-part problem. ...

"Progressively in recent times, unions—which in the beginning were originated by students themselves as instruments for shaping the conditions of their own life on the campus and which functioned, under a student or student-faculty governing board, largely independent of college direction (and still do in almost every country but the U.S.)—have been placed under the supervision of deans of students, business manager, directors of auxiliary enterprises. ...

"So, noting what the organization chart says, many students now perceive the union as part of the 'establishment'—something like the library or placement office. In consequence, if the union officers or board speak out, it must, other students think, be on behalf of the establishment, the bureaucracy which is anathema to the extremists and

Students march down Langdon Street at the University of Wisconsin–Madison in 1965, protesting the Vietnam War.

not overly blessed with admiration from other students. Union officers don't relish being tagged by their peers as errand boys for the administration, so more often than not they say nothing.

"And in consequence of this, when the college most needs an independent, influential student voice on behalf of orderliness and rational change—which it once had via the leaders of the union—it hasn't got it any more. But it has mainly itself to blame.

"The second part of the problem is that too many union boards and officers themselves conceive their role as 'providing programs.' They're not issue-oriented. The union, they say, shouldn't get involved in 'politics'; it should stay neutral because it concludes all students, or because its business is programming.

"Here an important distinction, sometimes hard for students and union staff members alike to grasp, has to be made—between partisan political activity, as with supporting a given candidate or aligning the union with a political party (on or off campus), on the one hand, and standing up for a principle or idea that is in harmony with the purpose of an organization, with the reason for its being, on the other. To illustrate:

"Unions themselves originally were the outcome of dissent. Students of Oxford and Cambridge wanted to come together to discuss and debate the issues of the day. They formed 'unions' to do it—and met with active disapproval, sometimes suspension, from university authorities who thought unwanted criticism might come out of such open discussion. So a union, considering its origin as a center of critical debate, should have no trouble deciding to be for dissent.

"But the early British unions never physically attacked university personnel, blocked buildings, resorted to violence, or deprived other students of their rights. The union purpose, rather, grew to include 'getting to know and understand one another,' providing a community center 'for all the members of the college family,' and 'serving as a unifying force in the life of the college' (Association statement of the role of the union). So a union has reason to be against—actively against—disruption, violence, 'student power' moves designed to separate students from the faculty and administration—all the antithesis of what a union stands for.

"The union of its nature—every student a member and 'taxpayer'—has to do with the welfare of students. So it has ample justification to be for, and work for, a vast range of propositions that enhance the welfare of students, and to be against conditions that hurt students.

"'The union is part of the educational program ... training students in social responsibility.' So it should have no hesitancy in declaring itself against deliberate interference with the operations of the university and of the union, against the forces that hinder learning, against irresponsible and dangerous demonstrations, against one-sided, undemocratic attempts to commit a student body by force to a position. And at the same time, no hesitancy in actively seeking for ways of sensible change.

"In short, there's a crucial difference between making a political commitment to the Republication party or the Students for a Democratic Society per se, and, contra, making a commitment to the good of one's community or the well-being of one's fellows. ...

"But despite the efforts of a few, despite the announced union purposes, and for whatever reasons, it is fair to say that most unions have not been heard from, or heard of, in the current overriding crisis on the campus. ...

"So what can the union now do?

"If we care about our stated goals—about the well-being of students and the campus of which we're a part—there's reason to embrace issues with which students are concerned, or should be concerned, as well as concerts and coffee houses, and to see to it the great middle majority is heard and felt as well as the minorities.

"The least we can do is to make sure we carry out the historic union tradition of providing not only the facilities but the impetus for free and open discussion of any and all issues, for everybody. And do it before the issue reaches the boiling point. This doesn't mean just providing a hall for others. It means the union picking up the issue and ventilat-ing it itself, in time; making sure there are speakers on all sides of the question; and, equally important, making sure the audience is representative. ...

"If the union board is itself persuaded the curriculum should be reformed, that more should be done for black students, or that social regulations should be changed, there is no reason why it shouldn't say so. There is great merit in sensible reform—'reform is the enemy of revolution.' ...

"Some say: 'That's the job of student government.' Maybe. Student government itself has often been taken over by an activist minority; or follows the separate student power line; or doesn't enjoy much support or respect from the student body or administration. In any case, building a better community and student satisfaction with it is the union's job, too. And it's likely to be listened to, because it does represent the mood of the majority, or can.

"But you won't get results by passing resolutions or firing verbal shots at the administration, let alone picketing the president's office. Assume (usually rightly) the administration and faculty are deeply concerned about these issues, too. Identify constructive measures that might be taken, go to the administration and say, 'We know you're concerned; we as students are concerned; how can we help?'

"It would be an electrifying change in the student approach; beleaguered faculty and administrators would be so shocked, and pleased, that something good is very likely to happen. We might even set a model of success for student government and the more sincere activists who are interested in more than an uproar. ...

"In short, in this crisis brought on by disruption by a few and the indifference of the majority, could not the union be a positive force, giving voice to the majority, working for a genuine—and peaceful—community of teachers and students in which education can happen, helping preserve the university as an arena of free inquiry and discussion, free from disruption and the threat of destruction?"

— "Crisis on the Campus ... and the College Union." The Bulletin of the Association of College Unions International, 1969.

"We talk of college unions and student leadership in the same breath. This is a time, if ever, for union leadership."

— The Bulletin of the Association of College Unions International, 1969.

"

The least we can do is to make sure we carry out the historic union tradition of providing not only the facilities but the impetus for free and open discussion of any and all issues, for everybody. **And do it before the issue reaches the boiling point.**

"

Above: The Tarrant County Junior College South Campus Student Center in 1967.
Below: The University of Waterloo Campus Centre in 1968. ACUI ARCHIVES

Above: The Wright State University Center in 1968.
Below: The State University of New Jersey, Rutgers Student Center in 1969. ACUI ARCHIVES

THE ▶

1970s

In the early part of the decade, ongoing activism and changing student demographics pose challenges for the union. While major concerts, outdoor activities, and the arts are significant programs, for some, the union is seen as little more than a "pool hall." Aging facilities, built shortly after the world wars, seek funding for capital improvements. In the later 1970s, students' role in the union also begins to transform as governance models change and the student workforce diminishes.

AGAIN, THE QUESTION OF CENTRALIZATION OF FACILITIES, OR DECENTRALIZATION

"Too often, I fear, the administration wants a union for the wrong, or partly wrong, reasons. Either the president has seen 'one of those' and wants one, to keep pace in the race; or the campus planner or dean of students reminds everybody there has to be a place to eat; or everybody agreed there's an acute need for a new bookstore, or a place for students, especially commuters, to be somewhere between classes.

"So the problem is now not so much one of selling the idea of having a new building as selling the idea of what a union might be.

"No one can take too great exception, of course, to the suggestion that students, like everyone else, need to eat, that they have to buy books, and that they ought to have a place to get in out of the rain. And if this sells a union project, fine.

"But before the college freezes on the concept of a union as a combination snack bar-cafeteria-bookstore, plus a few meeting rooms and offices, someone on the campus ought to assemble a docket of information on unions and go to the president and say: 'Won't you appoint a planning committee to study out all our out-of-class needs and make recommendations?'

"The president may think of this himself; a number have. But all too often the whole matter has been left in the hands of the business office; or an architect who has never seen a union is commanded to produce a preliminary scheme next month; or the planning office devises some formula that defines what the building is going to be. And this doesn't mean the job will be done well. ...

"The first task of the planning committee, I would suggest, is to familiarize itself rather fully with the historic purposes and the present potentials of a union. ...

"With background reading under its belt, the second task, I happen to believe, is to arrive at a controlling statement of purpose for the new building, or addition, so that all may have a common reference point, so that the basic functions of the building are understood by all—including by the administration, trustees, and student body. For if the fundamental guiding purposes of the building can be agreed upon, many corollary decisions regarding what facilities to include, site selection, and other campus planning will more readily fall in place. ...

"Basic to all planning throughout is the answer to this fundamental question: 'Should the new or expanded union, in principle, be conceived as a general community center to meet rather fully the institution's out-of-class needs, present and future, or as a facility designed mainly to take care of a few more pressing immediate service needs (i.e., expanded bookstore and food services) as a supplement to cultural, social, and service facilities in other buildings?'

"The answer most colleges, here and abroad, have arrived at after careful study has been to design the union as the major focal center of campus life and activity outside the classroom. ... To date, at least, the union as the campus community center is the basic concept in the U.S., borne of the belief that providing a general common meeting ground is the way you get the maximum interaction among the otherwise insular segments of the campus populations and gain some semblance of unity (the reason for the name 'union'), and the belief that in coming for one activity to a union which embraces the arts and social recreation as well as services, students will be exposed to, and perhaps inspired by, another activity. ...

Minnesota State University Moorhead's Comstock Memorial Union. ACUI ARCHIVES

"Now I am quite aware that some are questioning this centralization of community services and programs. A widely published report from a university in the Midwest, for example, says: 'Our plan rejects the notion of a single architectural utopia. ... The classic union building—a monolithic structure that is intended to be all things to all students—is no solution.' And then the report goes on to advocate a series of 'outposts' in scattered locations, small gathering places along campus or nearby commercial streets, and classroom building lounges or 'hangouts'—where students can rest between or after classes, get light snacks, study, play a game of table tennis, and wait for the bus. ...

"It seems to me somebody at this university hasn't heard what a union is. They're talking about washrooms, hamburgers, places to study, and bus stops. I have no quarrel with dispersing these; of course you don't put all the campus washrooms, vending machines, study tables, and bus stations in the union. You install them where people are; you make conveniences convenient. But you still haven't come anywhere near doing what a union does, or can do.

"What about students who want more than a snack day after day? What about group gatherings, large and small, that need catered food service? What about rooms for meetings everybody can readily find? What about the large assembly places every campus needs—ballroom, auditorium? What about student-faculty interaction—and special provisions for faculty and conference groups? What about a well-conceived social-cultural-recreation program, and a place for program staff and student committees to operate? What about a central place where students can find each other, broaden their acquaintanceships, meet the other students they might marry? What about enlarging the student's sense of belonging to something more than a street outpost or classroom lounge?"

— "Getting the Union Project Under Way." Association of College Unions Seminar in Planning a College Union, 1970.

"In planning facilities, consider fully that a union is no longer merely a place to eat and meet, but has to do broadly with the constructive employment of student time outside the classroom, that it represents an experience in a way of living. Hence consider facilities for cultural and creative pursuits (theater or auditorium, music rooms, library, art display space), for hobbies and crafts, for motion pictures, and for outdoor activity (outing headquarters and program) as well as for social and dining activity. ...

"Remember that students are rarely interested in just a place to sit down. Plan rooms and lounges in which students can do something."

— "College Unions—Facilities and Administration." College and University Administration. Published by McGraw-Hill, 1970.

Accommodating the Physical Growth of the Campus

Ideally, the college union was built to be near the center of campus. This provided easy access for the university community to utilize the programs and services provided within the college union. But as campuses grew, their landscape was not always equally enlarged on all sides, finding the college union in a remote corner. In planning for future development, some institutions looked at facilities to be built within the new growth areas, as at Oklahoma State University:

"Though much can be accomplished through the development of the community center concept with centralized social, recreational, and cultural facilities, located in close proximity to one another, and sharing multipurpose space such as meeting rooms, parking, auditoria, dining facilities, and lounge area, a part of this study should give consideration to the kinds of satellite facilities the unions should provide to serve the high-density population areas in the long range campus plan. Such satellite facilities should be anticipated and should become a part of the total union expansion."

— George Stevens, director of the Memorial Union at Oregon State University, 1970. Printed in "More than a Building: The MU at OSU," 1984.

The College Union in a Changing Society

"The number of college unions in the United States today is about 1,200. There are over 400 international unions in countries such as Japan, Pakistan, China, England, Finland, and Australia. There have been some reports of unions behind the iron curtain in Yugoslavia. Two-thirds of these unions have been built since World War II, and many of the older unions have had up to six additions.

"Not only does the college union continue to grow, but it also continues to respond to the changing needs of its society, and yet at the same time continues to satisfy its basic philosophy as a place where all members of the university family meet and identify with each other.

"Lifestyles of students are never static. However, the speed of the pendulum regulating changes has increased. ... Students today have lived through electronics and other technological advancement which makes them part of the world scene immediately and provides computerized answers to complex problems in seconds. The space program teaches them that nothing is impossible, providing there is commitment of human and financial resources. As a result, they are 'now' people, and they want to see change happen quickly. Their life experience tells them that change is necessary if one is to keep relevant. The college generation is concerned about the individual in our society. Students are concerned that as we grow in population and live closer together, we will lose a personal identity. Today's student is concerned about his environment and what we have done to it as we grew technologically. He is worried about how we will feed ourselves if our rate of population growth continues. Today's student is seriously concerned about his education and how it will prepare him for his future. The days of the university 'in loco parentis' philosophy are past. College students seek self-determination in where they live, in developing their sexual mores, in establishing their value structures, and in building a curriculum. Students no longer are spectators at a lecture, nor do they study only in the library or in their room. The involved student, as a part of his educational process, feels that learning about life and commu-

The University of Hawaii at Manoa Campus Center in 1974. ACUI ARCHIVES

nity responsibilities is as important to him during his educational years as the formal instruction which he receives in the classroom. I believe that today education must look to the broader campus and community environment for teaching stations, and should not restrict teaching to the traditional classroom. The college union, which early advocated education outside the classroom, is currently becoming one of the most important teaching stations in the university. Students tend to identify today with smaller special interest groups rather than the large school events. Dances are giving way to concerts where the individual can have his own experience as he listens—even athletics are coming up for criticism.

"Another important dimension affecting the design of the college union is the economy of 1971. Inflation has caused state governments, individuals, and corporations to examine priorities as they allocate money to education. Campus unrest last year caused people to ask for more accountability from students and educators, and to underline this, private schools raised tuitions and state legislatures are asking students to pay a higher percentage of their education. The college union is almost exclusively financed by student fees to pay for the cost of the building. Operating departments (food, recreation, etc.) are generally expected to break even—a feat most difficult in the present economy. All of this at a time when we find many of the established college union buildings in need of repair and renovation, as well as additional space needs to meet rising enrollments."

— Bruce Kaiser. "Student Life Styles and Their Impact on College Union Planning." Paper presented at the National Exposition of Contract Interior Furnishings, Chicago, June 24, 1971.

THE ACTIVIST LOOKS AT CAMPUS UNIONISM

"I would ask that you join me and the activist student—in taking a penetrating look at the campus union.

"My travels across the country during the last 18 months persuade me to believe that the seeds of disorder and uprising have in fact been implanted and are germinating at an alarming rate. And I fear that, in far too many instances, it may be past the time for changes designed to make our unions more responsive.

"But still, my journeys to almost 100 unions have convinced me that the college union can be a viable force in bringing about dialogue rather than destruction, education as opposed to confrontation, and light instead of heat. I believe—I truly believe—that the college union can aid in healing what Archibald MacLeish has termed 'this bursting pustule of violence.'

"First let's ask ourselves: 'What does the campus activist see when he looks at his campus union? ... When he examines the college union movement, in general?' Not a great deal, I fear. Far too often, he sees the same shallow and puerile programs that evolved in the post-World War II period ... programs that fail to excite his mind ... programs that fail to challenge and stimulate his intellect and the intellects of his terribly bright, worried, and skeptical peers. I'm afraid he regards us as a group who resists or runs from his ideas, his music, his beard, his skin color—perhaps his prophets, his heroes, and his anti-heroes. I'm afraid he feels apologized for, feared, mistrusted, misunderstood, and in general, rejected.

"What does the activist think about our college union role statement? Is he 'turned on' by references to the hearthstone, the amenities, enduring regard for the college, and a 'laboratory of citizenship?' I doubt it. Instead, he is doubtless disappointed that the union is not attempting to be a laboratory of liberal education, a free and open community of minds, a place where the trinity of peace, justice, and freedom seem more than the tedious cant of adult apologists—a temple of faith ... faith in the amazing abilities of our young Aquarians.

"The fall Association *Bulletin* devotes a great deal of space to the student/staff assembly held at Camp Mishawak, Wis., this past June. At Camp Mishawak, a portion of our time was spent in identifying—not solving—the paramount problems facing college unions in 1969. Clearly, the number one problem listed was an environmental problem, viz, the lack of an environment in which every individual has a sense of belonging and personal growth.

"What's happening at your school to create the kind of environment that is needed? An environment in which every student—including the non-conformist—feels a sense of belonging? Is this question being deliberated by your union board? Or do you even have a union board?

"If you agree with me as to the value of positive reform, and if you further agree that violence is an unacceptable instrument of reform, then I hope you realize that the unity we seek can be brought about—in substantial part—through and in our unions. And this is something that can happen here—and now. I am convinced that we have a rare opportunity to circumvent bull-horns in the quad, bloodshed in the plaza, and yes—even death in the streets."

— Robert A. Alexander. An address presented at the Region 4 Conference, Duquesne University, Pittsburgh, Pa., Fall 1969. Printed in the April 1970 The Bulletin of the Association of College Unions International.

In 1970, students at the University of Toledo hold a vigil (above) and occupy the top of the union (left) in protest of the Vietnam War.

The Union as a Place to Protest

"Students at the State University at Albany held a protest meeting today after an overnight stay in the Student Center after an administrative decision not to renew a popular faculty member's contract.

"The overnight stay by about 200 students followed incidents last night of snowball throwing followed by a flurry of window breaking when stones were added to the snow missiles."

— "State U Students at Albany Protest." The New York Times, March 15, 1970.

"Police arrested 132 young persons—most of them Michigan State students—after they defied repeated requests to vacate the MSU Student Union building at East Lansing, Mich. They were booked for trespassing and loitering. The removal of the occupiers was without violence. But some demonstrators earlier smashed windows of campus buildings and of at least one off-campus building not connected with the university."

— "Campus Arrests and Injuries Mount." The Washington Post, May 20, 1970.

"Seventeen black students were arrested at the University of Nevada at Reno this evening when they refused to end their occupation of an office in the Student Union Building. They had occupied the office for a week as part of a long-term effort to get space in the building for the Black Student Union.

"University officials had ordered them to leave by tonight. When they did not, sheriff's officers and city policemen removed a barricade the black students had set up, pushed open the door, and used chemical mace and a fire extinguisher to remove the students. There were no immediate reports of injuries.

"Outside the building, about 250 students had gathered, expressing sentiments both for and against the blacks, but they dispersed at the direction of N. Edd Miller, president of the state university's Reno campus."

— "Arrest of Blacks Ends Nevada Sit-in." The New York Times, October 29, 1971.

"An eight-day occupation of the Student Center at Pratt Institute by black and Puerto Rican students ended last night after the school's administration and trustees agreed to either implement or investigate the protesters' nine demands."

— "Pratt Students End 8-Day Occupation." The New York Times, May 18, 1972.

Dealing with Difference— A Union of People

Many campuses have seen the growth of unions serving different student populations. These groups have developed in response to a lack of existing support systems on campuses, not to compete with college unions. In many ways, their growth provides additional opportunities for programming and education around race and culture.

"Most large campuses now have Black Student Unions, which operate as separate entities to the union board, which is responsible for the major programming on campus. These unions have expanded to not only meet social and political needs but have also been instrumental in providing a new cultural dimension for the entire campus population."

— Floyd Flake. From a speech given at the 52nd Annual Conference of the Association of College Unions International, 1972.

"Since our early days as debating societies, we have been a part of the world around us. But more and more in recent years, we are inextricably intertwined with the larger, the changing society. ... We wonder if we can adjust to the accelerated change. And, we know we are a part of the continuous agenda of our society—war, poverty, environmental pollution, racial tension, the struggle for equality, the uneasy economy, the shifting morality, the war against physical and mental pain, the widespread disenchantment with institutions and rules, the raging conflict resulting from diverse philosophies, lifestyles, and values. Whether we chose to be or not, college unions are not isolated. We are involved. We worry."

— Shirley Bird Perry, from the University of Texas and the first woman to serve as ACUI president. From a speech given at the 52nd Annual Conference of the Association of College Unions International, 1972.

"The union is definitely a part of the academic establishment of the university. On the other hand—the opposite hand—the union is exactly what its name connotes, a union of people which provides programs and services all within an educational context."

— A. Robert Raineville. From a speech given at the 52nd Annual Conference of the Association of College Unions International, 1972.

Following the Civil Rights Movement, in the 1970s, a more diverse population had access to higher education.
WARD M. CANADAY CENTER ARCHIVES, UNIVERSITY OF TOLEDO

"Are the college unions ready to assume the roles they will play in this revolution, through awareness of change; through research activity; through adherence to your goals for student service, instead of institutional service; through planned action, instead of expedient reaction from obsolescence, or overreaction as a result of crises; through creating an image broad in educational concept, instead of narrow in the social life concept; through belief in the social-cultural needs which must be your prime goal? The college union must not be thought of as merely an auxiliary enterprise. It must be a social and cultural center."

— R. Buckminster Fuller, faculty at Southern Illinois University. "Focus on the Future." Proceedings of the 52nd Annual Conference of the Association of College Unions International, 1972.

"Musts" for Programming

"Encourage more programming on your campus for the following reasons. I call these reasons 'union musts,' none of which are mutually exclusive:

"To help make classroom learning more meaningful by assuming an important role in the educational process. How can we help make Asian Studies, American Studies, and Black Studies, for example, more significant and understandable through our programs? To relate to the concerns of the immediate environment and the world around us through talking about social issues, learning about other cultures, and bringing in the best of our world as representatives in the arts.

This promotional photo advertises The Kinks performance at Queens College during this, "the golden era of union concerts." MIKE DEL GAUDIO

"To help program participants to have more fun. Learning to have fun is becoming increasingly important for many reasons as we anticipate more and more leisure time. Americans have never been very good at relaxed sheer enjoyment.

"To help various groups satisfy personal desires to learn something basic (and sometimes by doing in contrast to the abstraction of the classroom) in the pursuit of the arts and crafts or interests of an avocational or practical nature.

"To enhance the useableness of physical facilities of the union and its service features such as food, drink, companionship, and information.

"To bring together as many interest groups as possible on a common meeting ground so that participants interact and their values are challenged through exposure to other lifestyles.

"To provide opportunities for service and leadership so that students can 'turn on,' help each other, and also participate in activities involving social responsibility."

— J.S. Sturgell. An Uncommon Guide to College Union Programming, 1974.

Big Names Come to the Union

The social programming of the 1970s took on many forms and continued to evolve with students' changing tastes. The decade was described as "the golden era for union concerts," for having "such comedic giants as Bob Hope, Jerry Lewis, Red Skeleton, Bill Cosby, and Lily Tomlin," and for "many outstanding programs, from the then-unknown Jimmy Buffet and the Coral Reefer Band to the first showing of the cult-classic 'The Rocky Horror Picture Show.'"

— K-State Student Union: From Concept to Creation—The History and Memories of Your K-State Student Union, 2006.

Also, a Focus on Outdoor Activity

"I think that the fascinating expansion in the union's outdoor programming area seems most to meet in a variety of exciting ways the union's primary aims."

— J.S. Sturgell. "An Uncommon Guide to College Union Programming." Proceedings of the 53rd Annual Conference of the Association of College Unions International, 1973.

"The philosophy of most outdoor programs epitomizes that of the college union. Participation by all factions of the academic community is welcome. This provides for an intermingling of age groups, interests, skills, and intellect. Important leisure time is utilized. Union programs functions as a counterweight, providing balance to the normal business-like classroom schedule of the institution."

- Greg Simmons. Proceedings of the 53rd Annual Conference of the Association of College Unions International, 1973.

A Perception Problem

The programs offered within the union were meant to have more than social value, although this was not always the perception. In planning the Campus Union Building, which opened in 1972, the University of Alaska Fairbanks noted the importance of eliminating the "pool hall" atmosphere to reinforce the educational use of the college union.

In a report to his staff about the 1973 ACUI conference, Jim Reynolds said: "One of the loudest frustrations I heard at the conference was: 'The administration just doesn't know what the union is all about,' 'They just don't appreciate what I do,' 'I have no contact with the president,' etc. ...

"The problem points up to the reality that college union staff members have either not performed or have not communicated their accomplishments and philosophies; and that college presidents have not seriously considered the value and role of a college union. In this area of accountability, when all aspects of college operations are being critically scrutinized, only those which have a purpose and which have accomplished that purpose will be maintained."

Reynolds said many administrators viewed the college union as a money-maker, highlighting another concern, this time regarding new emphasis on revenue generation. Fiscal constraints and the rise of campus auxiliary enterprises led many college union directors to decide how to continue services while generating much needed financial support. This became a profession for entrepreneurs—balancing the needs of students, faculty, and university administrators, while supporting our union boards and campus activities programs. Would we lose sight of our role as campus educators? Would we see students and university guests as mere customers? Union directors once were called "wardens," but the use of the title "commercial manager" in the 1970s signaled this transformation from college union to commercial union.

This transformation became visible as college union operations focused on developing marketing plans to attract new profit-driven services such as specialized dining outlets, conferencing, and travel agencies. In 1973, one conference presenter mused: "The college union of the future will be in the business of leasing space—much the same as real estate shopping center entrepreneurs do today. [Union] directors will manage business rather than hordes of people. Body count will no longer be a criterion for compensation—unless adversely so—and judgment of ability will be profit-oriented. The income will finance student services, programs, and functions."

In some instances, new consideration was given to old ideas. William Barrett wrote that the Rutgers University Student Centers were counting on the establishment of beer and wine bars to bail them out of serious financial difficulties. The Student Centers received operational funds from the state, which were being reduced. New Jersey had also lowered the drinking age to 18, and Princeton and Seton Hall Universities were seeing success with their campus bars. The Student Center at Rutgers University in Camden expected a $20,000 yearly profit from the proposed pub. At Rutgers–Newark, a $15,000 surplus was predicted.

Later in the decade, the identity problem of being a convenience center and a place to support the campus cocurricular continued. *The Washington Post* presented this struggle in its 1977 article "Student Unions: Juggling Money, Politics": "At many institutions, the student union is running into a familiar dilemma: how to deliver good and popular services without going broke, and how to allow students enough of a voice in running the place to keep them satisfied."

"

THE CAMPUS POPULATION IS DIVERSE, BUT ALL HAVE IN COMMON THE NEED OR DESIRE FOR EDUCATION. **THE UNION BY DESIGN SHOULD BE ABLE TO FOSTER THESE NEEDS IN A WAY NO OTHER COMMUNITY ORGANIZATION CAN.**

"

Students enjoy watermelon while waiting in line at a 1976 Boise State University voter registration drive.

Building Community through the Union at Two-Year Colleges

"The college union is a program which strives to bring all factions of the campus together in some form. It is the gray areas in which the needs of students, faculty, administration, and community can overlap, and with this overlapping, create a better understanding of each other and of each other's needs. ...

"The role statement speaks of the 'college family.' The interaction of students and staff can be a unique experience if the goals and motivations of each are to stimulate the other's intellect and creativity. The campus population is diverse, but all have in common the need or desire for education. The union by design should be able to foster these needs in a way no other community organization can."

— Thomas Lease. Proceedings of the 55th Annual Conference of the Association of College Unions International, 1975.

The Union and the Curriculum

"Unless there is an educational justification of a union on campus, there is no justification for it at all."

— John Wong. "The Union and the Curriculum." Proceedings of the 54th Annual Conference of the Association of College Unions International, 1974.

"The idea of union staff and/or the union being involved with the curriculum of the college or university is a nontraditional concept. Some may question the appropriateness of the union taking such a direction; after all, services and offerings of the union have traditionally been a part of students' spare time and on a voluntary basis with regard to their participation. Should students earn credit for such pursuits? ...

"I do not think the union's role with relation to the curriculum of the institution is to maintain the traditions of the classroom as past models have exemplified, nor must it be a duplication of that effort. But rather, it should be an attempt to deliver new areas of academic pursuit using challenging, stimulating, and rewarding methods and techniques in the endeavor to provide today's students with enriching and worthwhile educational experiences."

— Carole Hennessy. "The Union and the Curriculum." Proceedings of the 54th Annual Conference of the Association of College Unions International, 1974.

The Arts— An Expanding Commitment

"We have seen considerable growth in cultural activities in the last 25 years, which some say started with the traveling done by servicemen during World War II. ... The major booking agencies tell us that of the concerts booked in the country today, 70 percent is happening on our college campuses. ...

"In our planning, the challenge is to interest, attract, educate, develop the student. ... Do we give them just what they want? Meaning, the program has the same level all the time. We must look at and evaluate the program at all times and be sure that in the four-year college cycle, we include all areas of programming, dance, drama, pop, vocal and instrumental soloists, orchestras, chamber groups, opera, chorus, and not just a piano solo because it has been popular. The easiest thing to do is forget about the classics, especially the vocal soloists. When we look for a balance, there are often other considerations that cloud our thinking.

There are times when we have financial problems. It would be easier to have the house sold with solid box office attractions and not be concerned with appeal versus worth; box office versus quality. We should give our students only the very best in all areas of programming and if we have this approach we will see positive evidence of audience growth."

— James Wockenfuss, theater director of the LSU Union at Louisiana State University–Baton Rouge. "Why Visual and Performing Arts on Campus?" Presented in Houston, Texas, March 20–22, 1970.

"The purpose of art programming in the union continues to provide an alternative to the students' classroom situation, allowing the artistic process to be experienced firsthand through visual display and direct participation. However, the scope of the arts has increased to such an extent that confusion often prevails when a union attempts to develop and manage an ongoing art program. No longer is it necessary to just be committed to the arts; a union must now decide what art orientation it plans to pursue."

— John A. McCauley and Teryl Ann Rosch. "Logistics for Developing and Managing a Union Art Gallery." Proceedings of the 56th Annual Conference of the Association of College Unions International, 1976.

"The union is programming in the field of theater, it has been for years, and if we are smart and have an eye to the future, we will continue to expand this most exciting field."

— Ray C. Myers. "The Many Forms of Theater in the Union." Proceedings of the 56th Annual Conference of the Association of College Unions International, 1976.

End of the Student Protest Movement

"I am still asked from time to time to comment on the demise of the student protest movement. I agree with those who say that much was accomplished, in the way of helping to end the Viet Nam War and forcing a reexamination of values. What was, for me, a significant comment was made recently by S.M. Lipsett, the political sociologist: he points out that movements of this kind cannot be expected to last; they just run their course. If a revolution is expected to succeed, it must succeed quickly; otherwise, there is a natural regression toward the mean, as people drift away to take up neglected affairs."

— Nevitt Sanford. Proceedings of the 57th Annual Conference of the Association of College Unions International, 1977.

Contributions of College Unions to Student Development

"The development and expansion of volunteer programs on campus and in the community is one of the great contributions the union can make in developing competent, dedicated citizens in a democracy."

— Burns B. Crookston. "Student Development and Involvement in Governance." Proceedings of the 54th Annual Conference of the Association of College Unions International, 1974.

"The activities and organizations of college unions can play a strong role in this transition from reliance on parents; through reliance on peers, other adults, and organizations; to self-reliance. Many students come to union activities and organizations for the associations with fellow students and the support groups that are offered. And many of those who simply hang around, shooting pool, playing cards, drinking coffee, and talking endlessly are dealing with the same transition by developing close relationships and informal friendship groups with other students who are experiencing similar concerns. The union acts like the local street corner of the local hangout during the high school years and like the local bar, pub, or disco for those recently out of high school who have not gone to college. Every institution needs settings where students can find each other to pursue these development tasks and a union which creates these opportunities and encourages this kind of interaction makes a useful contribution.

"'Instrumental independence,' the ability to carry on activities and cope with problems without seeking help, is another major component of autonomy. In college much work is 'academic': right answers to rote problems are expected; prescribed ways to solve most problems are spelled out; assistance is to be sought if difficulties are encountered. Opportunities to develop a variety of other kinds of skills and knowledge are limited. And the chance to test oneself in action which calls for more than academic and verbal abilities is similarly constrained. To the degree that student union activities expand the range of possibilities for developing diverse

As in this 1973 photo, bulletin boards were a primary method of advertising programs. ACUI ARCHIVES

kinds of competence and practical know-how to that extent they also contribute to increased instrumental independence. ...

"When the student union becomes a meeting ground for diverse kinds of students and not just the turf for a limited few, it can be a central locus for freeing interpersonal relationships. When programs and activities are supported which bring persons from different racial, ethnic, and socio-economic backgrounds together to undertake a joint project or share an event, it creates the context where ... [positive changes] can be encouraged. When the union, through its service and community action activities helps middle or upper-middle class students enter environments different from the small towns or suburbs from which they came, and when it helps them meet and work with children and adults in

those new environments, substantial changes can be fostered. These changes in the persons may have more lasting significance than the actual services rendered, when they lead to greater sensitivity, awareness, self-understanding, and understanding of others. For then the soil has been cultivated so that there is greater receptiveness to other kinds of experiences and persons.

"The union also provides opportunities for working relationships between students and older faculty members or other persons in various positions of power and authority."

—Arthur W. Chickering, prominent educational researcher and student development theorist. Proceedings of the 57th Annual Conference of the Association of College Unions International, 1977.

A PLACE TO EXPERIMENT AND EXPLORE

"On a weekday afternoon, the Student Union Building at the State University at Stony Brook is a bustling arcade of special interest groups, and the impressionable undergraduate is the prize for whose attention they tirelessly compete. Some sell jewelry, some philosophy. But whatever they offer, they vie to attract the undergraduate, either to buy their merchandise or join their cause. ...

"'A college campus where such a wide range of interests are represented is an ideal place to experiment and explore,' said Edward Idell, a senior from Brooklyn. 'Merely going to classes and to the library leads to a dulling of the senses. While studying is important here, it is also important to become exposed to alternatives that may challenge what you've read in the textbooks.'"

— David Gilman. "To Catch the Eye and Ear." The New York Times, March 20, 1977.

"An active student organization, such as our Union Board, offers students a range of activities and a kind of involvement that builds loyalty to the institution and maintains high interest through what may be otherwise trying periods. Indeed the union, with its myriad activities, provides the best microcosm on the campus of the larger world into which students will soon pass upon graduation."

— Robert M. O'Neal. Proceedings of the 59th Annual Conference of the Association of College Unions International, 1979.

"The offerings that the union has complement the intellectual growth of the students, that's true. ... And students need special outlets. At the union an uptight engineer plays the guitar, a law student plays Hamlet, a math major makes a film, an accountant reads poetry, a musician debates politics.

"I believe that our university can offer education to the whole person. I believe that people learn in a variety of settings, in a variety of ways, from a variety of ways, from a variety of people. We learn in classrooms, in residence halls, in gymnasia, on athletic fields, in laboratories, in libraries, on mountain tops, in field houses, in religious foundations, and in college unions. Through our total program at the Texas Union, a student can meet and enjoy other people, explore new directions and ideas, and express himself in his own special way. We offer students a lot."

— Shirley Bird Perry. As quoted in The University of Texas at Austin Alumni Magazine, September/October 1975.

Art displayed on the top floor of New Mexico State University's Corbett Center. ACUI ARCHIVES

Students at Rhodes College. BY ED UTHMAN

A Shift from Governing to Advising the Union

"It is apparent that the policy boards and program boards continue to be a valuable attribute to the overall operation of the college union. However, these boards have decreased in their final jurisdiction areas and accepted the role more and more of advising the administrative unit."

— Tom Kennedy, Sam Beckley, and Bernard J. Pitts. "The Great Debate: Who Runs the Show?" Proceedings of the 58th Annual Conference of the Association of College Unions International, 1978.

Updating Existing Facilities

"Many unions were built after World War I as memorials. Some have kept pace with the years and are serving their campuses now better than they did a half century ago. Others are failures. ... A number of the older unions are conducting their own fundraising programs, usually using alumni who served on union boards as volunteer leaders. The union is an appealing target for 25- and 50-year class gifts, one that alumni can appreciate and which can be made meaningful to them by other alumni. Oregon State alumnus Jack Porter, for example, is completing 53 years of membership on the union board and is nearing his 400th board meeting. The University of Wisconsin Memorial Union is still a pace-setter with its development program now well-established. Most of the funds raised by unions are earmarked either for the improvement of physical plants, program development, or scholarships for union volunteers. ...

"Many of the older vital unions are involved in extensive refurbishment or renovation programs. Indiana University is putting nearly a half-million dollars into a new food service concept with almost all of the money being directed at converting the front-of-the-house facilities into a food shopping center. The Memorial Union at Iowa State is now planning its ninth building addition."

— Chester A. Berry, ACUI's first executive director. "State of the Union." The Bulletin of the Association of College Unions International, February 1978.

Increasing Accessibility

"Federal law now mandates that all campuses receiving government funds must eliminate, by the middle of 1980, those architectural barriers which prohibit accessibility to the nation's nearly 68 million citizens suffering from limiting physical conditions. ...

"It has been difficult to get attention focused on program accessibility because some people seem to skim over the regulations and explanatory materials and start fretting about the widening of thousands of doors or installations of high and low water fountains in every facility at every conceivable point. ...

"When it comes to adapting existing facilities, writes Dean McDevitt at Baltimore, 'college administrators should ask a handicapped student for advice.'

"However, if they started listing some of the things they have learned from these students and personally observed, 'they will realize that their own maintenance crews can correct 80 percent of the problems at minimal cost.'"

— "Overcoming Barriers to Higher Education: Program Accessibility for the Handicapped." Southern Regional Education Board, Winter 1978.

Problems on the Horizon

"American colleges and universities have fundamentally altered their conception of the importance of organized student activities. In effect, they have relinquished the idea that the 'extracurriculum' is a vital part of education. ...

"For several decades prior to World War II, student governments gave major attention to developing social activities for students, often with the active cooperation of the colleges. The decline in the importance and influence of student governments and the shift of their attention away from this traditional function has left a vacuum on college campuses, which only staff can fill. ...

"Participation in student activities and organizations has traditionally been a principal way in which students expressed and developed feelings of loyalty and allegiance to their institutions. This fact helps to explain why presidents and deans traditionally made their support of such activities visible

Trenton State College's Clayton P. Brower Student Center in 1976. ACUI ARCHIVES

to the campus (and alumni) and why they formerly assigned such high priorities to campus life. The present apparent neglect of this part of the life of the colleges is taken, therefore, at considerable risk to the well-being of the institution."

— W. Max Wise. "Conversations about Organized Student Activities in College." The Bulletin of the Association of College Unions International, December 1978.

"'The most significant single problem,' said the director of one of the world's largest and most venerable unions, 'is student labor'—or the lack thereof, he might have added.

"Considering his problems of 10 years ago—riots, disappearing student leadership, deficit budgets, limping programs, low staff morale, anti-intellectualism, this problem—one in which his colleagues concurred almost unanimously—did not loom large.

"Actually, the problem of a diminishing labor pool for the menial service tasks involves both student and full-time employees and it does seem to head the list of nuts and bolts difficulties. The overshadowing concern, however, centers around the quality of campus life. Inflation is diverting an ever-increasing share of collegiate dollars into academia. Unions are viewed as auxiliary operations not deserving of tax or tuition dollars, operations which should somehow earn enough money to keep their doors open. Through such open doors, students and others will come to pay for food or books or toilet supplies or recreation or entertainment. Forums, art shows, poetry reading, music listening, browsing, social interchange, or the hundreds of other activities that make a facility into a college union scarcely get lip service, let alone financial support."

— Chester A. Berry. "State of the Union." The Bulletin of the Association of College Unions International, April 1979.

The University of Nevada, Las Vegas's Donald C. Moyer Campus Student Union. UNLV PHOTO SERVICES

California Polytechnic State University's Julie A. McPhee University Union in 1971. ACUI ARCHIVES

A Rhodes College student works on The Sou'wester student newspaper in the basement of the Briggs Student Center.
BY ED UTHMAN

A campus radio disc jockey at the University of Southern California. EL RODEO YEARBOOK

1980s

As the university becomes more of a business, the union is increasingly seen as an auxiliary enterprise, confounding its core mission to educate. High-risk drinking becomes a common theme of the college experience with the union and others seeking to eradicate the behavior. A heightened awareness and acceptance of diverse populations calls for the union to be a campus leader in creating a sense of place for individuals and enhancing multicultural education. Professionals see their role as educators and encourage future generations to choose a career in college unions.

The 1980s heralded the introduction of the mainstream personal computer.

MENLO PHOTO BANK

ROLE OF THE COLLEGE UNION

"When is a union a union? I suggest a 1981 update to the 1956 role statement that goes like this: A union is more than a community center of the college for all members of the college family; it is, and must be, much more if it is to fulfill its institutional role. It must act as an important campus center for preserving and transmitting those goals and values that determine a college's community of interest and provide for the college's distinctiveness. A union is not just a building; it is also an organization and program. Through its program, it constantly seeks ways to enhance those elements that constitute a college's unique sense of community. It does this as an integral part of offering a considered plan for the community life of the college.

"In conclusion, it is my contention that it is a myth that our colleges are still closely knit social communities existing in isolation from each other. The reality is that most are not, and we must recognize this fact. We must also realize that the union today bestrides two worlds; first, the world of its origin, which still exists in some measure; and a second world of rapid change, change of a nature that threatens to undermine the basic assumptions upon which the union movement exists. The consequence is that the union itself must assume a major role in retaining and nurturing the sense of community essential to the academic process. In this role, the union itself may discover ways to link the union's past to its hoped-for future. This is the challenge, and if it is successfully met, it may well bring the union into the full bloom of its potential. This is when a union will truly become a union, as is inherent in the word union itself"

— Philip C. Chamberlain. "When is a Union a Union? Fiction vs. Reality." Proceedings of the 61st Annual Conference of the Association of College Unions International, 1981.

"When the student union becomes a meeting ground for diverse kinds of students and not just the turf of a limited few, it can be a central locus for freeing interpersonal relationships. When programs and activities are supported which bring persons together from different racial, ethnic, and socio-economic backgrounds to undertake a joint project or share an event, it creates the context where ... [change] can be encouraged. When the union, through its service and community action activities helps a middle or upper middle class student enter environments different from the small town or suburb from which they came, and when it helps them meet and work with children and adults in those new environments, substantial changes can be fostered. These changes may have more lasting significance than the actual services rendered when it leads to greater sensitivity, awareness, self-understanding, and understanding of others. Then the soil has been cultivated so there is greater receptiveness to other kinds of experiences and persons."

— Arthur Chickering. "Potential Contributions of College Unions to Student Development." College Unions at Work: The Impact of College Unions and Their Programs on Today's Students. Published by the Association of College Unions International, 1981.

Art and the Union: Education and Revolution

"As all of us are aware, each year we must, to some extent, justify our existence on our own campuses as a part of the educational enterprise. It has been established over the years that one of the most important functions that we serve is in the area of the arts and cultural programming. When we speak of the arts, we are talking about the fine arts, craft programs, the performing arts, literature, film programming, and concerts—all areas with which program advisors and program directors deal every day. ...

"Perhaps more important than any other reason for an emphasis on the arts in this period in our history is best expressed by the following quote by Romain Rolland from 'Musicians of the Past': 'The political life of a nation is only the most superficial aspect of its being. In order to know its inner life, the source of its action, one must penetrate to its soul by literature, philosophy, and the arts, where are reflected the ideas, the passions, the dreams of a whole people.'"

— Adell McMillan. Presidential remarks at the 61st Annual Conference of the Association of College Unions International, 1981.

"College unions are relatively modern manifestations of the long-held American belief that students are affected positively by participation in 'activities' which supplement instructional programs. College unions provide opportunities for the exploration of interests, the exercise of initiative, and the development of abilities to plan and carry out organized activities. Unions also promote the development of more informed social and political perspectives and the cultivation and appreciation of the arts. Since the days of our earliest colleges it was considered that student participation in campus activities developed important abilities. These were essential for the graduate in assuming his responsibilities in the common life of the country and in achieving a sense of personal fulfillment."

— W. Max Wise. Introduction, College Unions at Work: The Impact of College Unions and Their Programs on Today's Students. Published by the Association of College Unions International, 1981.

Reasserting the Importance of Programming to the Union's Mission

"Programming is our destiny. If you talk to any union professional for a few minutes, you find a programmer. Whether the area is food service, operations, or volunteer training, the focal point is the program. We have only to consider the role statement of our organization to realize that. A beautiful building with no activity is merely a shell. It is the program and its quality which attract people to the union. Nearly all of us have stories of the facility that used to be our union. It was tiny, perhaps in the basement of some building, had only one tennis table, took a long walk to get to, and was always full of students, faculty, and staff. Its programming budget was minuscule, but its programs were prolific, fun, and educational.

"Quality programming, then, is not dependent on facility or money. Too many of us have fallen in love with our buildings and expect them to captivate our public. Too many of us buy our programs from various agencies. While a good facility and reasonable budget certainly contribute to the quality of our programs, they are not the final word. Sometimes our very dependence on them inhibits the quest for quality programs. We are all, regardless of our particular jobs, responsible for the creation and maintenance of an overall quality program. Even in the face of slashed budgets, small staffs, and burnout, a quality program must be our goal. Mutual support of students and staff are required commitment and caring are indispensable."

— Wanda Yuhas. "Principles of Programming in the College Union." Proceedings of the 62nd Annual Conference of the Association of College Unions International, 1982.

"When students assume responsibility for planning and carrying out various student union activities they encounter real opportunities to test their abilities, to do things on their own, and to accomplish something observable by others. Successful accomplishment of this kind can help build a strong sense of competence and self-confidence, which in turn makes for increased readiness to take responsibility, increased willingness to risk self-esteem in new ventures."

The University of Calgary Students' Union in 1987. ACUI ARCHIVES

— Arthur Chickering. "Potential Contributions of College Unions to Student Development." College Unions at Work: The Impact of College Unions and Their Programs on Today's Students. Association of College Unions International, 1981.

"What are some direct benefits students derive from participating in union programs?

"Students can gain experience in making decisions as they plan and carry out activities.

Satisfying interpersonal and intergroup relationships, including improving one's tolerance and understanding of other people and their views, can be fostered.

"Students can apply knowledge and skills from academic work in a practical setting.

"Students can obtain experience in activities related to their chosen vocations.

"Bonding, affiliation, or a sense of belonging within the university community is facilitated.

"Self-understanding—understanding one's abilities, interests, and limitations—may be increased.

"Aesthetic sensitivity and appreciation of literature, art, music, and drama may be enhanced.

"Leisure-time pursuits, which have a lifetime value, may be discovered and refined.

"Opportunities for improving communication skills may be provided."

— James Marine. "The College Union's Role in Student Development." The Bulletin of the Association of College Unions International, February 1985.

The Human Perspective in a Machine-Filled World

"The first student union was founded at Cambridge in 1815. It played an important role in enabling students to participate in society. Since that time, unions have continued to serve as meeting places, as centers where students, faculty, administrators, and alumni can meet on common ground. The union programs provide essential and timely added dimensions to education and expansion of learning beyond the classroom walls.

"As you prepare students to sustain and improve our high-technology society, the unions will become even more important. The unions will provide an environment free from the professional and guild structure of the major courses of study; an environment where students will be free to explore and learn without the pressure of classroom measurement. The union is able to provide the means of self-expression—the toning of body and mind, the mental and physical hygiene that allow and individual to find some perspective of self, a perspective of self with a career field and within the board social structure. The union will also provide the vehicle for the pleasures of university life—social, sports, and personal—the social interactions that provide a necessary balance for the student who may be off-balance from the pressure of the classroom.

"Unions have an important role in preparing students to live and work in a future filled with high technology, a future where the emphasis will be on friendly man-machine interaction rather than on human-human interaction alone. The union is where students can try out a personal fulfillment and social perspective in a machine-filled world."

— Peter Cannon. "High Technology and the American Society." Proceedings of the 64th Annual Conference of the Association of College Unions International, 1984.

"Union and activities administrators have a wide range of responsibilities. The recently published 'Standards for Student Services/Development Programs' portrays the typical member of our profession as a cross between a 'jack of all trades' and some sort of super-being. One crucial aspect of union administration is human development, be that student, employee, or personal/professional. Computerization is frequently viewed as being somewhat dehumanizing. ... It is important to keep in sight the basic goals of our operations: education and service. The computer is an important ally in helping to improve the quality of our work."

— Robert Rouzer. ACUITION Computer Applications. The Electronic Union, 1985.

A New Debate: Contracting vs. Self-Operation

During the 1980s, as the union became home to a growing number of services, many campuses debated whether to staff their operations with university personnel versus a contact provider.

"Contracting started primarily with food services in the early 1970s as a method to replace faltering operations," wrote Donald Sabatino, director of auxiliary services and programs at the University of Akron, in a 1984 Bulletin. "... Our profession's early responses to contracting took the form of warnings. We heard repeatedly that by contracting we were admitting our inability to handle a job function."

However, Sabatino went on to itemize reasons why such logic was outdated, pointing to capital investments, specially trained personnel, higher staffing levels, quicker responses to changing needs, and more varied offerings as advantages of contract labor.

A year later, such claims were rebutted in a *Bulletin* column by J. Craig Harman, a campus dining services professional at Syracuse University who formerly had worked for a food service contractor. Harman argued that self-operated services benefitted from individualized training opportunities, better productivity, greater recourse in the case of poor performance, and no limiting clauses if institution wanted to change providers. He also stated that specialists, response time, and bureaucracy were characteristics of both contracted and self-operated services.

Sabatino and Harman were just two examples of campus executives weighing such decisions, which would become a mainstay of college unions and universities in general.

Is a Union's "Business" Business?

As budget constraints grew, having a clear sense of mission and purpose had never been more important for the union. What is our purpose? Why do we exist? Can our educational mission coexist with our financial mission? They can and they must. They are not at odds, but instead two sides of the same coin, each dependent on the other for success. Good business practices lead to good education and good education supports good business practices.

"The college union, founded on the principles of democracy and intellectual exchange—evolving into the campus community center, a place for sampling, recreating, sharing, questioning, playing, resting—growing into an individual—now finds itself increasingly concerned with financial survival. Decreases in enrollment coupled with the decline in institutional budget support have forced many unions to concentrate on increasing income-generating programs and services. Many unions formerly governed under a centralized union management have been subdivided to the extent of reporting to two or three offices with little or no coordination. Oftentimes internal bickering and quarreling seem to rule the day.

"Concern for striking a proper balance between the programs and business operations side of the college union is nothing new. Those unions which have been very successful have tended to be the ones that understood the differences and worked toward achieving a balance."

— Association of College Unions International Think Tank II Recommitment: What Business Are We Really In? 1984.

"

YOU HAVE OFTEN REFERRED TO YOUR UNIONS AS THE HEARTHSTONES OF THE CAMPUSES. THAT MAY BE AN OUTDATED PHRASE IN 1984, BUT IT CAPTURES MY SENSE OF THE TRIANGULAR RELATIONSHIP **AMONG UNION BUILDING, UNIVERSITY COMMUNITY, AND THE LARGER COMMUNITY OF CITIZENS.**

"

MAKING THE CASE FOR THE COLLEGE UNION

"During the past 30 years while the major transformation of faculty and presidential attitudes towards activity programs has occurred, most directors of college unions and directors of student activity programs appear to have been relatively unaware of the implications of these changes for their work. Some, of course, have attempted to maintain that their programs make an important contribution to student growth. But even these people appear to have assumed that reiterating their position would affect faculty and presidential attitudes. None, so far as I am aware, understood the very basis of their work—the three-century-old assumption that student activities were an integral part of collegiate education—was wasting away. Failing to grasp that fact, few directors have set about to collect evidence that their programs were effective influences on student development."

— W. Max Wise. Introduction, College Unions at Work: The Impact of College Unions and Their Programs on Today's Students. Published by the Association of College Unions International, 1981.

"The union building is in many ways the only structure on campus that can serve as a microcosm of the university and thereby help explain what a university is all about to the citizens who support higher education, most particularly institutions supported by the public sector. You have often referred to your unions as the hearthstones of the campuses. That may be an outdated phrase in 1984, but it captures my sense of the triangular relationship among union building, university community, and the larger community of citizens. ...

"You control what will happen to the functions of union buildings as we move toward the 21st century. If you cannot make the case, if you cannot persuade budgetary affairs committees of faculty councils or senates, student government organizations, chief executives of campuses, of how you contribute to the overall atmosphere and environment and life of an academic institution, then there will indeed be difficult times ahead. I am optimistic about what we face, but we must not be complacent."

— Kenneth R.R. Gros Louis, vice president of Indiana University Bloomington. Dialogue in the The Bulletin of the Association of College Unions International, April 1985.

Our Legal Responsibility

"During the past two decades, there has been a significant increase in the amount of litigation involving colleges and universities. Postsecondary institutions and the students they serve have become much more sophisticated with respect to the legal issues affecting their relationships to each other. Student groups and organizations are involved in a large portion of the litigation on campus as they exercise and define their rights."

— Donald D. Gehring. "Legal Rights and Responsibilities of Campus Student Groups and Advisors." A Handbook for Student Group Advisers. Published by the American College Personnel Association, 1984.

"Colleges and universities have struggled for years to define their liability for student activities, both on and off campus, especially those events where alcoholic beverages are consumed. A university's responsibilities for its students' action has been redefined since the late 1960s. ...

"The changes in the nature of the university and the role of its students has changed the liability incurred by the university. As students gained more freedom, they also earned the responsibilities and obligations of adulthood."

— Neil Gerard. "Who's Responsible when Students Mix Alcohol, Campus Activities?" The Bulletin of the Association of College Unions International, June 1982.

TO DRINK OR NOT TO DRINK: THE ROLE OF ALCOHOL IN COLLEGE UNIONS

"When college union and student activities administrators are asked what the major campus issue is, one response towers above all others. It's alcohol—and its impact on campus. Now that all but eight states have gone to the 21 drinking age, an expanded range of administrative worries has surfaced. ... Major research indicates that between 80 and 90 percent of students on campuses drink alcoholic beverages, between 10 and 20 percent drink abusively, and that these figures have not changed in the last two years. What has changed is a lessening university tolerance for unacceptable behavior and policy violations—a clear change in the last few years—and increasing university attention to substance abuse education and assistance for abusers."

— Richard D. Blackburn, ACUI's second executive director. "Trend Shifts Evident on College Campuses." The Bulletin of the Association of College Unions International, March 1987.

"Social learning theory views the drinking of alcoholic beverages as learned behavior. Whether a person abstains, drinks in moderation, or abuses alcohol, the idea that the behaviors are learned provides opportunities for student personnel workers to implement programs on campus which promote responsible drinking. The recent trend in literature is to develop alcohol awareness programs which promote the concept that drinking is an individual choice and informed consumers can make responsible choices.

"Student personnel workers planning changes in drinking patterns on a campus can select a 'pub' approach to student sponsored activities where alcohol beverages are included.

"The 'pub' experience is one in which the student is attracted by the atmosphere and physical environment. Soft lighting, alcohol alternatives, music, friends, and the opportunity to dance are part of the pub experience."

— Robert J. McBrien. "Facilitating Moderate Drinking on Campus." The Bulletin of the Association of College Unions International, December 1981.

High-risk drinking had become commonplace on campus as in this 1980 fraternity toga party.

"For educators, and especially for those involved in campus life and activities, the reliance of students on alcohol and the frequent abuse of alcohol appear to be excessive. The amount of drinking may not have changed significantly in recent years; what has changed is that students are entering college with more drinking experience. There is also the perception that the reasons for drinking and the drunkenness have changed to the extent that getting drunk is an end itself. What might reasonably be labeled as 'social drinking' appears as the exception rather than the rule.

"It is important to understand the background elements which explain and at the same time complicate the situation for those working in the area of campus activities and programs. In the early to mid-1970s, drinking ages were lowered in many states from 20 and 21 years of age to 18. This led to the development of college pubs on many campuses. For the first time on a large scale, colleges became involved in selling alcoholic beverages to their students. These facilities were promoted for a variety of reasons, ranging from economic factors to the development of places where members of the college community could gather in a pleasant atmosphere with some control.

"At the same time, major alcoholic beverage distributors, primarily those selling beer and wine, began massive promotional campaigns to place their products in front of the student audience. ... Professionals involved in student activities and college unions were also faced with student pressure to incorporate alcohol into other programs to ensure their success, increasing the popularity of beer blasts, inexpensive happy hours, beer with movies, and the like. Such internal and external pressure created ethical dilemmas for student personnel administrators and other members of college communities.

"The second challenge is to develop programs that do not resemble what people think of as alternatives—programs that stand on their own merits. ... The semantics and intentions of what we do are extremely important and should not be underestimated. Campus social life can be enhanced and enriched by opening up social options. On every campus there are those students who are looking for and will support such initiatives. ... The support exists for paving the road beyond; all that is needed are those who are willing to offer a new direction."

— Ruth Bradford Burnham and Stephen J. Nelson. "When 'Alternatives' Aren't." The Bulletin of the Association of College Unions International, October 1984.

Setting New Standards for Excellence

"The primary goals of the college union must be to maintain facilities, provide services, and promote programs that are responsive to student developmental needs and to the physical, social, recreational, and continuing education needs of the campus community.

"The college union is a center for the campus community and, as such, is an integral part of the institution's educational environment. The union represents a building, an organization, and a program; it provides services, facilities, and educational and recreational programs that enhance the quality of college life.

"Through the work of its staff and various committees, the college union can be a 'laboratory' where students can learn and practice leadership, programming, management, social responsibility, and interpersonal skills. As a center for the academic community, the union provides a place for increased interaction and understanding among individuals from diverse backgrounds.

"To meet its goals, college unions should provide: food services; leisure-time and recreational opportunities; social, cultural, and intellectual programs; continuing education opportunities; retail stores; service agencies that are responsive to campus needs; student leadership development programs and opportunities; student employment; and student development programs."

— CAS Standards and Guidelines for Student Services/ Development Programs. College Unions Standard, 1986.

Auxiliary Enterprises?

"Distressingly, many college unions in 1987 are viewed primarily in terms of revenue production. Most unions are not and never have been self-supporting when one takes into account student fee support and general university support. Earned income may come from certain operations in the union, such as bookstores, food services, retail shops, and recreation areas; however, many of the union's other services and programs are free and important elements in its educational and community development purposes. ...

"'Auxiliary enterprise' as a description of the function of the college union is plainly a misnomer. We should contend for a role of more transcendent importance. If we are willing to be complacently comfortable in having our purposes clustered with those of campus bus service, campus vending, and the parking lots, then 175 years of college union history and educational mission is headed for eclipse."

— Richard D. Blackburn. Dialogue in The Bulletin of the Association of College Unions International, November 1987.

New Construction, New Responsibilities

"Recently, the Commission on Educational Programs and Services of the Association of College Unions International surveyed member institutions regarding union renovation or expansion work presently in the planning stage or underway and received rather surprising information. Not only did the Commission receive nearly 100 responses, but more surprisingly, the number of projects presently in the planning stage or underway totaled more than $200 million in projected costs. Considering the restricted nature of capital funds on college campuses today, major renovation and construction of union facilities must rank among the top in terms of institutional priorities associated with physical plant enhancement or expansion.

"Whether related to a refocusing of institutional efforts in support of increased recruitment and retention, or a greater sense of maturity and understanding regarding the important educational role the union plays on campus, union professionals must take full advantage of the present opportunities available. Not only must the profession develop greater skills in effective coordination of physical plant renovation and expansion; there must also be a greater emphasis placed on the thoughtful and careful evaluation of institutional needs, and effective translation of those needs to facility design and function.

"Physical environments developed to support the social, recreational, personal, and developmental needs of today's campus population are significantly different from those even 10 years ago. Union professionals must take a contemporary approach toward identifying those needs, merging profes-

Hacky Sack, the game involving a small "footbag" kept in the air by an individual or multiple players, became a popular leisure activity in the 1980s. ACUI ARCHIVES

sional experience, and acknowledging the important aspect of longevity and quality interaction and input by users to effectively establish priorities and direction in physical plant renovation and construction. ... Considering the significant level of union renovation and expansion presently underway on campuses around the country and throughout the world, the opportunity to have a positive impact on the growth and development of campus constituencies is substantial."

— Manny Cunard. Renovation and Construction of Union Facilities Resource Notebook. Published by the Association of College Unions International, 1988.

MEETING THE NEEDS OF A MULTICULTURAL COMMUNITY

"During the 1980s, colleges and universities will be challenged to expand their scope beyond traditional academic endeavors, to education for lifelong learning and development of the whole person. College unions, within and beyond the boundaries of their own institutions, must be forerunners, providing opportunities for the practical an environment conducive to fulfilling the multidimensional needs of the community.

"In examining the concepts and tools necessary to take on this challenge, it is clear that multiculturalism, on all levels, is a key factor in our efforts to facilitate the education of the whole person. Multicultural education exposes individuals to the religious, sexual, lingual, and ethnic differences among people, and to the relationship of this diversity to society. The phenomena of cultural and ethnic traditions on college campuses and the resultant impact on lifestyles just cannot be overlooked. The influences on attitudes and actions are too great.

"The process, then, becomes one of constantly exposing our students and ourselves to opportunities for examining different value systems, lifestyles, and traditions that today govern the actions of the people in our society. Multicultural programming, as a part of this educational process, is a means by which we, as student development specialists, can provide diverse experiences that will facilitate growth in those we teach. There are as many of these activities and services as there are individuals to develop and explore them."

— Patrice A. Coleman. "Multicultural Programming: Teaching a New Meaning for Life." Proceedings of the 61st Annual Conference of the Association of College Unions International, 1981.

"The benefits of multiculturalism on the college campus and roles the college union can play are discussed. It is suggested that multiculturalism requires college union professionals to go one step beyond cultural pluralism by integrating the beneficial contributions of diversity. The following views are offered: (1) in addition to considering the needs, values, and culture of all its students in assessment and planning, the college union staff and the college's leaders need to respect those needs and values; (2) college programs should reflect the diverse interests of the entire campus population, lounges should be provided for interaction, and food services should offer a varied menu; and (3) before providing student activities that focus on social responsibility, staff and decision-making boards should be exposed to training/discussion that encourages them to appreciate, challenge, and integrate differences of opinion, values, and ideas. It is concluded that the college's environment and quality of the interpersonal development of students are enhanced when the college union adopts multiculturalism in its delivery of programs and services and in its staffing and decision-making boards."

— G. M. Stewart and J. A. Hartt. "Multiculturalism: A Prescription for the College Union." The Bulletin of the Association of College Unions International, November 1986.

Where Religion and Freedom of Expression Meet

"Court decisions suggest that religious programs advocating a particular religion or religion in general, when sponsored by a student government, union, or other official entity, should be avoided. However, it is legal to sponsor programs that examine values and in which religious lifestyles are compared and contrasted, as long as the religious lifestyles portrayed are only representative and not encouraged. Also, forced participation in religious exercises at private universities may constitute a denial of freedom of exercise.

Multicultural programming in the 1980s often included international food festivals, as at this Western Illinois University bazaar. ACUI ARCHIVES

Art was one way to offer students a multicultural learning experience, as at the Dittmar Memorial Gallery in Northwestern University's Norris Center. BY STEVEN HALL HEDRICH

"Issues that unions may face include: student demands to support a boycott (e.g., lettuce and grape boycotts) and the nature and degree of proselytizing and evangelizing that religious groups can engage in when using the student union. In considering the educative role of student activities and college union departments, active partnerships may be formed with the chaplain, campus ministry, and local clergy in developing ways to present basic information about religion, and tactics and dangers associated with aggressive cults and sects. Referral networks for counseling on religious issues and advisory groups to deal with religious concepts may also be formed cooperatively. It is suggested that while the college union is not engaged in ministry, per se, it can offer the space and environment for discussions of sensitive human issues."

— D. E. Johnson and S. J. Nelson. "Religious Uses of the College Union: Whose Temple Is It?" The Bulletin of the Association of College Unions International, October 1984.

The Glass Ceiling

As professionals who seek to educate and understand multiculturalism and diversity, there is an awareness that diversity extends beyond race into gender, socioeconomic status, sexual orientation, religion and every other part of the human existence that make up who we are as individuals. These issues present themselves in different and unique ways on college campuses and in college unions mirroring the issues seen across the country and around the world. There are still many miles to go before we achieve gender equity in the union and on our campuses.

"Although more institutions have affirmative action policies than 12 years ago, about the same percentage of women report feeling discrimination in the workplace, according to a recent survey conducted by the ACUI Women's Concerns Committee. Comparable pay and lack of opportunity for advancement persist as major concerns of women in college union and student activities fields.

"Almost one-third (31.9 percent) believe their salaries are not comparable to those of men in similar positions: 44.6 percent believe that they are, and 24.2 percent do not know. ... Race seems to have little effect on perceptions of comparable pay. ... The majority (69.1–79.8 percent) indicates they have felt no discrimination in the workplace. Of those who have felt discrimination, the most frequent complaint is in the

area of pay scale, followed by job/project assignment and workload."

— Terri Delahunty. "Women Concerned about Pay, Opportunity." The Bulletin of the Association of College Unions International, August 1985.

Out of the Closet and into the Union

"As college campuses move towards a multicultural environment, lesbian and gay students are becoming more open about their sexual orientation and more assertive in securing their niche in the campus culture. Union and activities professionals are called upon to work with group of students about whom they may know little. College union and student activities professionals need to develop a knowledge base for working with gay and lesbian students. This base should include an understanding of various theories of sexual orientation development: the unique developmental tasks gay men and lesbians face, legal sanction and rights, and the AIDS epidemic. ...

"Lesbians and gay men must also learn how to deal with outright discrimination on the college campus. Whether it occurs in the classroom, employment, housing, or health center, they must either choose to accept it or fight it. Institutional policies and procedures, counseling, and offers of personal support by faculty and administration will all influence which options a person chooses. ...

"One way college union and student activities professionals can have an impact on the lives of lesbian and gay students is by structuring the campus environment to be more responsive to the needs of those students. This can be done through developing and implementing policies, through influencing the attitudes of campus personnel, and by taking steps to eliminate harassment of individuals on campus. ... Inclusion of sexual orientation in the institution's statement of nondiscrimination and in its statements on sexual harassment is an important step. ... Institutions can incorporate language into their personnel policies that will give recognition to same-sex relationships.

"The college union and student activities staffs can produce a variety of programs that will aid lesbians and gay men in their academic pursuits and personal development and that will educate non-gay students about homosexuality and related concerns."

— Dick Scott. "Working with Gay and Lesbian Students." The Bulletin of the Association of College Unions International, March 1988.

Nurturing Racial Diversity

"Many nonminority students, particularly at white institutions of higher education in this country, come from environments that are racially homogenous. When they come face to face with someone different from themselves, the interaction is often negative, as they attempt to assert their experiences (with which they are most comfortable) onto the other individual. Many minority students experience culture shock when they arrive on a predominantly white campus—due in part to the environmental isolation of their pre-college experience—that they don't last more than a year at the institution.

"If we do not provide students with what they need (in this case, multicultural education), we will not be fulfilling our role as educators: we will not be developing students to their fullest potential."

— Patrice Coleman-Boatwright. "Creating a Multicultural Perspective." The Bulletin of the Association of College Unions International, March 1986.

"The 1987–88 academic year was a nightmare for minority college students, many of whom lived in fear and uncertainty about the racial climate on campus and suffered pervasive, systematic, and obstinate discrimination. On many campuses, administrators sat idly by blaming black and minority students for their protest against racism, doing nothing themselves to change the situation. ...

"The future rests with us. The college campus must create an environment in which ethnic, religious, and racial groups can live and study side by side. The love of learning must replace the love of hate. The dignity of humankind, respect for self-expression, and the contributions of the entire community of learners must be enhanced. As educators, we must teach by example. We must depart from the old traditions and create new and exciting social conditions on campus. Activities that familiarize the campus with the unique cultural differences of people should be incorporated into the academic and extracurricular experience. Our stand must always be proactive, and our energy levels should invigorate others toward social change."

— Sherwood Thompson. Dialogue in The Bulletin of the Association of College Unions International, July 1988.

An increasingly diverse student body called for more varied retail and services in the college union.

ACUI ARCHIVES

Recreation was still an important part of the college experience. ACUI ARCHIVES

GLOBAL CONCERNS

"'Our investments entrench the repressive minority regime!' These words, in bold, are the focal point of a flier that advertised a November 1986 rally outside of Armstrong Hall protesting Colorado College's investments in South Africa during apartheid. The phrase embodies the sentiments of the divestment movement that targeted college and university endowments from the 1970s into the early 1990s. At the bottom, the flier directs the CC community to the rally: 'Display your disgust of CC's involvement in South Africa. Bring friends!'

"One in a series of student-led protests held at Colorado College in the 1980s, this rally was a manifestation of a national divestment movement targeting South Africa during apartheid that sought to prevent American funds from supporting the South African government. ...

"According to a position paper released by the Colorado College Community Against Apartheid in March 1987, the divestiture movement aimed 'to convince the South African government that economic security and growth is dependent upon their initiating serious dialogue with legitimate black leaders concerning the dismantling of apartheid and the implementation of power-sharing mechanisms. ...'

"The divestment movement took off on campuses across the country. Four undergraduates at Brown University conducted a nine-day hunger strike. Two hundred Smith College students occupied an administration building for six days. UC Berkeley's student government decreed that the school's computer stores could not purchase from companies doing business in South Africa, including IBM. Another two hundred University of Wisconsin students occupied the capitol in Madison demanding divestment, and students erected shanty towns on campuses across the country. By 1987, Soule writes, 21 states and 68 cities had some type of divestment policy, and 167 institutions of higher education had divested partially or in full between 1977 and 1989."

— Lizzy Stephan, Colorado College. "Watering the Quad with Blood Money." CampusProgress.org, posted July 19, 2011.

"Efforts have intensified to make the international students feel welcome and secure in the student union. There are more differences than similarities among international students. Political, economic, and social differences in many cases cause friction among these groups. The various struggles and battles that frequently rage in their home countries cause friction among these groups on campus. An example is the friction between the General Union of Palestine Students and the Palestine Students Association or the friction that exists between the Iranian Student Organization and the Lebanese Student Union. By providing space and support for each group and by providing the groups an opportunity to work together, we are able to assist with the understanding of the cultures and their values and problems. It is through understanding that mutual respect develops and genuine positive growth is possible."

— Dallas L. Garber. "How One Union Retains International Students." The Bulletin of the Association of College Unions International, May 1988.

"

By providing space and
support for each group and
by providing the groups an
opportunity to work together,
we are able to assist with the
understanding of the cultures
and their values and problems.
**It is through understanding
that mutual respect develops
and genuine positive growth
is possible.**

"

Top left: Russel Sage College's Albany Campus Center in 1980. **Top right:** A student provides music at a 1985 program held in the University of Maryland's Stamp Student Union. **Bottom left:** The University of Pittsburgh Program Council meets in 1986. **Bottom right:** The Thwing Center atrium at Case Western Reserve University in 1987. ACUI ARCHIVES

Indiana University of Pennsylvania's S. Trevor Hadley Student Union in 1985. ACUI ARCHIVES

The University of Texas at San Antonio University Center in 1986. ACUI ARCHIVES

Campus professionals needed to learn how to use computers to keep up with current students. ACUI ARCHIVES

A student works in the Graphics Center at the University of Minnesota St. Paul. ACUI ARCHIVES

Able-Body Bias

"As student services professionals, we feel an obligation to improve the human environments of our campuses. Part of this improvement centers on the comfort level of nontraditional students, whose numbers are growing yearly. A percentage of these nontraditional types are students who have disabilities. In the last decade, increasing numbers of disabled individuals have sought college educations, and campuses across the nation have worked steadily to become accessible to these students in every way.

"By now, colleges and universities have eliminated most of their architectural barriers. But those obstacles were only the visible and, in some ways, the easiest impediments to break down. Much more pervasive and harmful are the attitudes and prejudices of able-bodied people against people who have disabilities. These kinds of subtle barriers are what keep disabled people from participating fully in society."

— Jeantz Martin and Martin M. Armato. "Sensitize Yourself to the Subtle Barriers." The Bulletin of the Association of College Unions International, November 1987.

The Rise of a Profession

"Most of our graduate students come with a very vocational orientation towards graduate school. They want to know everything they could possibly know about advising students and managing college unions. There is a danger in becoming so practical that we turn our graduate programs into vocational/technical training programs. It is important for students to take enough courses of a philosophical nature so that they understand why we do what we do. Students should understand the American higher education system and the support role that college unions and campus activities play within our institutions.

"A graduate education should continue to help students with value clarifications, learn to think through complex situations, develop their communication skills, and understand relationships between various phases of the higher education enterprise and between departments in which they may find employment. Business management, organizational development, and program planning and ad-visement are all areas in which our graduates will find themselves engrossed. Thus, our graduate programs should address each of these."

— Association of College Unions International Think Tank II Recommitment: What Business Are We Really In? 1984.

"We should continue to upgrade the quality of the professional staff members who work in the co-curriculum through an insistence on professional preparation through graduate work and continuing education (i.e., workshops, professional associations and conferences, and in-service training).

"Allow me a slight parenthetical digression at this point. It seems to me that it would be desirable for colleges and universities to establish student affairs career ladders that are not dependent upon promotion via administrative titles and responsibilities. Using roughly the same criteria and ranks as are now applicable to faculty, a student affairs adviser, for example, should be able to advance to higher rank and more salary by becoming very good at his/her job, by researching and writing in the field, and by serving the campus community through governance and committee service."

— Paul A. Bloland. Introduction. A Handbook for Student Group Advisers, ACPA, 1984.

"Student groups are important elements in campus extracurricular life, and advisors can affect both the quality of those groups and the learning experience they offer their members. First and foremost, advisors are educators. They intervene in groups to affect the behavior of individuals in the groups and/or the groups themselves."

— Richard McKaig and Sharon Policello. Group Advising Defined, Described, and Examined. A Handbook for Student Group Advisers, ACPA, 1984.

"Faculty and staff members who serve as advisors are invaluable. They become role models and enrich students' lives both within the organizational setting and, perhaps more importantly, within the broad collegiate experience. Often in very casual yet meaningful ways, membership in student organizations provides students with long-remembered opportunities to interact with respected scholars and academicians outside the classroom."

— M. Klein. "Preparing Faculty for Out-of-Class Experiences." The Bulletin of the Association of College Unions International, September 1989.

THE UNION AS COMMUNITY BUILDER

"The role of the college student union is discussed in this review of what makes a union successful. It is suggested that the truly successful one combines the concepts of unifying force, common meeting ground, and community in order to educate as well as generate revenue. Issues considered include: hiring and training employees; competition with local businesses; matching activities with student interests; diversity of programs to combat racism and changing demographics of college student bodies; facility space; bans on alcohol; safety and security issues (e.g., date rape, AIDS, smoking bans); food service; revenue generation services (e.g., copy centers, video stores); and outlook for the future."

— Richard D. Blackburn. "Back to Basics: Unions Reaffirms their Campus Roles." The Bulletin of the Association of College Unions International, March 1988.

"I love the word 'union.' I've been thinking about it for quite some time, and asked the past presidents to provide me with spontaneous definitions, and I rather like what was returned.

"Union: A joining together; unification, bonding; uniting for a commons or uncommon purpose; the coming together of similar and diverse people to participate as a community for specific and similar purposes; U-United, N-Nurture, I-Individuals, O-Organizations, N-Network; the unification and nur-turing of individuals and organizations, thereby developing a network to focus on and to foster desired outcomes; diversity with understanding. And then I received this very special definition from Porter Butts: 'College union—The center of social, cultural, and educational activity outside the classroom, giving the diverse population of the college a sense of belonging to the same community, thus serving as a unifying influence.'

"There's that 'community' word again. It certainly has been bantered about lately. But this is not a new discussion. Plato spoke of utilizing legislation in developing community: 'It makes them share together the benefits which each individually can confer on the community; and its purpose in fostering this attitude is not to enable everyone to please himself, but to make each a link in the unity of the whole.'"

— Carol Prior. Proceedings of the 68th Annual Conference of the Association of College Unions International, 1988.

"From the beginning, from the first brick, we should continue to reinforce, in broad institutional terms, the mission of the college union, and how closely it is aligned with the larger mission of the university. Our practices will be judged on a daily basis. We do not get enough opportunity to 'place' or

The University of Maryland, Baltimore County University Center in 1982. ACUI ARCHIVES

'position' our operations in the context of their value to our institutions and the educational process. We are mostly perceived as a profession of 'doers.' While this is very respectable and somewhat accurate, we should also be perceived as a profession of thinkers and contributors to the educational process.

"In a presentation in 1976, John Wong stated that 'the strength of the union lies in its diverse range of peoples, talents, services, and facilities.' Wong asks questions which relate to the union concept and a diverse population.

"'Can different cultures coexist and benefit from each other?'

"'How can the union capitalize on differences rather than work towards uniformity?'

"From my perspective, I see the 'union' as bringing together the increasing diversity of our institutions and our students. If there is a challenge to the mission of the college union, it comes more from the pressures of the future than from diversity. Winston Shindell, in a recent ACUI *Bulletin* 'Dialogue,' wrote: 'These are interesting times because many of our institutions are struggling with reaffirming, redefining, or in some cases, even defining what the role and mission of college unions ought to be. We find ourselves caught in the middle—squeezed by administrative dictates demanding more self-

sufficiency and revenue generation while at the same time kowtowing to the private sector which is screaming unfair competition and demanding congressional relief at the state and federal levels.'

"We are currently seeing an increase in harassment and physical violence on our campuses, pitting student against student, male against female; racism, sexism; and the list goes on. We are seeing more isolation, more compartmentalization. All these things destroy community and are counterproductive to the long-term health of our institutions. We need to be developing a sense of community through our programs and services. We need to be forcing groups who are different to start interacting with each other, not building separate centers into which they can flee to interact with those who appreciate the same culture, the same principles, and the same ideas.

"College unions have never been more important to the welfare of their campuses than they are now. If we truly do provide a sense of community and if we truly do have an impact on unification, then we truly need to be carrying this message to our individual campuses."

— Proceedings of the 68th Annual Conference of the Association of College Unions International, 1988.

1990s

The union promotes experiential education through programs, employment, and the arts. Architecture focuses on a "town square" concept, offering services, meeting space, and activities. Training, post-graduate education, and a specific knowledge domain give rise to union work's classification as a profession. The Carnegie Foundation report sparks great discourse on the concept of building campus community, and union leaders advocate for their authority in this task. Again, the mission of the college union is discussed and restated.

In 1998, students gather to watch a basketball game in Marquette University's Union Sports Annex restaurant and bar.

ACUI ARCHIVES

EXPERIENTIAL EDUCATORS: THE ROLE OF COCURRICULAR PROGRAMMING

"Students' time, interest, financial status, and other factors have shifted their commitments away from college union and student programs. ... Expectations include dynamic change, a variety of learning settings, student consumerism, shifting markets, and interactive/competitive environment.

"Adding to demographic forces and changes in higher education, programmers face significant issues of competition from outside the institution. Whether it be outfitted raft trips, music and comedy events at local bars, films at local theaters, community organizations, or other leisure options, the campus no longer has an exclusive on students' free time.

"To meet the challenge of this environment, programmers will have to respond to students needs in different ways. Programs will have to become more instrumental, their outcomes more measurable. ...

"To make our effort truly cocurricular, we must understand what are the major outcomes for activity programs versus curriculum. Student activities programming results in four identifiable outcomes. These are leisure pursuit, student development (both by the planners and the participants), cultural enrichment, and knowledge/skills. Curricular outcomes are generally in the area of knowledge and skill development. The curriculum demonstrates these outcomes through measures of assessment such as grades and evaluations. Cocurricular does not imply duplication of the academic program but instead developing a complementary relationship in support of the curricular outcomes.

"An administrator once described student affairs as the 'soft underbelly of the university' in comparison with the rigid, structured, inflexible backbone of the institution. Student affairs has the ability to change quickly. It can respond to changing needs of students without going into a long, involved process with a curriculum committee. It is market-oriented.

In student activities, if we don't receive a response from our efforts, we change our approach to find the market and the need. Best of all is our ability to be flexible in how outcomes may be achieved. We are flexible in how we provide our programs, how we design our programs, the content of our programs, and their duration. As experiential educators, we can create learning environments that the faculty can only dream about.

"Whatever strategy is used, it is important to demonstrate the cocurricular nature of our programs. Many programs are labeled cocurricular but have weak or nonexistent ties. Is a homecoming event cocurricular? For the participants, probably not. For the planners, possibly so. What are the specific outcomes of the planning process in relation to gains in knowledge and skill? Can they be demonstrated?

"Greater involvement in student activities programs will become a reality when student needs are met and activities complement their major purpose for being on campus—the academic program. Shifting to a more instrumental mode does not imply abandoning the development of a sense of community and the values of a normative culture. There is room for events that are not cocurricular and are merely entertaining. Leisure is valuable and should not be downplayed in providing only measurable outcomes. But at the same time, the reality of the changing higher education environment must be recognized. Our student development foundation must be defined in broader terms, reflective of the changing needs of a diverse student population and the reality of gaining student involvement in all aspects of our operations."

— Jim Rennie. "The Challenge of Cocurricular Programming." Proceedings of the 70th Annual Conference of the Association of College Unions International, 1990.

Customer Service in Distinguishing the Union

"Some elements of service management, which are being touted as essential survival techniques for business in the '90s, can be readily implemented in college union operations. Survival may not depend on how well a union meets the needs of demanding customers, but it may be more significant in unions competing for the attention and discretionary income of students, faculty, staff, and alumni. This may be especially true for unions operating food or other retail services and for those located on urban campuses.

"More importantly, if a college union is to fulfill its role as a community center, living room, and unifying force in the life of the college in the '90s, then it must meet the needs of campus community better than the competition.

"A customer is anyone who has any contact with a union in person or by phone. Therefore, training employees to improve customer services means training all employees, part-time and full-time including cashiers, housekeepers, information desk attendants, kitchen workers, secretaries, supervisors, managers, assistant directors, and directors. As Karl Albrecht and Ron Zemke said in their book 'Service America,' 'If you're not serving the customer, you better be serving someone who is.'

"The delivery of high-quality customer service is possible for every college union operation. It becomes easier to institute and maintain customer service standards when training programs become educational programs. With an educational focus, these programs help employees learn not only what they do, but also who they are and, more importantly, who they can become."

— Bart Hall. "College Unions and Customer Services: Perfect Match or Perfect Strangers?" Proceedings of the 70th Annual Conference of the Association of College Unions International, 1990.

A Common Purpose for Union Operations and Student Activities

"If a facility is defined by its function, the whole union exists as no more than an extension of academia. Facility is defined as 'the means by which an accomplishment of anything is rendered easier' (New Webster's Dictionary). The whole facility is an educational tool and all its employees' contributors. But even by a more narrow interpretation of function, we are all programmers and/or hall managers. A meeting room is a lecture hall if a speaker and audience join there, a lounge a museum, a hallway a gallery. Service is more than just building care; it is providing environments for learning and discovery. The operations' role becomes much more programmatically oriented in this perspective.

"Ultimately, function ties together space, service, and programs. We are a unity of service and space that are greater in sum than in parts. A union is not a conference center, food service, hotel, amusement arcade, or banking center. We are a collection of services, spaces, and events that transcend individual limitation to serve the greater mission of 'developing people as well as intellects.' In that function we are all programmers and educators."

— David Mucci. "Student Activities versus Operations: An Arbitrary Distinction." Proceedings of the 70th Annual Conference of the Association of College Unions International, 1990.

Sharing the Union's Relevance

"In 1982, at our reunion conference in Dallas, Shirley Bird Perry shared a secret concern she had developed after working for three years with college presidents and other high-level administrators across the country. To quote Shirley, 'They are not talking about you. I fear they do not view you as the important resource I believe you are and can be.'

"Well, Shirley, it is now eight years later, and I would say the good news is that they are talking about us—the bad news is they are talking about us for all the wrong reasons. I fear too often we are seen as nothing more than a service center which should be paying more of its own way instead of a unit devoted to student development, a unit that can and does make positive contributions to the quality of campus life and thereby influences recruitment and retention. They fail to appreciate the connections we make with students who later become alumni and who, because of those connections, support the institution through private gifts. They fail to understand our commitment to community and our continued support of multiculturalism through the programs and services we provide. ...

"John Gardner has stated: 'In some measure, what we think of as failure of leadership on the contemporary scene may be traceable to a breakdown in the sense of community.' Our Task Force 2000 report notes that, 'What is needed is reconceptualized model of community which builds on the commonality of individuals across cultures while simultaneously focusing on the benefits found in diversity.' As the 'living room of the campus,' the college union can play a significant role in reconceptualizing community.

"Let there be no misunderstanding. We have a very important role to play in the life of our institutions as we move toward the next millennium. This can be our 'golden gate!' To achieve that level will not be easy. Again quoting from Task Force 2000, 'If we are to survive as a part of the educational process, then the educational role played must be understood by others inside and outside the academy. Ways must be found to demonstrate what is being done and how such actions serve students and institutions in valuable ways.'"

— Winston Shindell. Presidential remarks at the 70th Annual Conference of the Association of College Unions International, 1990.

Declining Focus of the Arts in the College Union

"The college union and student activities professional is not as committed to the arts as before. The college union has experienced a distinct, persistent, and pervasive erosion of arts programming, facilities, education, and advocacy over the past several decades. Unfortunately, union professionals believe they either are not technically capable of or philosophically committed to presenting the arts. ... The college union must restore or develop its art facilities, and professional staff must regain the confidence to advise student art programming."

— Arts in the College Union. Task Force 2000 Final Report, April 1990.

"For the college union, the arts represent an anchor that is firmly embedded into the foundation of education. The systematic transmission of culture from one generation to another is part of the mission of formal education. The means by which this is achieved, however, is often debated. An appreciation of art, literature, philosophy, music, film, and other forms of expression appears to have little to do with structured educational experiences and more to do with persuasion by mentors, association with peers, or personal involvement—in other words, more to do with the domain of the college union."

— Terrence E. Milani. "Reaffirming the Role of the Arts in the College Union." The College Union in the Year 2000, 1992.

"The college union mission can be communicated readily through arts programming in the building. It illustrates the interconnectedness of the facility and the program while drawing on the part of the mission that is devoted to enhancing each student's development through education and opportunities. Many opportunities for students can be realized through involving students in the decision making process so they can become the program initiators and implementers. Whichever components of the programming model are combined for each institution will result in a successful venture achieved for the facility and the students."

— Brian Keintz and Julie Rowlas. "The Art of Student Development." Proceedings of the 75th Annual Conference of the Association of College Unions International, 1995.

A teambuilding activity in 1998 as part of outdoor programming offered at Truman State University. ACUI ARCHIVES

Stonehill College holds student leader training in 1998. ACUI ARCHIVES

IN SEARCH OF COMMUNITY

"Since the demise of in loco parentis in the '60s, no new theory of campus governance has emerged. Unsure about what standards to maintain, college administrators have sidestepped the issue while parents and the public still assume that students will in some general manner be cared for by the institution.

"Responding to this void in governance, the Carnegie Foundation for the Advancement of Teaching last spring proposed 'six principles that provide an effective formula for day-to-day decision making on the campus, and taken together, define the kind of community every college and university should strive to be.' The Carnegie Foundation report, *Campus Life: In Search of Community*, discusses how each of the following principles contributes to new framework for higher education governance:

- A college or university is an educationally purposeful community.
- A college or university is an open community.
- A college or university is a just community.
- A college or university is a disciplined community.
- A college or university is a caring community.
- A college or university is a celebrative community.

"A strong case can be made that college union and student activities professionals have been using these six principles as a guide for day-to-day decision making since 1956 when ACUI adopted 'The Role of the College Union' as the profession's statement of purpose. These principles were relevant then, they are relevant now, and as the report suggests, they might provide a future framework that 'not only could strengthen the spirit of community on campus, but also provide, perhaps, a model for the nation' (Carnegie Foundation, 1990, p. 8).

"Community has become a universal goal for campuses. An American Association of Community and Junior Colleges report, *Building Communities—A Vision for a New Century* (1988), calls for involvement of nonfaculty in discussions about college goals and priorities and for a commitment to build community beyond the classrooms. Porter Butts, in 'The College Union Idea,' states that, 'It may well be that the union has its highest value as a community center.'

"The parallels between the Carnegie Foundation's *Campus Life* and ACUI's 'The Role of the College Union' demonstrate the value of college unions and student activities on campus life."

— Winston Shindell. "The College in Building." The Bulletin of the Association of College Unions International, January 1991.

Performing Arts in the College Union

"As C. Shaw Smith would state, the right program creates a house of serendipity. Webster's says that serendipity is the faculty of making desirable but unsought discoveries by accident. Much of what we do is informal in purpose. We come to the union for a cup of coffee and find the music listenable and we want to hear more of it. That's serendipity. We come to read a newspaper and see a painting on the wall that excites our mind and heart and we are never quite the same again. That's serendipity. ... A quality performing arts program can also develop positive leisure-time habits. We need to spend leisure in constructive ways. Performing arts programs provide us a wonderful opportunity to cooperate with academic departments such as those in music, art and theater. The union can provide the venue for a dinner theater featuring students from the theater department or community theater."

— William E. Brattain. Proceedings of the 71st Annual Conference of the Association of College Unions International, 1991.

A Noble Profession

"The American Heritage Dictionary defines a profession as 'a body of qualified persons of one specific occupation or field' and professional as 'one who has an assured competence in a particular field or occupation.' Another source describes leadership as 'the ability to infuse value into an organization.' It is these two concepts that will serve as the basis for my comments tonight. The terms 'qualified,' 'assured competence,' and 'infuse value' are not limited to college union/student activity professionals but are those distinctions that separate a professional from a mere manager or administrator. ...

"Several standards of professionalism have emerged over the years that must be a part of a successful college union. Much the same way a surgical procedure or legal principle is applied consistently from locale to locale because it is inherent to the practice of medicine or law, there are some fundamental precepts that characterized college union/student activity work, which, if followed, transform a field of employment into a profession.

"These maxims symbolized what our work has come to represent to the campuses and the students we serve. All true professions are given authority over their own affairs because of the existence of standards such as these. They are chronicled by our colleague Shirley Plakidas in 'Standards for Professional Staff Preparation' and documented again in such works as the CAS Standards. All professions are given such a full measure of latitude because they ascribe to a code of ethics that governs their behavior and conduct. ACUI's Code of Ethics exists to foster high standards of performance, service, and professionalism among its members.

"One final criterion, a profession is granted public trust and great latitude to practice its craft based upon its ability to monitor and certify the consistent high standards of its colleagues. ... My friends, for me this is the crux of what we are about. If we are indeed educators, if we are indeed proficient managers, if we indeed subscribe to the precept we hold before us and as represented in our role statement, we must accept these as the icons of our daily work and view lesser efforts from ourselves as well as our colleagues as an affront to our profession that serves to erode public confidence in our chosen work. Ours is a noble undertaking that has withstood the challenges of nearly two centuries of evolution. For many of us, this is what we choose to do, not merely a means to provide sustenance as we pass through on our way to a perceived higher calling. It is our professional organization, likewise which must oversee qualifications, and assure competencies, and infuse value throughout its many its many programs and services.

"We are engaged in a noble profession, perhaps with a little less opportunity for frivolity than in years past, because of a greater sense of urgency to respond to environmental, economic, and social concerns. The one element the students bring to the table, which humanizes and softens the urgency, however, is the sense of community that demonstrates we are all in this together. The union has continued as that unifying force through wars, economic crises, tumultuous growth, protests, and ultimate downsizing because it offers all members of the campus the opportunity to meet on common ground."

— J. William Johnston. Presidential remarks at the 71st Annual Conference of the Association of College Unions International, 1991.

Education of the Whole Person

"Perhaps the simplest way to understand the role of the college union is to regard it as the education of the total person. This view reflects the basic philosophical tenet that the quality of students' out-of-class life is an important ingredient of a higher education. The domain of the college union is the education of the complete person: mind, body, and spirit.

"First and primarily, the college union is part of the educational program of the institution. Its organization, facilities, services, and programs exist to enhance the intellectual, social, and personal development of students through the extracurricular arena of campus life. As important as its role, the manner in which it is fulfilled is also an integral part of the college union idea. To achieve its ends, the college union serves as the community center, offering services, conveniences, and amenities needed in daily campus life and providing the source for the building of community though its organizations, programs, and facilities. In all its activities and the means used to accomplish them, the union promotes student involvement in leading and participating in its programs and operation. It strives to maximize opportunities for personal development and self-discovery through self-directed activity and emphasizes the constructive use of leisure time for immediate and lifelong benefit. It endeavors to instill in students a sense of the meaning of citizenship, social responsibility, and service, as well as an obligation to accept the mantle of leadership in our society. Perhaps as much a result of these roles as the fulfillment of any goal, the college union cultivates an enduring regard for and loyalty to the institution that enriches and unifies campus life and helps develop bonds that tie graduates to the institution as active alumni."

— Terrence E. Milani, J. Thomas Eakin, and William E. Brattain. "The Role of the College Union and the Future." The College Union in the Year 2000, 1992.

Students discuss upcoming University Council elections at the University of Georgia. ACUI ARCHIVES

Students at a West Virginia University late-night program enjoy the games room's video arcade.

ACUI ARCHIVES

COMPETING INTERESTS: BALANCING COMMERCIAL AND EDUCATIONAL NEEDS

"'We have to better respond to the needs of our population, and become fiscally responsible, too,' says Manuel Cunard, director of Colorado State's Lory Student Center. As enrollment in higher education grows only modestly from about 13.6 million students currently, schools will have to scramble for extra funds in coming years.

"'The idea of comparing student unions to shopping centers is one that's caused some people to bristle—it's too crass, too commercial, and lacks the educational component,' says J. William Johnston, assistant vice president, student affairs, at Southern Methodist University and president of the Association of College Unions International. 'But philosophically, they're the community center of campus, and malls have become that in our society.'"

— Pauline Yoshihashi. "Retailing: Colleges' Student Unions Face Big Test and the Answers Are on the Bottom Line." Wall Street Journal, March 16, 1992.

"The pressure to create income is compounded by organizational problems that can drive a wedge between building and program. The existence of student activities offices apart from the college union and often part of a different division of the institution can strip the union of its responsibility for extra- and co-curricular student life. Despite problems with funding and organizational jurisdiction, the college union is responsible for presenting a well-considered plan for the community life of the institution. It cannot achieve its goal by being a vessel that is filled by first-come, first-served users and money-in-hand consumers. Although food services, bookstores, banking, travel agencies, computer stores, copy centers, and other revenue-producing services are part of the union, they are incomplete without its cultural, social, and recreational programs. Revenue-generating programs and services must complement the union's role of developing community, enhancing student development, affecting students' values, and contributing to the institution's educational offerings."

— Terrence E. Milani, J. Thomas Eakin, and William E. Brattain. "The Role of the College Union and the Future." The College Union in the Year 2000, 1992.

"There has been effectively through the 1980s a drive for financial self-sufficiency; and the pursuit for income generation there has effectively developed almost different divisions (standards of students' unions) and, within that, different types of models. ... The typical models are Model A, where the students' union has attempted to embrace the issues of service delivery, income generation, and also fulfilling its noncommercial mission, and Model B, where the drive toward income and commercial services has taken over the organization and the noncommercial model has been lost. That is most clearly illustrated in terms of the space allocations within different students' unions. ... Typically, in many situations the unions have devoted space to income generation that in an ideal world could be devoted to recreation, to leisure space, to lounge space, or simply to study space.

"A critical element in the 1990s is the evolution of the concept of student activities. This is a concept that has prevailed in the United States for many years but is something that is now being actively embraced by a growing number of local students' unions in the United Kingdom. This whole area looks at the empowerment of students as individuals and groups and looks towards student development as an issue, both in relation to the following: employment, involvement in the guild/union, involvement in clubs and societies, and individual training and development."

— Ian King and John Windle. "Towards the Millennium: Student Unions in the 21st Century." Proceedings of the 75th Annual Conference of the Association of College Unions International, 1995.

The renovated Marist University Student Center opened in 1994 at nearly double its original size. WIKIMEDIA COMMONS

The Architecture of Community

"Our physical environment profoundly affects how we think, act, and feel. In fact, research by architects and campus planners shows that particular design elements of buildings and the spaces around them inspire people to interact with each other. We call these elements the 'architecture of community.'

"The town square, that icon of small-town America, is a good example of the architecture of community in action, for it provides a broad range of community services and activities, including commerce, government, and religion.

"Traditionally, town squares combine civic (city hall, public library, community center) with commercial uses (post office, bank, shops, offices, and professional buildings). These uses were usually grouped around a central plaza that served as a meeting place for residents. If you needed to see the tax assessor, take out a book from the library, go to the post office, or just catch up on the latest gossip, you were drawn to the town square, to the heart of community life.

"College unions do the same thing for their campuses. Because the union serves all students, its form and function help shape a campus's overall identity more than any other facility on campus.

"Bringing these issues together can create a true town square right on the campus, especially if they are grouped around a well-planned plaza."

— Sandy D'Elia. Sidebar. "The Architecture of Community." The Bulletin of the Association of College Unions International, March 1993.

Societal Influence on Union Architectural Design

"Over the years, WTW has developed a philosophy of what a student union should be. 'We try to make the building work like the town square,' says Mr. Knell. 'The building is for students first.' The firm has found that a certain kind of construction works for hormone-charged students—multistory atriums surrounded by balconies with open railings where students can check out who is on the floor below or across the building. It's sort of a '90s version of cruising the strip. 'The whole idea is to show off,' Mr. Knell says. 'Students want to see people, see other kids.'"

— Andrea Petersen. "Architects Who Still Think Like Teens." Wall Street Journal, March 3, 1997.

Profile of a Profession

"The profile of the college union director, and thus college unions, is in a state of transition. Although a general definition of the modern director and union can be developed, many variations exist. Catalysts of change, although specifically undetermined, may be institutional growth, educational preparation programs, philosophical transition and execution of both ACUI and institutions, changing dynamics of the university environment, etc. Regardless of cause, change appears to be the norm. ...

"Looking ahead, are we appropriately positioned to move into the future? To meet fiscal, facility, and other needs? To alter pertinent services and programs? This profile suggests we no longer operate major auxiliary services, and that we expend more energy on student development, facility maintenance, and budget development than in the past. What does this all mean?

"The statistical data composing this profile of the college union profession may not be exciting reading. However, the dryness of the subject matter should not prevent us from examining who we are and how we have matured. As a profession, our persona may be very different from our individual parts. Understanding our similarities and differences, our past and intended future is paramount to ensuring a smooth ride and purposeful journey."

— Daniel A. Habrat. "Profile of a Profession, Part II." The Bulletin of the Association of College Unions International, July 1993.

The Critical Element of Community

"In 'The Different Drum: Community Making and Peace,' M. Scott Peck cites many of the same characteristics that the Carnegie report *In Search of Community* uses. But Peck describes in greater depth the nature, process, and patterns of community building. Using Peck as a primary source, I would like to offer a definition that looks at community more as a process or journey than a product or destination: 'Community begins with good communications, where we speak and listen to each other openly and honestly. It requires both courage and patience as we learn to confront, understand, and accept differences in cultures and experiences. It calls again and again for objectivity because it constantly challenges our traditions, attitudes, lifestyles, behaviors, preconceived notions, and expectations. It is exciting and rewarding as the barriers of misunderstanding are dropped and acceptance changes to respect, and ultimately to a celebration of cultures and differences.'

"If we can accept this definition of community, then we may see a different challenge for the activities, programs, and services of college unions and student activities. I am not sure we have thought of ourselves as being responsible for the process of community building among people with differences, helping them transcend their own cultures and experiences in order to understand, respect, and celebrate the culture and experiences of others. We need to be sure this concept permeates all levels of our organization if we are to build bridges on campuses. We need to remember that we are partners in education and we need to be more than passive participants in enhancing campus life. We need to recognize that campus life is more than services and programs and that we must be more than shopping centers or service stations. We need to think seriously about the phrase from 'The Role of the College Union' that states we are more than buildings, that we are a 'well-considered plan for the community life of the college.'"

— Susan Yung Maul. "Communication: The Critical Element of Community." The Bulletin of the Association of College Unions International, July 1993.

"

INVOLVEMENT
AS A STUDENT
LEADER IN
THE STUDENT
CENTER
ENHANCES
THE PRESENT,
FUTURE, AND
PAST MEMORIES.

"

In 1994, a brewery was renovated and reopened as the Tivoli Student Union, serving the Community College of Denver, Metropolitan State College of Denver, and University of Colorado Denver. BY JACKIE SHUMAKER

Experiential Education for Many Careers

"Although union and activities exist on virtually every campus, Hood and Arceneaux (1990)* describe as all too frequent the view of some faculty that student activities on campus is 'strictly the sideshow.' This view demonstrates the need to better communicate the ways in which involvement outside the classroom provides a value-added dimension to education. This attitude of faculty is clearly in conflict with the beliefs held by many students and alumni who feel greater learning takes place through their involvement in out-of-class activities than through classroom and laboratory experiences. Educating through programs and experiences, as well as being at the center of one of the most intensively utilized facilities on campus, is the exciting, challenging role of many union and student activities professionals."

— J. Thomas Eakin. "Preparing for the Future: The Profession in the '90s and Beyond." A report prepared for the ACUI Executive Committee, March 1993.

"'Never in my life have I seen a building full of so many faces—the doctors, the lawyers, the judges, the teachers, the scientists. All had a unifying message: the Student Center created an important network of people and experiences that can never be diminished—not by the decades nor by new life goals. Involvement as a student leader in the Student Center enhances the present, future, and past memories."

— Mary Beyer. "Memories of the Student Center." M&M, November/December 1994.

*Hood, A.B., & Arceneaux, C. (1990). Key resources on student services: A guide to the field and its literature. *San Francisco: Jossey-Bass.*

Students make their own music video during a late-night program at West Virginia University. ACUI ARCHIVES

Responding to Change—Again

"At various points in its 150-year history, the college union movement has weathered all of these issues—changing student demographics and values, programmatic revolution, financial stress, competition in the marketplace. The challenge for the college union in the 21st century will be to contend effectively with all of these factors simultaneously. By melding its historic role as campus community center and its programming heritage with the power of information and technology, the college union will be equal to the task."

— Bart Hall. Dialogue in The Bulletin of the Association of College Unions International, December 1994.

Restating the Role of the College Union

In 1996, an ACUI committee looked into revising the The Role of the College Union statement. The original statement had been adopted in 1956, and some felt the language needed to be modernized and perhaps even the core mission of the college union examined. The dialogue stemming from this process led to the following philosophical comments.

"The issue, as I see it, is that for a lot of different reasons, many colleges and universities do not subscribe to the union model that the statement envisions. We see campuses that do not have any physical facility that could be considered a union, or that perhaps have several different facilities that collectively attempt to fulfill a union's function. We see organizational restructuring that separates the business/service component of a union from its student activities/development function. And even in cases where the functions noted in the role statement stay together organizationally, we see reporting line changes that easily give the impression that a union is no longer considered part of the cocurricular education, but instead is some sort of amorphous conglomeration of profit centers and cost centers. ...

"To somehow embrace those institutions who have not made the investment in a physical union facility, and also those institutions who have separated the business/service functions from the student activities/development functions, what kind of message would that send to high-level university administrators, many of whom seem to always be on the lookout for 'new trends' in organizational structuring? I believe it would just accelerate what I find to be an already disturbing trend. Certainly this can be looked at in two ways: one way is to say, 'Hey, look around and smell the roses, things are changing and you can't run and hide from it.' Another way of looking at it is to say, 'This is troublesome, and let's not do anything to further promote it.' I'm clearly in the latter camp."

— Susan Yung Maul. Memo from Ted Crabb to Neil Gerard regarding the ACUI role statement. Sent March 15, 1995.

"My sense is that some within the profession are uncomfortable because they consider the statement to be too 'pedestrian' in content and beneath the call of the profession. To this, my response is, 'bunk.' Others may feel the words no longer have meaning in our culture, and/or that being a campus force for the creation and maintenance of 'community' is unimportant or immaterial within the context of the 21st century campus, to which I say, 'bunk.' Yet others would aim, through the mission statement, to commercialize the union's purpose."

— Rufus Simmons. Memo from Ted Crabb to Neil Gerard regarding the ACUI role statement. Sent March 15, 1995.

"To fail to address the union as a structure is to fail to address the role of the union; to fail to mention those things which the union does without a building is to fail to address the soul of a union."

— David E. Johnson. Memo from Ted Crabb to Neil Gerard regarding the ACUI role statement. Sent March 15, 1995.

Top: An advertisement for a 1991 Nirvana concert produced by University of Kansas Student Union Activities. ALICE DAER

Above: The Wayne State University Student Center in 1999. ACUI ARCHIVES

In the 1990s more campuses looked to student fees as a way to fund union and activities events such as concerts.
PHOTOS BY SAM RICHE

The Functions of the 1990s Union

"If libraries are the temples of learning, the student unions are the agorae and forums. Campus unions today serve the following functions:

- The sale of goods and services, either as a convenience to the campus community or as a necessity (when the campus is too remote from local shopping centers).
- Provision of facilities for supervised social activities and indoor recreation.
- Provision of facilities for extracurricular student activities and organizations, such as student publications, hobby groups, and political clubs.

"On some campuses the student union may serve as the central dining hall, achieving economies by combining several kinds of food operations under one roof, particularly when there is insufficient volume to support or warrant such functions individually.

"On the denominational campuses, because they are centrally located facilities, student unions are also convenient places for chapels, which are sometimes constructed as a wing to the student union. The offices of the deans of men and women can be advantageously located in the student union, close to the pulse of student life. Institutions with large enrollments may have several buildings devoted to the purposes which are embodied in a single building on a smaller campus. ...

"Campus unions are excellent foreground buildings, and their special purpose affords the opportunity for a display of architectural dexterity. Outdoor spaces surrounding the student union building deserve equally elaborate treatment as they are likely to be the crossroads of the campus. The higher costs for special design effects may be justified on the basis of the income which attractive student unions can yield. In fact, on many public campuses, self-liquidating bonds rather than public appropriations are used to build campus unions. Beyond the point of convenience, campus unions have to compete with off-campus recreation centers for a clientele. In some ways, good architecture and generously designed buildings and space are essential to bolster the economic support for the campus union."

— Richard P. Dober. Campus Planning, 1996.

Promoting Student Development amid Economic Reality

"College union professionals are now faced with the challenge of responding to that campus community beyond providing a comfortable gathering place for socialization. They are faced with a campus generation which demands convenience, service, and multiplicity, while still anticipating the exposure to social experiences.

"Economic reality has made it necessary for college unions to look at alternative and creative funding sources as expenses continue to escalate. Quite naturally, a strong retail emphasis is evolving as retail enterprises in the union are seen as a way to create positive revenue streams, while reacting to the broadening needs of the campus community. In this evolution of responsiveness, however, it is imperative that the focus remain on the goal of enhancing student life through provision of these services and goods, rather than solely on the production of income."

— Barbara Weiske. "Economic Reality in the Middle of Student Development." Proceedings of the 76th Annual Conference of the Association of College Unions International, 1996.

The University of Warwick union information desk in 1998. ACUI ARCHIVES

THE COLLEGE UNION AS HOME

"'This is clearly a building where students can come to do business, to study, to eat ... to connect with each other,' said James Studer, vice president for student affairs at [Southwest Texas State University]. The student center is named for SWT's most famous alumnus, LBJ, who graduated in 1930. Luci Baines Johnson, LBJ's daughter, spoke at a special reception honoring the opening of the center. 'This is a magnet; it is a place that people will want to come,' Johnson said before a full auditorium of alumni, faculty, students and regents. 'This is a place to call home.'"

— Cara Tanamachi. "A 'Living Room' Named for LBJ: New SWT Student Center Offers Food." Austin American-Statesman, May 1, 1998.

"The college union and the home share similar roles and perform similar functions. In most homes, the living room is the center for its residents' cultural values. It is in the living room that the family perception of the world via television viewing, reading, and conversation are generally decided. It is in the living room that the open or closed nature of our family relationships is most directly expressed. The furniture and decorations in the living room stand as the best testimony to the role of are beauty, taste, and practicality in any particular family. The number of times nonfamily members enter the living room is an excellent indicator of how much a family values interaction with others.

"My conviction is that the college union family and the home family unit have the opportunity and responsibility to provide guidance on dealing with authority, managing one's impulses, maintaining self-esteem, developing healthy values, and ultimately, liberating attitudes. The college union can be a major contributor in shaping and improving multicultural campus environment, as the home is also where bigotry starts. In the home or in the union, we are exposed to certain situations and attitudes both directly and indirectly. We learn values and skills, openness, decision making, and respect for individual difference. We learn about the dignity of the individual and the appreciation of good literature, good music, or art, and other expressions of the human condition. We learn personal accountability for actions and the importance of the freedom of association."

— Bernard J. Pitts. Presidential Perspective. "Home-away-from-Home Spells U-N-I-O-N!" The Bulletin of the Association of College Unions International, March 1997.

Promoting Inclusion and Cultural Understanding

"Appalachian's 105,000-square-foot Plemmons Student Union has a fitness center with rows of high-tech exercise equipment, an art gallery with sophisticated displays of student designs, and a computing center. It's the hub of campus activity, with 7,000 people a day using the building, compared with 500 a day for the old union. Appalachian junior Fernando Little says the renovation, which added a multicultural lounge, is helping to draw more minority students, only 6 percent of the student body, into campus life. 'Before the addition of the new union, a lot of minority students went home on the weekend,' he says. 'Now we feel a little more comfortable staying in town.'

"With more students living off campus or in special-interest groups, campuses need more and better space to bring people together. 'There is a great deal of division in society. The student union is a place where everyone can feel welcome,' says Timothy McDonough, vice president of the National Association of Independent Colleges and Universities, which represents 880 private schools. Indeed, many student unions are shedding the name 'student union' in favor of the more inclusive 'campus' or 'university center.'"

— Andrea Petersen. "New Marketing Magnets: Student Unions." Wall Street Journal (Eastern edition), March 3, 1997.

The College Union's Role in Recruitment

"Student unions have become increasingly important marketing tools because, along with residence halls, they are the buildings most students and parents ask to see. 'You need an attractive union to be competitive with other institutions that are pulling out all the stops,' says Wayne Anderson, president of the Associated Colleges of the South, a group of 13 regional liberal arts schools. 'Parents and students are increasingly asking, "What am I getting for my payment?"'"

"A state-of-the-art union played a role in the college choice of Joe Leventhal, a sophomore at the University of California at San Diego, which recently renovated its union. 'In deciding between two schools that are academically equal, the beauty and the warmth of the union was a major factor,' he says. 'Everything about it was just "wow."'

"Student unions can also help solve another campus problem: keeping students out of mischief off-campus. 'There are other kids there, there are other adults—it's a real strong support system,' says Betsy Herrscher, mother of a senior at Northeastern University in Boston, which recently spent $13 million renovating its student union."

— Andrea Petersen. "New Marketing Magnets: Student Unions." Wall Street Journal, March 3, 1997.

"'There's been a real shift in expectations and nobody wants to blink,' said Ray Ritchie, vice president for enrollment services at Philadelphia's La Salle University, which has added fully equipped townhouses for undergraduates. 'Families are looking for bells and whistles, and a student union that looks like the lobby of a cruise ship is going to make a more profound impression than a biology lab that has the latest microscope.'"

— Jon Marcus. "Across Nation, Colleges Building to Attract Students." The Patriot Ledger, Sept. 2, 1997.

A Campus Center at the Campus's Center

"Lisa Campbell, Gannon's director of student organizations and leadership development, stressed the vital importance of the location of a campus center. 'Physically, you want a campus center to be as close to the dead center of the campus as you can get,' said Campbell, who is instrumental in planning the center and who will direct operations of the facility. 'A campus center should be the heart of the campus, something the rest of the campus cannon function without, someplace you keep coming back to throughout the day. The architects really studied our campus and incorporated that.'"

— Angela Brooks. "Something New! Gannon University Embarks on First Campus Center Project." College Services Administration, 1999.

A PLACE FOR REMEMBRANCE

"On Wednesday evening, Oct. 5, 1998, about three miles east of Laramie, Wyo., a 21-year-old University of Wyoming student from Casper, Wyo., was found robbed, severely beaten, and tied to a fence. Two Laramie residents soon were charged with attempted murder in the attack that has been labeled a hate crime. In addition, the defendants' girlfriends were charged with accessories after the fact in connection with the crime.

"On Thursday evening, Oct. 6, the beating of Matthew Shepard was the headline story on the Denver NBC-affiliate television station. In the scene behind the TV reporter, viewers caught glimpses of the Wyoming Union. By Friday, Oct. 7, the story was broadcast nationally on the three major networks. It was at this point the union, in addition to being a hub of the campus community, became a focal point for local, regional, national, and international media.

"Like any other college union, the Wyoming Union is a central part of daily campus life. The union is located in the heart of the campus with about 10,000 people passing through on a daily basis. At first news of the attack on Shepard, the Wyoming Union provided a foundation for university's and students' reactions. ...

"Monday morning, Oct. 12, brought news of Shepard's death. Union Director Bill Fruth contacted Campus Activities Center (CAC) staff members to share this news and request they report to work by 7 a.m. to provide support and make preparations. Despite previous planning, no one was prepared to deal with the news of Shepard's death or the presence the press had on campus that day. It was easily the most difficult day the union staff has ever worked.

"It is impossible to describe the circumstances that quickly unfolded within a matter of a few hours. While the mood was somber, the CAC maintained a high level of activity. By 9 a.m. the CAC staff, in conjunction with student government and student organizations, developed and promoted a program titled 'Remembering Matthew.' The program was intended to allow the campus and Laramie community an opportunity to pause, reflect, and grieve.

Following the 1999 murder of Matthew Shepard, this memorial was given to his parents to represent the University of Wyoming community's intolerance of violence. BY JIM STOWERS

Throughout the day, hundreds of telephone calls, emails, and faxes were received expressing sympathy and support, but on occasion some were hate focused. Students continued to make and distribute armbands. Gay Awareness Week activities began. At dusk, an estimated 1,500 people gathered to participate in the 'Remember Matthew' program on the main university mall. It was truly a community-building experience."

— Bill Fruth, Susie Arnold, and Cindy Haarstad-Darrow. "Wyoming Union Leads Grieving, Recovering Efforts." The Bulletin of the Association of College Unions International, May 1999.

"

IT WAS EASILY THE MOST DIFFICULT DAY THE UNION STAFF HAS EVER WORKED.

"

THE ▶ 2000s

The union sees more competition or partnership opportunities with the rise of online communities and mini and satellite unions on campus. National tragedies influence how the union is perceived and operated. Greater accountability for learning achievement among students and competency among union personnel become common themes and at times are directly linked to funding. Amid broad understanding of a union as a facility, the task of communicating the role of the college union as an organization becomes more difficult.

Students recruit for their organizations at the University of Minnesota Duluth in 2009

COURTESY OF
CORBIN SMYTH

225

The Union Left Behind?

"In recent years, as campuses grew, unions often found themselves no longer at the physical center of campus. As the institutions grew—sometimes quickly—in new directions, some grew away from their unions and came to look upon them as part of 'the old campus.' It's a quiet and subtle move. No one says, 'We're leaving the union.' Instead they gradually turn in new directions that don't always involve the union. And the challenges don't end there. People don't always share or understand the values on which the college union movement was built."

— Perry Metz. Remarks at the Indiana Professional Development Seminar, 2000.

The Union as a Symbol

"For most institutions, it is important the union symbolizes the school. Officials want the union to be a center of pride for the campus. On some campuses, the college union is seen as the institution's face, front door, living room, or 'home page.' However, unlike many places that have obvious archetypes (such as hospitals, city halls, banks or schools), the union does not have an archetype, which is part of the excitement of planning and designing one. The notion that the union belongs to everyone has an impact on the design process. Building a new union or redesigning an existing one is a situation that offers a series of opportunities for the planning and design teams to define what the idea of the union means to that particular institution. How can it welcome people, provide a gateway to campus or be a link between campus and community? How can it come to feel like the obvious place to go?"

— David C. Evans, Steve Clark, Trudi Hummel, and Elizabeth Mullins. "Using a Participatory Process to Design a College Union." Vision to Reality: Designing and Building College Unions to Meet the Needs of the 21st Century Student. Published by the Association of College Unions International, 2001.

The Campus Community Center

"The college union profession can celebrate success in being the community center for our campuses. Each of us can identify examples of how our union program welcomes and promotes diversity, encourages freedom of expression and celebrates, and promotes institutional spirit. All of these community-building efforts tend to be somewhat passive. We provide the lounge space, or perhaps we even provide a program that attempts to bring people together. We might gain some greater recognition on our campuses if we did a better job of telling our story, defining the characters of the plots that we weave. ...

"We should revisit Butts' ideology and other founders of the college union philosophy and explore the relationship between community building, civility, and citizenship. It is within those concepts that we find our contribution to the educational mission of our campuses in preparing students for social responsibility and leadership."

— Ed Slazinik. "Defining the College Union's Community-Building Role." The Bulletin of the Association of College Unions International, January 2001.

Debating Societies Continue to Have Relevance

"The times have moved debating beyond a male-only pastime for students in the United Kingdom. Now it is an international pursuit, with students from Africa, Southeast Asia, and Eastern Europe vigorously participating in this long tradition. In addition to continuing to provide a forum in the college union for disputation and argument, debate now presents a forum for international discourse and sport. It continues to build students' skills in critical thinking, oration and argumentation, and engages campus audiences in considering different perspectives."

— Jennifer Hamilton. "Be It Resolved: Debating Is Still an Integral Part of the College Union." The Bulletin of the Association of College Unions International, September 2001.

A POST-SEPT. 11 COLLEGE UNION

University of Iowa students watch news coverage in the Iowa Memorial Union, Sept. 11, 2001. PRESS-CITIZEN

The morning of Sept. 11, 2001, confusion spread as Americans intently watched television screens and listened to contradicting news reports. During the chaos, college unions became important places for the campus community to gather as a center for information and comfort. It was the place of for sharing sadness; it was the place for building community.

"Our student body became united that day, united in fear and a feeling of mourning. The K-State Student Union was the place where this coming together occurred. I'll never forget the eerie feeling of belonging that I felt that day and in the days to follow. The union was a common gathering place where students, faculty, and staff came together to watch the news, discuss the tragedy, and come to terms with it."

— K-State Student Union: From Concept to Creation—The History and Memories of Your K-State Student Union, 2006.

"The events of Sept. 11 stunned the world by destroying the façade of invulnerability that covered daily life in the United States. The attacks perpetrated on the highly concentrated business center left thousands injured and killed. According to Steven L. Fordice, retired criminal investigator for the Oregon State Police, this international terrorist action was intended to create fear by attacking symbols of America and killing large numbers of innocent people. Fordice postulates that the threat of international terrorist attacks against college unions is remote, despite the fact that they meet two terrorist target criteria, symbolism and people.

"While international terrorism is unlikely to create havoc in the heart of campus activity, the social forum that the college union represents may be attractive to domestic opposition in the form of terrorist activities or civil unrest. Campus activism continues to thrive on campuses throughout the country, focusing primarily on human rights and environmental issues. Sit-ins, demonstrations, and other forms of protest over a broad spectrum of controversial issues are not relics of the 1960s and 1970s. Campuses across the United States continue to experience student political expression. While they are generally prepared to deal with the expression of the First Amendment, the potential for calamity exists.

"Other emergencies caused by weather, fire, hazardous materials, or infrastructure failures represent additional safety issues for the highly trafficked college union facility. Regardless of the nature of the crisis, timely response is of vital importance to avoid injury and save lives. Therefore, it is imperative that a staff is well trained to take the correct course of action when problems arise."

— Kim I. Savage. "Safe at Home: Keeping the College Union Secure." The Bulletin of the Association of College Unions International, March 2002.

"While we are in a more complex and difficult era managing college union operations on campuses, college union professionals must stay current and connected to keep our venues safe and secure. The terrorist threats, including those to higher education institutions, will likely remain. As such, we must rely on the common-sense approach and developmental methods to teach students, staff, faculty, and visiting members of our communities how they can play a role in working to protect, defend, and secure our campus facilities. Despite the real threat, our responsibility, duty, and desire to maintain an open and safe environment is a critical element of higher education's core mission. This may cause the role of the college union to continue to evolve. While no institution can ever guarantee protection against a threat or incident, good planning and preparation can only add to the ability to move forward in a progressive, positive manner to recover and adjust after a crisis has abated."

— Peter Konwerski. "College Union Security Two Years After Sept. 11: A Case Study." The Bulletin of the Association of College Unions International, November 2003.

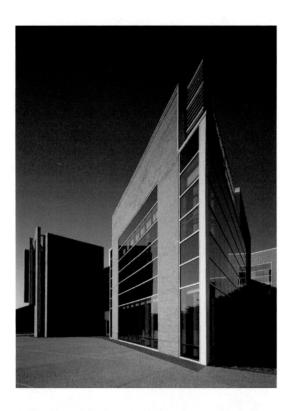

Top left: The $14 million, 113,500-square-foot Hampton University Student Center was completed in 2001.
BY MICHAEL HOUGHTON – STUDIOHIO

Top right: Genesee Community College's $1.8 million, 10,000-square-foot Wolcott J. Humphrey III Student Union opened in 2006.
COURTESY OF CLIFFORD SCUTELLA

Bottom left: The $37 million, 126,000-square-foot Northern Kentucky University Student Union opened in 2008. NORTHERN KENTUCKY UNIVERSITY

Bottom right: The $34.5 million, 106,600-square-foot Christopher Newport University Student Union opened in 2006. COURTESY OF SHAUN MCCREADY

Alternatives to High-Risk Drinking

"So many students find alternative ways to relax such as binge drinking, campus vandalizing, and visiting online communities. As college union professionals, we must be intentional in our efforts to offer recreation programs as a substitute. Simply having a recreation center in the union is not enough. Competitive events, relaxing, and blowing off a little steam are valuable in fostering individual development within our students. We must strive to be the providers of choice for recreation and leisure-time activities."

— Jack Voorhees. "Recreation Still Has a Place in the College Union." The Bulletin of the Association of College Unions International, July 2002.

"Since the early days of American higher education, student activities have always been a part of college life. Out-of-class activities and programs were organized at first by students to provide a social outlet and break from the 'pious' rigors of the academy. At the same time, alcohol and tobacco use has been a rite of passage practiced by college students since the days of the Colonial college of America. So what has changed?

"Over the past decade, binge or high-risk drinking has increased to where it is estimated that, of the 10.4 million 12- to 20-year-olds who drink alcohol, 29.4 percent are classified as binge drinkers, and 6.0 percent are classified as heavy drinkers (U.S. Department of Health and Human Services, 2000). ... The need to provide alternatives to high-risk drinking behavior and our commitment to promote programming that helps to support the developmental growth of students have created an impetus to support late-night programming on many campuses. ...

For example, the mission statement at Penn State for LateNight reads: 'To provide students quality late-night entertainment during prime social times, LateNight provides an alcohol-free environment with opportunities for programming experience, leadership development, and responsible social action.' ...

"Whatever your reason for encouraging a late-night program, it seems clear that it not only can reduce behaviors associated with high-risk drinking, it's the right thing to do for the ongoing development of students."

— Stan Latta. "Late-Night Programming Can Reduce High-Risk Drinking, Provide Quality Student Development." The Bulletin of the Association of College Unions International, September 2002.

Funding Concerns

"Ninety-seven percent of the annual $23 million budget is self-generated. Institutional funding support has dwindled while at the same time dependence upon the unions by the university has increased. The institutionally mandated Administrative Service Fee is 6.5 percent of all externally generated revenue. A long-range view of the unions' income and expenses demonstrates how perilously few extra dollars there are to establish fiscal planning and avoid deferring building maintenance and capital projects."

— Dan Adams. Director's Statement. The University of Arizona Student Unions Annual Report, 2005-06.

"As this continual evolution toward viewing the college union as a revenue-driven auxiliary continues, it is evident that it has become more and more difficult to tell our story. At this year's meetings, significant time was spent discussing the age-old philosophical question: 'What business are we really in?' Student fees seem to be tapped out. College unions are constantly challenged to find new monies. Unhealthy competition takes place between college unions and other auxiliaries as well as university departments. College unions, athletic facilities, residence halls, and academic colleges are duplicating services such as renting rooms, catering events, and selling soft goods. ...

"Ultimately how we choose to respond to these conditions becomes profound and determines not only our success, but how we choose to live our lives."

— Marsha Herman-Betzen, ACUI executive director. "Spring Hopes Eternal." The Bulletin of the Association of College Unions International, May 2003.

A CRITIQUE OF THE MODERN UNION FACILITY

"Has any American college not yet built a new student center? If so, it is probably interviewing architects at this moment. All across the country, from Bowdoin to Pomona, colleges are scrambling to renovate, expand, or replace aging student unions, with their battered billiard tables and subterranean TV lounges. ...

"The modern student center is a versatile breed. It might be a sprawling creation, like the $75-million, 330,000-square-foot leviathan at the University of Massachusetts at Boston. Or a restrained and subtle affair, like the taut, 50,000-square-foot building at Sweet Briar College, which cost only about $14 million. But large or small, it is certain to contain a multistory atrium, cafe seating, and the obligatory food court. And it boasts an extravagant quantity of glass, so that it can blaze away cheerfully in those nocturnal views that are so often used to depict the buildings. Such is the state-of-the-art student center in 2003. ...

"The atrium preserves in vestigial form some of the features of the great hall, like its visible roof construction and its baronial fireplace. But where the great hall was a discrete room, snug within comfortable walls, the modern atrium is a permeable space, open to the main channels of circulation. It is a place of lively movement and serendipitous collision, less like a room than like the outward swelling of a broad river. Such is the formula of virtually every major new student center, and woe to those that stray from orthodoxy. ...

"The student center has dispensed with the essentially private character of its predecessors, as epitomized by Penn's Houston Hall. Not only do the modern center's public spaces open onto one another, but they unfold to the world outside as well. The place is extroverted to the point of exhibitionism. Having lost its sense of being a rather oversized living room, the student center has assumed something of the impersonal quality of a visitors' center at a national park, or a bus terminal—buildings whose task it is to orient strangers. And, in truth, the student center is designed in large measure for strangers. It must serve not only college students but also prospective students. And while it is the former who will use the building regularly, it is the latter who, in the scheme of things—even though many will visit it no more than once—matter most.

"The essence of the modern student center is to be a recruiting instrument, a fact that pardons its many infelicities: its self-consciousness, its nervous unctuousness, its relentless transparency. If its character is shaped by the world of commercial architecture, that is because it is itself an advertisement. It is the principal highlight of the standard college tour, along with the fitness center. And it communicates exceptionally well. Directors of admissions note that a quick meal in the student center conveys more information about life at a college, and with more credibility, than the lengthiest formal presentation. There the visitor can observe at a glance how students act and interact, how they

California State University, Dominguez Hills' Loker Student Union in 2008.

dress, their relative stress level, and how they relate to their professors. As one admissions director told me, 'It's a veritable vibe fest.' ...

"The modern student union also expresses startling changes in the nature of student life. Since the American campus was wired for computers, a process essentially completed a decade or so ago, studying is no longer a private affair of reading and typing, which involved prolonged and quiet concentration. Studying has become more intermittent, more gregarious, and more mobile. As workstations and terminals have been dispersed across the campus, the clear hierarchy between public and private spaces has dissolved. That, too, is written across the eloquent face of the modern student center—hospitable, industrious, and somewhat prone to insomnia. ... Movement rather than repose is its leitmotif. Here the student center is no longer the gentleman's clubroom but a kind of medieval market square, under a glass roof rather than a tent.

"If the student center increasingly caters to consumers, then consumers have shaped them in turn. No academic building has ever been subjected to as much student involvement. Students have played crucial roles on building committees, as is apparent on the large number of websites devoted to student center projects. Not only are these sites used as clearinghouses during the planning process, but many of them charmingly provide webcams, which broadcast the subsequent course of construction in real time (surely one of the more esoteric species of Internet entertainment). Some campus centers can even be said to be student-designed, to the extent that their functions were democratically chosen.

"Fashions in architecture, as in clothing, are ephemeral, and every building eventually takes its place in the great faceless mass of nondescript, somewhat dowdy structures that compose most older institutions. But nothing grows so soon stale as novelty, and commercial architecture is predicated on novelty. The Piranesian ramp at Columbia, the skylighted viaduct at Smith, the countless atriums with their granite fireplaces and cafe seating: It is not at all clear whether they are destined to be the beloved landmarks of the next generation or as outdated as the fern-and-pastel décor of 1980s nightspots.

"It was once true that the buildings of each college bore a family resemblance to one another, linked by a common scale or palette of materials and textures, and a shared sensibility. The new student center, with some exceptions, tends to be a stranger. It is more likely to resemble distant student centers at other colleges than its immediate neighbors. Let us give it its due. It is a lovely object, and it speaks with unerring honesty about the college today. But its tragedy is that in seeking so frantically to be state-of-the-art, it very likely will wound that most fragile of artifacts, the state of the place."

— Michael J. Lewis, chairman of the art department at Williams College. "Forget Classrooms: How Big is the Atrium in the New Student Center?" The Chronicle of Higher Education, July 11, 2003.

Friends and Neighbors Day for University of Southern California students in 2009. COPYRIGHT STEVE COHN

The Importance of Student Centers

"College unions are more than buildings; they are the community center or gathering place of the campus. The union provides services and conveniences, but more importantly, it complements the academic experience through an extensive variety of cultural, educational, social, and recreational programs. If the modern architectural element that allows for these experiences to occur happens to be an atrium, whether or not that form is appealing to us is secondary. ...

"Many of us as well as Lewis feel great nostalgia for the days when stained glass, marble, terrazzo, and brick were widely used in campus architecture. This is why many colleges devote time and effort to maintaining the integrity of their campus architecture by retrofitting historical buildings even though the infrastructure will be state-of-the-art. ...

"It is critical that the college union be relevant to the community it serves. For this reason, it is by design, not by default, that students have always been involved in the union's creation and administrative processes. This participatory involvement is not a flaw; it is a core value.

"College unions provide a laboratory for students to acquire skills and interact with others from diverse backgrounds, enabling them to develop responsibility and citizenship to become future leaders."

— Michael Henthorne and Marsha Herman-Betzen. Letter to the Editor. The Chronicle of Higher Education, September 5, 2003.

A Nerve Center

"Some 30 years ago, the student union was not designed to accommodate conferences or to create a sense of community. When President R. Thomas Flynn first joined Monroe Community College in 1974 as vice president of student services, the campus looked quite different. He understood then, as he does now as president of the college, the importance of a "nerve center" that supports the college's mission to serve the students and the community."

— Richard H. Ryther. "Community—the First Word in Community College." College Services Administration, August 2004.

"

College unions provide a laboratory for students to acquire skills and interact with others from diverse backgrounds, enabling them to develop responsibility and citizenship to become future leaders.

"

College Union Facilities Must Be Flexible

"As the major player on campus that engages the entire community, the college union, more than any other facility, must constantly reinvent itself to keep pace with evolving services and programs. Traditional student life services, such as social, recreational, and dining facilities, are being transformed to accommodate the increasingly diverse, on-campus, and commuter student populations. Some unions are now open 24/7. In addition, the union has taken on a host of new services. Some unions serve as the campus visitor center or include classrooms. Others are merged with the undergraduate library; include the college chapel, or the campus recreation center. As union professionals constantly rethink how to deliver these enhanced programs and services, they are charged with creating space that not only accommodates today's needs, but also address as yet unknown needs of the future."

— Thomas Kearns. "Flexible Spaces: Strategies for Flexible Design on the Evolving College Campus." The Bulletin of the Association of College Unions International, May 2003.

Creating "The Third Place"

"Recently, in reading 'Celebrating the Third Place' (Oldenburg, 2001) as part of my department's training and staff development program, it became apparent to me that the work we do in building community on our college campus goes hand in hand with recognizing the third places created by our union facilities, programs, and activities. ...

"Our facilities provide shared space where informal gatherings can take place from the earliest parts of our day to the last minute that the lights are on before we lock up for the evening. Our college unions and programs provide individuals a place to go, to learn, to be involved, and to be engaged in their community. For some, our facilities are multiuse spaces that bring cross functions/departments together like multicultural activities next to a bookstore, or student organization space adjacent to a food court, or administrative offices for various campus leaders near a lounge or art gallery. The space itself and those who use it through programs, functions, and campus-wide activities, draw members of the community together. What some may not see is the companionship that is promoted, the civic pride of being involved, the ability to gear up or wind down depending on what is going on, and the chance to have some ownership in the development of their respective community."

— Daniel Maxwell. "Builders of Community through the Creation of the Third Place." The Bulletin of the Association of College Unions International, November 2004.

Competition and Community Building

"Besides contribution, most would define competition as rivalry and cooperation as working or acting together toward a common purpose. As college union professionals, you face the increasing phenomenon of mini-unions now popping up across campuses. Like in my philosophy course, you must weigh the theoretical differences and applications between these two concepts. Do you view this trend as competition or cooperation when considering your role as a campus community builder?

"This spreading of services typically found in the college union most likely began with the expanded food service found in residence halls when they went from the standard cafeteria fare of meat loaf, mashed potatoes, green beans, and all the soft-serve ice cream you could eat to reinventing themselves with branded franchises such as Krispy Kreme, Pizza Hut, Subway, and Starbucks. Branded concepts became the rage as students became far more sophisticated, savvy consumers who knew what they wanted and were willing to pay to get it. More importantly, these same students demanded convenience, seeking alternatives to shopping on the periphery of campus to the union where they could purchase all of their favorite items. In fact, it was the identical transformation that occurred in the college union in the early 1980s as unions began to outsource and brand their food service operations from similar self-op fare into scramble-system food courts, borrowing from private sector's concept readily seen in shopping malls and airports.

"Residence hall food service was just the beginning of this bleeding of amenities and services that have spread over the campus, as this centralized concept once found only in college union is catching on like an epidemic. Smoothies and protein bars have become staples of recreation centers. Buying a Sharpie, an aspirin, or a quarter pound of Gummy Bears is now possible at the library. Scheduling a meeting or attending a lecture by some well-known speaker at the health center is not uncommon. In fact, what campus has not witnessed the proliferation of conference centers, lounges, meeting rooms, convenience stores, and expanded satellite food operations in such places as the college of business, engineering, or medicine? And I believe this trend will continue and expand as higher education continues to find ways to make campuses more appealing, persistently finding competitive ways to wow the best and brightest students.

"So where does this leave college union's role statement when it states: 'Traditionally considered the "hearthstone" or "living room" of the campus, today's union is the gathering place of the college? The union provides services and conveniences that members of the college community need in their daily lives and creates an environment for getting to know and understand others through formal and informal associations.'

"The college union might heed the often-used and familiar quote by United States Army Gen. Eric Shinseiki: 'If you don't like change, you're going to like irrelevance even less.' ... It is time to quit beating around the bush and address the question that begs to be asked: 'Are college union managers just managers of buildings or are college union managers in fact builders of community?' And if the latter is true, and we truly believe a college union is 'not just a building; a college union is building community,' then what will each of us do to ensure we are actively engaged in building and enhancing community on campus? How will our organizations prepare to do what needs to be done? How can we embrace the change that is happening in higher education and find ways to offer our expertise, while enhancing our role as community builders? Finally, when will those who have chosen college unions and student activities as their life's work be willing to begin? It is incumbent on all of us to make sure that the sentiment that has become the mission of our profession, does not just become something on paper that hangs neatly framed on the walls of our unions and nothing more."

— Marsha Herman-Betzen. "Competition or Community?" The Bulletin of the Association of College Unions International, July 2006.

The College Union in Cyberspace

"Quite simply, Facebook is a college union in cyberspace. ... Facebook gives students the opportunity to meet each other, share interests, share notes about classes, plan gatherings, and even form common interest groups. The most recent Horizon Report calls this 'social computing' and lists it as one of the technologies to most immediately be universally adopted in the educational arena. The report says what makes the phenomenon most interesting is 'the way it facilitates an almost spontaneous development of communities of people who share similar interests.'

"If this is the case, are online communities such as Facebook becoming a competitor of the college union? At one time the union could almost exclusively provide social interaction for students on campus, yet Facebook seems to be taking on this role. Will college unions see less building traffic as online communities continue to become more popular? As professionals, how do we convince students that face-to-face interactions are still important, and even more important, than relying on communication through online forums?

"We have heard claims already that interest in online communities will fade, but that is a misguided notion. E-mail, instant messaging, mobile phones, and blogging are a way of life for college students. Sure, student interest in Facebook may decline, but online communities and communication are here to stay. Therefore, we must take an active role in being among the first campus to embrace new technology to further our mission as campus community builders."

— Kera McElvain and Corbin Smyth. "Facebook: Implications for Student Affairs Professionals." The Bulletin of the Association of College Unions International, March 2006.

Students participate in Wright State University's Take Flight Leadership Program in 2008.

WRIGHT STATE UNIVERSITY

Students enjoy billiards at the University of Texas, San Antonio. JEFF STEBAR FOR PERKINS+WILL

"

IF THIS IS THE CASE, ARE
ONLINE COMMUNITIES
SUCH AS FACEBOOK
BECOMING A COMPETITOR
OF THE COLLEGE UNION?
AT ONE TIME THE
UNION COULD ALMOST
EXCLUSIVELY PROVIDE
SOCIAL INTERACTION FOR
STUDENTS ON CAMPUS,
**YET FACEBOOK SEEMS TO
BE TAKING ON THIS ROLE.**

"

The textile art by Gina Phillips hanging in Tulane University's Lavin-Bernick Center identifies 596 institutions in which students enrolled following Hurricane Katrina in 2005.

AFTER THE STORM: HURRICANE KATRINA

"Nearly six months after Hurricane Katrina destroyed much of their beachfront campus, administrators and faculty members from the University of Southern Mississippi's Gulf Coast branch held a ribbon-cutting ceremony last week to celebrate the opening of two double-wide trailers near their temporary campus at a former hospital in Gulfport.

"One trailer will serve as a student center, which will give students their first opportunity to buy hot food on the campus since the hurricane hit and will include places for studying and socializing. The other trailer will provide faculty members with office space and meeting areas, which are scarce inside the hospital facility."

— Sara Hebel. "Steps toward Recovery." The Chronicle of Higher Education, February 24, 2006.

"Charles, a private institution administrator, remarked about the status of student affairs in general and how it changed after the storm: 'Whether people want to admit it or not, student affairs is last, lowliest, and least, period. People don't really understand the importance because it is hard to measure. How do you measure community building? How do you measure the sense of connectedness to the institution? It's like the storm probably did a world of good. It washed away a lot of stuff and the sun is shining now and people go, "Oh, yeah, what we do is important. It's not just, you know, games out on the quad."'"

— Susan K. Gardner, Kristy Miller, Marco J. Barker, Jennifer Loftin, Marla Erwin, and Kay Maurin. "Student Affairs and Hurricane Katrina: Contextual Perspectives from Five Institutions of Higher Education in New Orleans." NASPA Journal, Vol. 44, No. 1, 2007.

Opened in 2007, the University of Vermont's Dudley H. Davis Center was the first LEED-Gold certified union in the United States.

COURTESY OF BOB HANDELMAN, JEFFREY WAKEFIELD

"Ultimately, the college union, as a place where all members of the campus community can congregate informally, provides a unique opportunity to engage the students, staff, and faculty on the subject of sustainability. ... Unions not only provide space for visioning sessions and charrettes, but can in themselves be one of a campus's most visible demonstrations of environmental awareness. Incorporating sustainable features into the union, both structurally and operationally, can be important in effecting a general shift of mindset—bringing green logic into decisions made at all levels, from custodial workers to the university president, from students to faculty. A thoughtful, conscientious approach to our daily decisions can yield substantial long-term change, and a college union can be an important factor in reinforcing this approach, ultimately helping to create a cohesive, intellectually vigorous, and sustainable campus community."

— John M. Rossi and Josh De Florio. "Campus Sustainability and Green Building: Design that Makes Sense for Today and Tomorrow." The Bulletin of the Association of College Unions International, May 2005.

Unions as Examples of Sustainable Practice

"Based on the founding principles of being the social center of campus, the college union can be a living model for all of sustainability design. Having a union that is LEED certified provides yet another working 'tangible model' for the university community to experience. It allows for a greater understanding of sustainability and the impacts that building has on the larger world and not just on the footprint of the building or the university's skyline. Buildings affect everyone and everything, from the extraction of raw materials from the environment to the way the building interacts with the area in which it is built. There are many ways to incorporate sustainability within the college union; it can be through educational programming, changes in the products that are used for dining services and cleaning, or even further when constructing a new building."

— TJ Willis. "Sustainability in Higher Education: College Unions Take the LEED." The Bulletin of the Association of College Unions International, May 2005.

A More Diverse Student Body

"One important trend influencing unions of the 21st century will be demographic diversity. College campuses will see greater influence from Hispanic, Asian, and other ethnic cultures. Unions also will need to respond to growing numbers of nontraditional students by providing an expanding array of multigenerational services. People from all generations continue to join traditional-aged students (18–22 years of age). The union is more appropriately assuming the identity of a true 'university union,' serving the broader needs of nontraditional students, faculty, staff, and older alumni. As a response to the diverse needs of the ever-evolving campus, college unions are increasingly incorporating wellness and fitness facilities, faculty outreach programs, community service opportunities, and other special programs."

— Paul Knell and Stan Latta. College Union Dynamic: Flexible Solutions for Successful Facilities. Published by the Association of College Unions International, 2006.

NEW COMPETENCIES
FOR UNION
PROFESSIONALS

"Many challenges face the 21st century college union. Simply paging through recent issues of *The Bulletin* can generate a quick list: privatization, financial management, facility maintenance and renovations, technology, and managing a multigenerational workforce. Senior college union professionals must effectively lead their organizations to meet these and many other challenges. In fact, recognizing the significant role the college union plays in providing services and experiential learning for the campus, institutional expectations may be justifiably high. Success or failure of the college union may be related to the leadership behaviors and characteristics of the senior professionals responsible for operations and activities."

— John Taylor. "A Study of Senior-Level Professionals' Leadership Practices." The Bulletin of the Association of College Unions International, July 2007.

"Fundraising is something that many college union professionals are being asked to master in a time of state budget cuts and resistance on many campuses to continually raising tuition and student fees. However, this is often not a skill set formally taught in graduate school. The good news is that the most critical aspect of fundraising is fostering relationships—an area of expertise for campus community builders."

— Carolyn E. Farley. "Fundraising 101: Learning on the Job at the University of North Carolina-Wilmington." The Bulletin of the Association of College Unions International, January 2009.

"Traditionally, empirical research has not been a high priority among college union professionals. However, concrete data is perhaps the most effective bargaining tool to convince stakeholders of unions' vital contributions to student life, growth, and development. But how do we begin to measure and document the learning that is occurring around us each day? The key is to connect (abstract) desired learning outcomes with (concrete) measurable workplace experiences that have been demonstrated in prior research to relate with learning."

— Jonathan Lewis and Sebastian Contreras Jr. "Research and Practice: Connecting Student Employment and Learning." The Bulletin of the Association of College Unions International, January 2008.

"For many facilities professionals, it can be difficult to see how their role in assuring the college union is clean, functional, and exciting with adequate services might also provide strong student development opportunities. But today, these same union professionals, along with other campus administrators, are required to meet higher standards and face an increasing amount of evaluation measures related to student learning."

— Prairie L. Burgess and Jerrid P. Freeman. "Facility Professionals Develop Outcomes-Based Education for Student Employees." The Bulletin of the Association of College Unions International, May 2008.

In 2005, ACUI introduced 11 core competencies for successful practice in the college union and student activities profession: Communication, Facilities Management, Fiscal Management, Human Resource Development, Intercultural Proficiency, Leadership, Management, Marketing, Planning, Student Learning, and Technology. Those were followed several years later with skill sets outlining the knowledge and experiences necessary for a professional to be proficient in the core competencies. The core competencies and skill sets provide a framework for education and defining the profession.

Springfield College's Richard B. Flynn Campus Union in 2010, featuring a food court and gathering commons with views of Lake Massasoit. BY PAUL SCHNAITTACHER

Student Employment as a Learning Experience

"Student employment program administration can be rigid or nebulous, but more programs are on a continuum of intentionality between these two extremes. Some organizations may utilize an administrative structure based on deliberate planning. However, in attending to administrative concerns, the significant philosophy of cocurricular education can be lost. Does it matter? Is not any program better than none? Yes, any pro-gram is better than none—even if the only thing it accomplishes is offering students a way to earn money while they are going to school. But if given the chance to make the program more than this—to make it educational, rewarding, preparatory, and grounded in theory—this approach is beneficial to both employer (i.e., the university or department) and employee (i.e., the student).

"With more and more emphasis on accountability and a focus on integrating all institutional programs to the academic mission, it seems that there really is no question at all. Administrators must make student employment programs relevant and substantive if students are to achieve success and if institutions are to offer more than just a paycheck to students."

— Z. Paul Reynolds. In Brett Perozzi (Ed.) Enhancing Student Learning through College Employment. Published by the Association of College Unions International, 2009.

Following the April 2007 shootings at Virginia Polytechnic Institute and State University, a candlelight vigil was held and cranes to symbolize peace for the vicitims were displayed in the union. VIRGINIA TECH MARKETING AND COMMUNICATIONS

Challenges of a New Century

"The 21st century presents new challenges to institutions of higher education. Whereas, historically the focus of colleges and universities was teaching, research, and community outreach, it now includes campus security. In the past century, higher education expanded its scope from nurturing the mind to educating the whole student—body, mind, and spirit. Colleges and universities provide health centers, student unions, an active campus life, and much more. ... The past decade spawned the rapid growth of concern for physical safety, financial security, and protection of data and created the need for emergency managers in higher education ca-

pable of designing, implementing, and updating emergency management plans in a dynamic environment. This is, in part, due to the attacks on Sept. 11, 2001, Hurricane Katrina, Hurricane Rita, and the shootings at Virginia Polytechnic Institute and State University (Virginia Tech). The picture of the student sitting on a grassy knoll conversing with his tutor no longer reflects the modern college campus. Today's students are more likely to be sitting in their room chatting with a virtual 'friend' through Facebook while listening to their iPod and talking on a cellular telephone. The traditional slow, deliberative approach to change in higher education cannot continue to be the way colleges and universities react to the challenges they confront in the 21st century."

— Shirley Kathleen Rowe. Doctoral dissertation. "The Influence of Shootings on Change in Emergency Planning at Texas Four-Year Colleges and Universities." University of Texas at Dallas, 2009.

WHY NOT CALL IT A "CENTER?"

"As part of the five-year appraisal by the Council for the Advancement of Standards (CAS), I had seen the first revision of the College Union Standard and Guidelines several weeks earlier. In reviewing it, the thing that stuck out the most for me was that 'College Union' had been replaced by 'College and University Center' in our name. I knew this standard was a first draft and the process was to include distribution, discussion, dialogue, and debate by an extensive and respected group of reviewers. Yet I still became apoplectic at the very sight of this change in print and had to be talked off my second-story ledge by several staff members.

"Before I get any of you professionals who work in campus centers mad at me, let me differentiate between what I hold to be a philosophical tenet and what I believe to be contextual statements regarding the various names given to a college union. This is a very important distinction. It is not my intention to disenfranchise in any way institutions that do not have 'union' in their name. Rather, the story I want to tell is intended to offer an appreciation of where we came as a profession and as an association. I hope this bone-deep idealistic precept will serve as a foundation for the prolongation of the principles for which both were founded and will remain as part of our legacy.

"It is important to note that, depending on the college union's mission and that of the institution, your college union may be known as 'Student Union,' 'Student Center,' 'Memorial Union,' 'Campus Center,' 'University Center,' 'University Commons,' 'Student Guild,' or 'Student Association.' On campuses without a union building, the student activities department or program fulfills the role of the college union. As ACUI's role statement so poignantly says, 'By whatever form or name, a college union is an organization offering a variety of programs, activities, services, and facilities that, when taken together, represent a well-considered plan for the community life of the college.'

"So what is the difference between a student union, student center, college union, student guild, university commons, and university center? The word 'union' implies a bringing together, a goal of unity for the institution—its students, faculty, staff, alumni, and guests of the institution. As Blackburn (1990)* says: 'Union refers not just to a facility or place but to uniting members of the campus community' (p. 2). In this time of renewed importance on a sense of community and as community builders, the word 'union' is exactly the sentiment we are trying to convey. ...

"Blackburn (1990) acknowledges the possible confusion surrounding the term 'union,' but still finds it preferable to 'center': 'Even though the word "union" has been around since the early 1800s, we still struggle with a confused identity with labor unions. This concern, more than any other, is why some institutional governing bodies have avoided its use. Many have sidestepped that troublesome word "union" by using "center." "Center" implies only a place. It should be noted if the word "union" sometimes leads to mistaken identity; the use of the name "center" does so to an even greater extent.'

"Certainly I would agree that 'center' creates confusion, mostly because, while college unions are just confused with labor unions, 'centers' abound everywhere we look. Just on a college campus we find the: health center, computer center, counseling

---

* Blackburn, R.D. (1990, October). *What's in a name.* Union Wire of the Association of College Unions International.

center, audio-visual center, arts center, recreation center, placement center, alumni center, adult education center, research centers, and medical center. Go outside the campus, and you can add shopping center to the list. This ubiquitous word dilutes any identifying reference to the living room of the campus community and hub of student life.

"There are many esteemed colleagues who think 'center' is a better term. Perhaps because they want a building instead of just the organization, or because there is a confusion with labor unions or other organizations like the Black Student Union, or because the campus community is already familiar with 'center' and does not need to be taught the terminology, or because they feel 'center' better suggests that it is the center of campus life, or even to further the agenda of wanting their center built in the heart of the campus as opposed to being on the outskirts where land is still available.

"And while some believe that 'union' is a dated term, there are institutions that have built new college unions and chosen to have union in their name like Iona College, Slippery Rock, SUNY–Binghamton, University of Nevada at Reno, and Texas Christian University. ...

"Union best expresses the philosophy that the union building, organization, and program exist to serve the entire institutional community.

"What many still don't realize is that the name college union is a generic name that represents an ideal, something to strive for. The most important thing about a union, by far, is not the building but the program within it. The bricks and mortar are the bones; the community of a union provides its spirit. ...

"As an organization, we need to continually work to add language explaining the choice of name in the contextual statement for the CAS College Union Standard; in fact, the standard and the contextual statement should always be jointly distributed so that campuses without a 'union' can help their communities understand the college union idea.

"As Shakespeare's Romeo said, 'A rose by any other name would smell as sweet,' and many believe the same holds true for a college union. For those individuals, what matters is what something is, not what it is called. Whatever the name, let us never be so perfunctory to forget the college union ideal, for in the final analysis there are few that would argue this is what we truly strive to be."

— Marsha Herman-Betzen. "A Rose by Any Other Name." The Bulletin of the Association of College Unions International, May 2008.

Union Flatterers

"Other campus buildings are becoming more like unions every day. My opinion is that other departments are replicating what we do because of the excellent model we've created for spaces and environments on our campuses. Campuses have libraries with lounges, group study spaces, and even food. New dining halls are attached to residence halls and recreation centers. And art galleries and small bookstores are even found in some academic buildings.

"I think union and activities folk also are good at intentionally making spaces lively to help attract and engage students in the community. That doesn't just happen. The art you choose to hang on the walls or the space you dedicate to advertising campus events adds to the feel of the space. The names of student groups on office doors validate the inclusiveness of our community and our desire to recognize and celebrate differences. We have used the phrase, 'Living room of the campus,' to describe the type of space we want to be. We're not a mall or an airport or a museum. Our users are much more connected to our spaces. They are not just consumers; they are members of community. We offer students a gathering place for the development that comes from being a member of a community."

— Don Luse. "Buildings that Build Community." The Bulletin of the Association of College Unions International, May 2009.

Decentralizing the One-Stop Experience

"College unions are experiencing a new twist on the one-stop shop concept. Large institutions, colleges divided geographically by academic components and existing buildings that cannot be expanded because of historic or site limitations are finding satellite, 'mixed use' or 'mini-unions' as the answer. This model permits common functions within either a stand-alone facility or existing campus buildings. Satellite facilities provide a limited range of union functions in a stand-alone facility. A mixed-use building space is shared with another primary

Thousands of students raise money to fight pediatric cancer by participating in the two-day Dance Marathon at Pennsylvania State University. COURTESY OF MARY EDGINGTON

function such as a library or classrooms. The third type, mini-union is where a familiar service such as lounge or dining space is located within a building whose primary function is different from a college union. Although funding is a typical reason for the creation of mixed use and mini-union models typically the organizational structure allows for all functions to be managed under union leadership. This provides a complementary range of services to the campus."

— Erik Johnson and Bill Clutter. "Decentralization: Mini-, Satellite, and Mixed-Use Unions on Today's Campuses." The Bulletin of the Association of College Unions International, July 2009.

More than a Building

"'I have never, ever been to a union with as much spirit and life as this little place here,' [North Carolina Central University Chancellor Charlie] Nelms said. 'This is more than a structure. This is more than a building. This is more than a respite, more than a place to get your pizza or meet your significant other or get a pedicure. This is a platform for the development of character. It's a place where you form bonds, where you make friendships that will last for a lifetime.'"

— Neil Offen. "NCCU Celebrates Student Union Makeover." The Herald-Sun, Oct. 19, 2010.

The University of North Carolina at Charlotte
Student Union in 2009.

STU

TELLING THE STORY OF THE COLLEGE UNION IDEA

"Although I believe the Role of the College Union, and the core values are still right-on, I am concerned that a course correction might be needed to reach our envisioned future. ... For us, I am concerned that in too many instances we are perceived on campus as no more than an auxiliary enterprise that is rarely coupled with the educational mission of the institution. The course correction involved would be a recommitment to the educational mission of the institution, regardless of the funding base. The responsibility is ours. ...

"If no one understands what the union does, who better to beat the drum than you? If faculty questions the importance of student engagement or the out-of-classroom experience necessary to educate the whole student, you better have the assessment data at your finger tips to prove otherwise. There is no silver bullet, no panacea, no simple remedy, other than rolling up your sleeves and deciding you will have the steadfastness to accomplish the things you are too tired to get done. If you don't advocate for the college union idea, then who will? If you don't continue to tell the college union story, no matter how many times you have told it in the past, then you have failed to do your part for all those who will come after you."

— Marsha Herman-Betzen. "State of the College Union and Student Activities Profession." Keynote at the Annual Conference of the Association of College Unions International, 2010.

ABOUT THE EDITOR
PORTER BUTTS

Porter Butts arguably did more than any other individual to advance "The College Union Idea." Throughout his lifetime, he was known as "Mr. Union," "The Father of the College Union Movement," and simply as a legend to the profession.

In our research to update the adventure story of "The College Union Idea," it became evident that Porter's fingerprints are everywhere in our profession. From adding the "I" to ACUI, to initiating the concept of consulting on college unions (which he did for 125 organizations by 1970), to the books he wrote, Porter Butts' influence was pervasive.

As a student employee at the University of Wisconsin–Madison, Porter became involved in campus programming. After championing the fundraising campaign to build a union facility, Porter served as director of the Wisconsin Union from 1927 to 1968. However, during that time he held firm to the concept that a union is not just a building; rather, a union is an organization aimed at bringing together the campus community and enhancing student learning.

Porter was also instrumental in shaping the Association of College Unions International as we know it today. He served as president of the Association in 1932; editor of Association publications for decades; and member of the ACUI Executive Committee from 1936 to 1970. In 1967 he was the first recipient, along with Edgar A. Whiting, secretary/treasurer of the Association from 1941 to 1968, of the Butts/Whiting Award, established by the Association "to recognize outstanding college union leaders for distinguished achievement." Following that occasion, J. Burgon Bickersteth, former warden of Hart House, University of Toronto, and first president of the Association, wrote: "He has by his tireless efforts given to the Association form and substance. Indeed, more than anyone else he can be said to be, in one important sense, the founder of the Association."

Porter was not just an accomplished author in the college union profession but also in the study of Wisconsin Art. In 2004, Porter was honored as part of the inaugural class of the Wisconsin Visual Art Lifetime Achievement Awards. The organization cites his 1936 work, "Art in Wisconsin," as still essential to the study of Wisconsin art history. His passion for art led him to establish both the nation's first art gallery and first craft center in a college union.

In 1991, at Porter's memorial service, Richard Blackburn, former ACUI executive director and long-time friend of Porter, stated: "Armed with a solid philosophy, a strong conviction, and a gifted power of the pen, Porter Butts guided us, served us, and challenged us. He was a crusader for us, with a mind like a steel trap, and a possessor of uncanny administrative and organizational skills. He was a master of the now-disappearing art of letter writing. Being on a committee with Porter Butts was to receive a blizzard of perspective—well-reasoned documents always signed in his familiar green ink.

"Porter, by example, forced us to question, to examine, to analyze. He made us return again and again to our fundamental philosophies, to the basic enduring goals of the college union in the educational process."

In a 1970 special issue of *The Bulletin* about Porter Butts, Duane Lake, director of the University Center at the University of Florida, said: "Look to the union and observe the 'Porter Principle' operating ... a true partnership of students, staff, and administration." In the same issue, A.L. Ellingson, director of the Hemenway Union at the University of Hawaii, wrote in summary that: "Porter was our Aristotle, Herodotus, Pericles, and our Aristophanes—and we need more like him."

With that in mind, no greater tribute can be made to the author of "The College Union Idea" than to instill his philosophy in future generations of college union professionals, which is what this updated edition of his most well-known text aims to do.